CONTEMPORARY AMERICAN POLITICS

Contemporary American Politics

Edited by
ALAN GRANT
Oxford Brookes University

Dartmouth

Aldershot • Brookfield USA • Singapore • Sydney

Published by
Dartmouth Publishing Company Limited
Gower House
Croft Road
Aldershot
Hants GU11 3HR
England

Dartmouth Publishing Company
Old Post Road
Brookfield
Vermont 05036
USA

British Library Cataloguing in Publication Data
Contemporary American Politics
    I. Grant, Alan R.
    320.973

Library of Congress Cataloging-in-Publication Data
Contemporary American politics / edited by Alan Grant.
        p.   cm.
    Includes bibliographical references and index.
    ISBN 1-85521-492-X : $57.95 (U.S. : est.). — ISBN 1-85521-501-2
(pbk.) : $24.94 (U.S. : est.)
    1. United States—Politics and government—1945–1989.   2. United
States—Politics and government—1989–   I. Grant, Alan R.
JK21.C735 1995
320.973'09'045—dc20   94-32768
                                                                                        CIP

ISBN 1 85521 492 X (HB)
ISBN 1 85521 501 2 (PB)

Printed and bound in Great Britain by
Biddles Limited, Guildford and King's Lynn

Contents

Notes on the Contributors

Nigel Ashford is Principal Lecturer in Politics at the University of Staffordshire. He is the co-editor of *A Dictionary of Conservative and Libertarian Thought* (1991) and *Public Policy and the Impact of the New Right* (1993) and author of articles and chapters on Reagan and conservatism.

Peter Falconer is Lecturer in Public Administration at Glasgow Caledonian University. He is the co-author of *Local Government Charges: Policy and Practice* (1993), as well as articles on Congress. He is currently writing a book on Congressional oversight of environmental policy.

Alan Grant is Senior Lecturer in Politics at Oxford Brookes University. He is the author of *The American Political Process* (1979, 1982, 1986, 1991, 1994) as well as articles on American parties, elections and PACs.

Tim Hames is American Studies Research Officer at Nuffield College, Oxford. He is the co-editor of *A Conservative Revolution?* (1994) and co-author of *Governing America* (in preparation).

Richard Hodder-Williams is Professor of Politics at the University of Bristol and has been a visiting professor and scholar at the University of California, Berkeley. He is the author of *The Politics of the U.S. Supreme Court* (1980) and a large number of articles and chapters on the US Constitution and Supreme Court.

Dean McSweeney is Senior Lecturer in Politics at the University of the West of England, Bristol. He is the co-author of *American Political Parties* (1991) as well as articles on political parties and elections.

David Mervin is Senior Lecturer in Politics at the University of Warwick. He is the author of *Ronald Reagan and the American Presidency* (1990) and *The President of the United States* (1993) and is working on a new book on the Bush Presidency.

Nicol C. Rae is Associate Professor in Political Science at Florida International University, USA. He is the author of *The Decline and Fall of the Liberal Republicans* (1989) and *Southern Democrats* (1994). He is co-author of *Governing America* (in preparation).

Introduction

Alan Grant

The 1992 Presidential election saw the Democrats gain control of the White House for the first time in 12 years and obtain only their second victory in the last seven such contests. Despite his comfortable Electoral College lead over incumbent President George Bush, Bill Clinton won just 43 per cent of the popular vote, while a maverick independent candidate, Ross Perot, gained the backing of almost a fifth of the electorate. This was hardly a resounding mandate and the election had been primarily a referendum on Bush's handling of the economy. At the same time the American people seemed to be sending a message that they were tired and frustrated at what appeared to be the gridlock of Washington politics. Bill Clinton promised that, if elected, he would end the immobilism of 'divided government' and work constructively and cooperatively with the Democratic majorities in both houses of Congress to improve the economy, reduce the federal deficit and pass reform measures on key political priorities such as health care. At the same time Clinton campaigned as a 'new kind of Democrat' who was not committed to the 'tax and spend' policies of his Democratic predecessors or wedded to the traditional concepts of 'big government' and New Deal politics.

With this more moderate image among the public, Clinton was able to win key groups of voters who had deserted the party in recent Presidential elections back to the Democratic fold. Clinton's apparent move to the middle ground as well as the recent experience of the Bush Presidency's relationship with Congress gave voters less incentive for ticket splitting.

Despite the heady optimism following his November victory, Clinton and his team soon found out about the harsh realities of governing the United States in the modern era. With the distraction of peripheral matters such as whether homosexuals should be able to serve in the US military and the problems of filling the position of Attorney General, Clinton's first few months in office were little short of disastrous. An inability to focus on his own key priorities – the economy and health care reform – was exacerbated by what appeared to be vacillating and uncertain responses to foreign policy crises. The President's public approval ratings, which began the year as the lowest recorded for any elected President, were, by mid-summer, in free-fall. Changes at the top that led to the former Reagan adviser, David Gergen, returning to the White House stabilized a badly shaken administration and key Congressional victories, albeit with narrow majorities, on the budget and the North American Free Trade Agreement substantially improved Clinton's reputation for effective leadership.

It is ironic that, just as President Clinton was demonstrating some mastery of the complexities of governing in Washington, the relatively simple world of politics in Little Rock, Arkansas from which he had graduated came back to haunt him. Allegations of impropriety in the business transactions of Bill and Hillary Clinton (known collectively as the Whitewater affair) and of indiscretions in the personal life of the former Governor of Arkansas, including an accusation of sexual harassment by a state employee, dominated the news media in the first months of 1994. The ineptitude of White House officials in appearing to want to hide the details of these issues, the routine denials of wrong-doing by the President's staff, the hearings before a grand jury and the appointment of a special counsel to investigate Whitewater produced echoes of the Watergate scandal of 20 years earlier.

President Clinton's problems mounted during the year and the failure of Congress to pass his much vaunted health care reform plan, as well as other proposals including welfare and campaign finance reform, seriously damaged both him personally and the Democratic party in the eyes of the electorate. The sweeping Republican victories in the 1994 mid-term elections demonstrated the voters' disillusionment with the failure of the Democrats to end the deadlock in Washington as they had promised. What is more many politicians and commentators believed that Clinton had tried to govern by moving to the left while in the White House, giving up his pledge to be a 'new kind of Democrat'. It is clear that the President, in dealing with the first Republican controlled Congress since 1954 and a new form of divided government, will have even more problems passing his political agenda in the second half of his term.

The task of political scientists is, of course, to rise above the day-to-day events, the trivia and minutiae of detail which is so often the stuff of media coverage of politics and to seek to identify and analyse trends that are affecting and will influence in the future the working of the political system. As far as the United States is concerned, the remarkable continuity and stability created by the constitutional framework established by the Founding Fathers in the eighteenth century is the backdrop to the analysis of contemporary political developments. Evolution within the structure of government institutions based on the principles of the separation of powers and federalism makes the work of the political scientist examining the United States less hazardous than it is for those seeking to write on developments in, for example, the former Soviet Union or Eastern Europe, while at the same time we need to recognize the often large-scale and significant changes taking place in the wider society and economy that affect the political system.

The origins of the present volume are to be found in work I was starting to do for a new fifth edition of *The American Political Process*. As with all textbooks that seek to give the reader an introduction to and overview of the working of a political system, the need to be as comprehensive as possible in covering all the main governmental and political institutions inevitably leads to a situation where the author can only deal briefly with topics and themes that are important enough in their own right to deserve fuller discussion and analysis. At the time I had been carrying out research into the role of political action committees (PACs); I was able to devote a few pages within the chapter on 'Pressure Group Politics' to PACs but knew that this was only touching the surface in terms of explaining how and why the phenomenon of PACs had become so important and indeed controversial in American politics. Thus was born the idea of *Contemporary American Politics*. It offers the reader in-depth analysis of some of the key themes and issues surrounding the working of the American political institutions and in this respect complements existing textbooks. I have been most fortunate in securing contributions to this volume from a number of distinguished academics on American politics who have written chapters on specialist areas in which they have particular expertise.

The book is organized around significant contemporary developments in the 1980s and 1990s that have affected or are influencing the working of government, political movements and political ideas and the electoral process. In Chapter 1, David Mervin has examined the limits on and use of Presidential power. He argues that different Presidents approach the responsibilities of their office with different strategies and leadership styles derived from their personal characteristics, their view of the world and their previous experience. The chapter focuses on the Reagan and Bush Presidencies and concludes with an afterword on Bill Clinton.

In Chapter 2, Peter Falconer looks at the way Congress carries out legislative review, the different approaches by which committees discharge their responsibilities in this area and the shift that has taken place in recent years from oversight to micromanagement and its implications for legislative–executive relations. He also examines oversight in the context of 'divided government' and the Congressional response to President Clinton's problems with 'Whitewater'.

Tim Hames focuses on the key area of the budget process and deficit politics; an understanding of contemporary American politics is impossible without recognition of the fact that budgetary decision making and the federal deficit have dominated the agenda in Washington over the last decade. He examines the process of creating the US budget, why very high deficits have become a fact of life and what the political repercussions of this have been. He also surveys some of the alternative proposals for reform that have been debated in recent years.

Chapter 4 analyses a political phenomenon of the 1990s that could possibly have radical effects on the way legislative bodies work at both federal and state levels. Grassroots activists have tapped the mood of public disillusionment with 'politics as usual' by passing referendums in a number of states that would limit by law the number of years legislators could remain in office. The chapter outlines the origins of the movement, the political and constitutional debates over the issue, the way campaigns have been fought in the states and the possible impact such changes may have on legislatures and the wider political system.

Richard Hodder-Williams discusses the Supreme Court nominations of Presidents Reagan and Bush. He argues that all nominations to the US Supreme Court, which are recognized as having very important long-term effects on the working of American government as well as the wider society, are made within the White House and Washington contexts. In examining the nominations of Reagan and Bush, Hodder-Williams attempts to evaluate how successful they have been in producing different policy outcomes.

Nigel Ashford examines the state of the conservative movement in the 1990s in Chapter 6. With the defeat of George Bush and the charge that he had failed to build on the Reagan legacy, Ashford critically examines the thesis that the conservative movement has splintered and is unlikely to be an effective political force in the 1990s; he argues that, on the contrary, a revival in the Right's fortunes is a more likely scenario.

In Chapter 7 Nicol Rae looks at the other side of the political spectrum and examines the different factions within the Democratic party. He focuses in particular on the Democratic Leadership Council and why moderates within the party were able to secure the nomination of Bill Clinton in 1992, while also examining how the new President has worked with the various Democratic groups during his first year in office.

The chapter on political action committees in American politics discusses why the growth of PACs took place in the 1980s in terms of both numbers of such organizations and the amounts of money they contributed to election campaigns. It explains their donation strategies and their role in relation to the overall funding of elections and investigates their influence on the legislative process. The chapter concludes with an analysis of recent attempts to reform election campaign finance.

Dean McSweeney provides an interpretation of the way in which the process for selecting Presidential candidates has changed since the late 1960s in Chapter 9. He argues that there have been two phases in the history of the nominating process in the period since 1972 and that many of the criticisms made, particularly by political scientists about the reformed system, are more persuasive in relation to the first phase up to 1980 than to the contests that have taken place between 1984 and 1992.

Finally Chapter 10 is a revised and expanded version of an article that appeared in *Parliamentary Affairs* in April 1993. It surveys the nominations campaigns within the parties, the rise of Ross Perot and the general election itself, while providing an analysis of voting behaviour and the impact of candidates and issues on the electorate. As a post-script to this chapter I have included a brief survey of the 1994 mid-term elections.

I should like to thank my co-authors for their support and cooperation in the development of this project, American friends and, in particular, Sara Morningstar for their help during my visits to the United States and also all those at Dartmouth Publishing for their efforts in bringing the project to fruition.

1 Statecraft in the White House: The Reagan and Bush Presidencies

David Mervin

Presidents of the United States are expected to provide the nation with leadership; it is incumbent upon them to develop policies that meet the country's needs and to display the management skills required to put those policies into practice. At the same time, however, those elected to the White House face many impediments to the exercise of leadership, obstacles so large and so difficult to surmount as often to create an appearance of ungovernability.

Statecraft, or governance, requires that American Presidents demonstrate the capacity to overcome the difficulties posed by a notoriously intractable political system in order to translate policy goals into policy realities.[1] Different Presidents approach these obligations with different strategies or leadership styles derived from their personal characteristics, their view of the world and their previous experience. Later in this chapter we will outline and contrast the leadership styles of Ronald Reagan and George Bush. First, however, we will discuss some general considerations, surveying the constants that confront all Chief Executives before briefly noting the variable elements that help to determine the unique combination of circumstances bestowed upon any given incumbent.

The Limits on Presidential Power

Statecraft is not easy anywhere, but why is the United States so exceptionally difficult to govern? To begin with the obvious, the country includes within its borders a large population, scattered over a considerable land mass and marked by an unusual degree of ethnic and cultural diversity. These sociogeographic factors, in conjunction with the American historical experience, have helped to bring about a political culture where government and all forms of authority are widely regarded with scepticism and suspicion, gut feelings that even yet make leadership particularly difficult.

The Founding Fathers responded to these attitudes and otherwise sought to meet the needs and aspirations of this new nation by devising an instrument that provided for a centrifugal distribution of power and made for weak, unthreatening leadership. By deliberate intent, in other words, power was fragmented and placed in many different hands, in contrast to the centripetal arrangements and recipes for strong leadership found in traditional polities. Two constitutional principles, federalism and the separation of powers, contributed much to the extreme fragmentation of power that, to this day, marks the American political system and stands as a daunting obstacle to effective leadership from the centre. Without doubt the federal principle has been subject to erosion in the twentieth century, yet the continued significance of the states as a limit on the power of the national government cannot be underestimated.

Constitutional development has also undermined the separation of powers to some degree, but the structural division between the branches of government remains largely in place, especially in the realm of domestic policy. Chief Executives endeavouring to meet their responsibility to lead are obliged to seek the cooperation of an awesomely powerful national legislature armed with control of both the purse-strings and the legislative process. Congress, moreover, is itself a chronically decentralized, individualistic and undisciplined body, full of members notoriously close to their constituents, beholden to interest groups and generally unresponsive to the demands of party loyalty. And even if Congress can be brought to order the separation of powers also provides for an independent federal judiciary that can, in some circumstances, become a major player in the policy process.

Elsewhere in the world, parties facilitate coherence and direction in a political system; they provide means whereby leaders can gain the agreement, the cooperation, or at least the acquiescence, of other leaders in that system. In the United States by contrast, parties have great difficulty in fulfilling such functions. In the late twentieth century they lack the patronage resources they once commanded, they are largely bereft of serious programmatic commitments and are denied control of the processes whereby candidates are nominated. It should not be concluded from this that American parties have become irrelevant, but it has to be recognized that their role in the organization of government is far more limited than in other polities.

A vast, amorphous federal bureaucracy presents another major area of difficulty for Presidents attempting to gain control of the policy-making machinery. The bureaucracy participates in both the formulation and the implementation of policy; however it is a body led by political appointees whose loyalty to the White House may be questionable and staffed by career civil servants far less amenable to central direction than many of their counterparts elsewhere in the world. 'Post-modern' Presidents are also constrained by forces outside the United States; this is the case not only in foreign affairs, but also in domestic policy, most notably in their efforts to manage the economy.[2]

In the present era the media in the United States provide further potential obstacles to the exercise of Presidential power. Presidents now conduct public business and much of their private lives under the constant surveillance of television cameras. News broadcasts have supplanted parties, political meetings and peer group discussions as sources of voting cues for the electorate and television news executives have assumed agenda-setting functions. Meanwhile journalists, from both the print and the electronic media, armed with First Amendment freedoms and energized by investigative zeal, have, in recent years, repeatedly penetrated the walls of secrecy behind which policy makers are allowed to work in other political cultures.

In addition to the constants discussed above, every Chief Executive must deal with a unique set of circumstantial variables. Even allowing for the weakness of American political parties, a President with comfortable majorities in Congress stands a much better chance of achieving his agenda than if the legislature is controlled by the opposition. Similarly some Presidents are elected with a large popular vote, while others fail to win even a majority of the votes cast, a variable that will affect the chances of success or failure in the White House. The performance of whoever sits in the White House will also turn on fluctuations in popular support as revealed by public opinion polls. In addition the combination of opportunities and constraints facing any given President will be dependent on the ethos of the time, with President-led governmental action much more acceptable to the American people in some periods than in others and 'greatness' likely to be denied, so we are told, to Presidents not fortunate enough to be in office in 'great times'.[3]

The Reagan Presidency

Background and Experience

The prospects for effective leadership from the White House did not appear to be especially encouraging when Ronald Reagan took office at the beginning of 1981. In the 1980 election he had secured a ten percentage points margin of victory over President Carter, yet had won only a bare majority of the votes cast in the three-way contest. Moreover public opinion polls taken during the campaign had shown little enthusiasm among the electorate for any of the candidates and the election result was widely interpreted as a vote of no confidence in Carter rather than a positive vote for his principal opponent.

It is true that in that same year the Republicans won control of the Senate for the first time for many years, but the House of Representatives remained firmly under Democratic control, Congress, moreover, was in an even more recalcitrant state of mind than usual. The 1970s had been an era of Congressional reform, with various changes creating an even more fragmented and less manageable legislature than before. To add to all this, public confidence in political institutions was at a disastrously low ebb, with the office of President, in particular, suffering from a large loss of credibility.

For many commentators it seemed most unlikely that Ronald Reagan possessed either the background or the talents required to master an extraordinarily complex and problematical political system. He was seen as a rather simple-minded, conservative ideologue with an agreeable manner, who, aided by wealthy corporate sponsors, had made his way into politics after an undistinguished career as a film actor.[4] In fact there was much more to Reagan than his critics allowed. His origins were undeniably humble; his father left school at the age of 12, eventually becoming a shoe salesman who moved his family around a succession of small towns in Illinois. Reagan himself was educated at a small church-related college, after which he sought a career in radio before heading for Hollywood. Given the doubts later raised about the quality of Reagan's mind, it is worth noting that there were those who worked with him as a film actor who remembered him as a voracious reader with a photographic memory and a consuming interest in politics.[5] It was no doubt the latter that led Reagan to become an active trade unionist; he joined the Screen Actors Guild in 1937 and became its president for six years after World War II. As a trade union leader during a particularly tumultuous period of industrial relations in Hollywood, Reagan gained experience highly relevant to his future work in politics.

As his career in films was winding down, Reagan was employed by General Electric (GE) to host a series of television plays, in some of which he also starred. The same corporation then used Reagan as a public relations spokesman; at first he visited GE plants up and down the country to make speeches and raise morale among employees. Subsequently, under GE sponsorship, he spoke to a range of business, civic and other groups, usually extolling the virtues of the free enterprise system and the American way of life. These assignments gave Reagan the opportunity to hone his public speaking skills while further developing his political ideas, and it was in this period that he appears to have moved sharply to the right, abandoning his earlier enthusiasm for the New Deal.

The Reagan who successfully ran for Governor of California in 1966 was not a political novice with nothing to commend him apart from celebrity status and a pleasing manner. He had behind him many years of relevant experience in the communications industry, working first in radio, then in films and more recently in television. For a long time he had been deeply interested in politics, he had served as a trade union leader and had made himself into an accomplished and influential public speaker.

When Reagan became President in 1981, his greatest disadvantage was his lack of background in foreign affairs. This was undoubtedly a handicap, but, in other respects, Reagan went to the White House better prepared than many of those who have occupied the office in recent decades. He had, after all, been for eight years Governor of California, arguably the most important state in the union, with a GNP greater than all but six nations of the world. Most of the domestic policy problems that Presidents face in Washington exist on a smaller scale in California and in addressing those issues the chief executive of the state must overcome many comparable obstacles. The state legislature, for instance is, as prone to fractiousness and indiscipline as Congress and while Reagan was in the state house it was for six of the eight years controlled by the opposition.

Governor Reagan began unimpressively as a rather unworldly ideologue, deeply distrustful of professional politicians and with little understanding of the way the California political system worked. Before long, however, he began to come to grips with the realities of policy making and to develop the style of executive leadership that he took with him to the White House. He came to understand the importance of striking a balance between firmness and flexibility, adhering as far as practicable to his simple conservative beliefs while recognizing that bargaining and other forms of compromise had a vital part to play in the policy making process. In Sacramento, Reagan learned about negotiating with legislators while also discovering how to appeal over their heads directly to the people when necessary. He also experimented with a chairman of the board management style, delegating details to trusted aides such as Edwin Meese and Caspar Weinberger without surrendering control over the direction of his administration.

When Reagan began offering himself to the electorate as a Presidential candidate he was hardly a political amateur. He may have lacked the background appropriate for a British Prime Minister and even in American terms there was some reason to doubt his credentials. Nevertheless he had certainly had much experience highly relevant to executive leadership in the late twentieth century. Natural aptitude and a long career in radio, film and television had helped him become an outstanding communicator – a strength that equipped him not only for campaigning, but also for the business of government in the television age. Then in Sacramento, he had undergone a lengthy apprenticeship in the arts of executive leadership that allowed him to become a reasonably successful Governor of an important state.

Leadership Style

As was observed earlier, Presidents bring a distinctive style of leadership to the task of mastering the American political system; that style reflects their personality and their view of the world and is shaped by their life experience. In trying to understand something of Reagan's personality it should be noted that Presidents as a class, like politicians in general, tend not to be especially attractive, well-balanced human beings. Most are afflicted by hubris and delusions of grandeur, yet at the same time, and notwithstanding their high levels of achievement, more than a few of those who have sat in the White House appear to have been rather poorly adjusted, unhappy individuals, wracked by self-doubt and unable to derive satisfaction from their accomplishments.[6] Reagan is certainly not without hang-ups, yet he does appear to be a fairly well adjusted person. Commentators have remarked on his optimistic, upbeat approach to life and have seen him as a man of considerable personal charm, with a well developed sense of humour, a relaxed and self-effacing manner and a rare talent for putting others at their ease.[7]

Reagan's attractive personal qualities were not, as far as some critics were concerned, sufficient to offset doubts about his intellect, reservations which first surfaced in California and then returned with added force when he ran for the Presidency. However far too much has been made of Ronald Reagan's intellectual limitations. There have, to be sure, been many Presidents who would have scored more on an IQ test, but, as the examples of Herbert Hoover, Jimmy Carter and Richard Nixon confirm, intelligence alone is by no means sufficient to guarantee successful Presidential leadership.

In any case, leaving aside the many media pundits and caricaturists, there are those in a position to make an informed judgement who deny that Reagan lacked intelligence. One admittedly important voice to the contrary is that of David Stockman, Reagan's first budget director, who in his memoirs made some scathing comments about the quality of the President's mind.[8] However Stockman's analysis is remarkably blinkered and politically naïve and no doubt coloured by his disaffection. Moreover, to offset Stockman's remarks, there are the published views of observers such as Martin Anderson, Caspar Weinberger, Edwin Meese and Donald Regan, all of whom knew the President far more intimately. Meese characterizes the

'Reagan-as empty-vessel-theory' propounded by media gurus as 'ludicrous', while Weinberger says the President 'read voluminously and quickly... he was easy to brief and his memory was phenomenal'.[9] These comments by two men who worked closely with Reagan over many years are confirmed by Anderson, who describes the President as

> highly intelligent with a photographic memory. He has a gift for absorbing great amounts of diverse information, and is capable of combining parts of that information into new, coherent packages, and then conveying his thoughts and ideas clearly and concisely in a way that is understandable to almost everyone.[10]

Even Donald Regan, Reagan's first Secretary of the Treasury and later his Chief of Staff, who was by no means reluctant to criticize the President's style of leadership in his memoirs, does not share Stockman's excessively low view of his intellect, seeing him as 'a formidable reader and a talented conversationalist' whose 'grasp of economic theory as it had been taught in his time was excellent'. The notably hard-headed Regan believed that the President had a 'formidable gift for debate' and reported that he had seen him 'defend his ideas and critique the proposals of other heads of state with the best of them at six international summits'.[11] Those who persist in regarding Reagan as no more than an 'amiable dunce' really need to set aside the gaffes and the media caricatures to pay heed to the readily available opinions of those who knew the President well.[12]

Nevertheless, even if he was far from being the empty vessel proclaimed by so many of his critics, Reagan clearly did have intellectual limitations which had a bearing on his style of leadership. He did have a preference for anecdotes over analysis; his approach to matters of great complexity could be alarmingly simplistic and he was often shown to have a decidedly shaky grasp of the detail of policy making. Such shortcomings troubled the President's allies, to say nothing of his opponents, but weaknesses can simultaneously be strengths and there was a positive side to the very ordinariness of Reagan's mind. It struck a favourable chord in a society where government and politicians are not held in high regard; it seemed to confirm that government was not really that difficult, that even a man with a limited intellect could do the job, provided he had the right instincts and the courage to adhere to them.

A related feature of Ronald Reagan's personality was his modesty, a quality that answered anxieties prevalent in a political culture ambivalent about leadership. Those who sit in the White House must be careful to avoid arousing age-old suspicions and resentments; their standing will be weakened if the perception gains ground that they are 'power mad' and not properly respectful of the constitutional and other limits placed on Presidential power. As Woodrow Wilson, Franklin Delano Roosevelt, Lyndon Johnson and Richard Nixon were harshly reminded, such allegations can have devastating negative repercussions.

By contrast, Reagan was relatively immune to the charge of megalomania. His willingness to delegate his authority and his 'relaxed nine-to-five style ... made him seem less "Washington", less power hungry and less menacing'.[13] Unlike many of his predecessors he did not let his head be turned unduly by the trappings and the myths attached to the Presidency; he did not take himself too seriously, was not 'puffed up' by his high office and did not 'treat himself like a statue of himself'.[14] George Reedy has written convincingly about the corrupting, court-like atmosphere of the White House where a President is treated like a quasi-monarch and is surrounded by sycophants only too willing to flatter their master's ego.[15] However Reagan, in contrast to the likes of Lyndon Johnson and Richard Nixon, seems to have remained largely unaffected by the fawning attention and the deference that surrounded him. He put on no airs and graces and left people with the impression that, despite his high office, he remained essentially one of them. This relaxed, non-threatening style of leadership was attuned to the American political tradition and helped President Reagan to retain both popular support and his credibility with other political leaders. His unassuming manner, his non-intellectual attitudes, his propensity for wisecracks and for telling stories, almost always derived from Hollywood films, helped him establish an enviable rapport with the American people while also facilitating productive relationships with legislators, bureaucrats and other leaders. To put it another way, Reagan conveyed an image of a rather likeable man and likeability, it should be understood, is a valuable leadership resource not granted to all Presidents.

The widespread perception of Reagan as a likeable man, even among those who disapproved of his policies, provides part of the explanation for his tenacious hold on public opinion. This is often overstated; his standing in the polls fluctuated and never reached the heights temporarily enjoyed by his successor. For all that, Ronald Reagan's public approval ratings, when taken over the whole of two terms, were unusually high; they allowed him not only to be re-elected in a landslide, but also to survive numerous setbacks unscathed and to come back triumphantly, in terms of public approval at least, from a catastrophe like the Iran Contra affair that would have destroyed other Presidencies.

The fact that Reagan survived a number of disasters could in part be explained by the 'easy ride' that he was allegedly given by the media, one of the greatest obstacles, in the modern age, to the exercise of Presidential power. Journalists, cameramen and their colleagues warmed to Reagan in a way that they had not to other Chief Executives and this was a valuable political bonus. 'Sheer likability ... has been a great asset to Ronald Reagan ... news coverage of a public figure can be affected by the personal feelings of the press corps'.[16]

The fact that Reagan was a man easy to like was also of incalculable value in his dealings with legislators, whether via telephone calls, meetings with groups of members, or in one-to-one situations. His relaxed, amiable, self-effacing manner put legislators at their ease and inclined them towards cooperation. Deliberately using anecdotes and wisecracks to defuse tension, Reagan did not bully or overpower Representatives and Senators in the manner of Lyndon Johnson; he may have shared Nixon and Carter's contempt for Congress, its personnel and its methods, but he wisely kept such feeling concealed by a mask of affability. In contrast to Carter, his immediate predecessor, there was no danger of Reagan humiliating or intellectually upstaging Congressional members who met him in the Oval Office: 'His demeanour was one of cordiality and respect.'[17] He came across as a modest, decent, agreeable man anxious to like and be liked by his visitors. Thus, according to his main adversary in the legislature, the Speaker of the House, Tip O'Neill, Reagan was 'an exceptionally congenial and charming man. He's a terrific story teller, he's witty, and he's got an excellent sense of humor.'[18]

Reagan's view of the world was that of a neo-populist conservative; he was anti-government, anti-tax, pro-markets and virulently anti-communist. At his inauguration Reagan famously said 'Government is not the solution to our problem; government is the problem.' Checking or, if possible, reversing the gargantuan growth of government in recent decades was, the President believed, essential to the recapturing of economic prosperity for the United States. Minimizing the role of government would contribute to the liberation of market forces, an end that would also be achieved by cutting taxes, reducing government domestic expenditures and deregulating the economy. Reagan's brand of conservatism also included reviving federalism by devolving more responsibilities to the states, a social policy agenda, a substantial strengthening of the nation's defences and the pursuit of a more aggressive foreign policy. These were broad policy objectives that Reagan had been articulating for years and upon which his 1980 campaign was based. Unlike most Presidents, in other words, he entered office with a clear-cut programme of aims that he had laid before the electorate and which gave his administration a rudder to steer by. Neither political elites nor the public had been left in any doubt as to where Reagan stood and where he aspired to take the country. This possession of 'vision' constituted one of the great strengths of the President's style of leadership.

His conservatism was, moreover, marked by an activist thrust. Eisenhower, Nixon and Ford had all more or less accepted, or had not felt strong enough to challenge, the assumptions which clearly underlay the New Deal consensus that enveloped American politics for close to half a century. But Reagan was different; tinkering with the status quo was not enough for him, he was a quasi-revolutionary seeking a fundamental change in the terms of political debate.

The operational methods of any President are influenced by his previous experience and we indicated earlier some of the continuities between Reagan as Governor and as President. In Washington, as in California, Reagan made extensive use of delegation. In theory there are obvious advantages to delegation. The President's primary responsibility is to lead, to provide direction and, arguably, he is better able to do that if he is not distracted by matters of detail. In addition the mind-boggling complexity of the problems of modern government prohibits Presidents from coming to grips with all the detail and it is foolhardy for them to even try to do so. Those who make the attempt place at risk their physical health, their sanity and their sense of perspective.

Nevertheless democratic considerations demand that Presidents who delegate do so in a responsible manner. Overall direction and control must remain in their hands. The electorate places a President, not his staff, in charge of the government and if accountability is to have any meaning he must retain overall control. It has been suggested that Reagan singularly failed to meet this test; his was supposedly a 'no hands' Presidency where no one was really in charge and 'policy making was literally up for grabs'.[19] Stockman contemptuously declared the President to be 'as far above the detail work of supply side as a ceremonial monarch is above politics' and complained bitterly of a lack of direction in economic policy.[20] Donald Regan made similar complaints: 'The President never told me what he believed or what he wanted to accomplish in the field of economics. I had to figure these things out like any other American, by studying his speeches and reading the newspaper.'[21]

These charges are rejected by others such as Martin Anderson and Terrel Bell, Reagan's first Secretary of Education. Anderson insists that the President made all the important decisions and had enunciated his position on hundreds of policy issues long before he set foot in the White House.[22] Direct contradiction of the Stockman/Regan allegations of a lack of direction in economic policy is provided by Bell, who says,

> I never felt that his policies were aimless or wandering or lacked clear focus. ... Reagan was a decisive leader and it is inaccurate to portray him otherwise. ... He knew how to delegate and when to monitor. He had a laid back style, but this did not mean he was not effective. Indeed, it enabled him to be effective.[23]

Nonetheless there seems little doubt that Reagan delegated excessively and failed to recognize that delegation was not appropriate in all areas of policy making. In particular it was not suitable in complicated foreign policy matters, as the Iran Contra débâcle was to demonstrate. In the judgement of the Tower Commission, 'setting priorities is not enough when it comes to sensitive and risky initiatives that directly affect US national security'.[24] A more 'hands on' Chief Executive would not have allowed egoists and adventurers on the staff of the National Security Council like Oliver North to have such influence in the determination of US foreign policy.

It is also the case that extensive delegation makes a President unhealthily dependent on his staff. In Reagan's first term this was not a problem, for he was surrounded by a particularly talented White House staff led by a troika of outstanding senior aides; Edwin Meese, James Baker and Michael Deaver were keenly aware of the President's idiosyncrasies and manoeuvred skilfully to protect his interests. The second term staff operation led by Donald Regan was much less effective and has been widely blamed for some of the disasters that befell the Reagan administration in its later years.

President Reagan's intellectual limitations, his legendary affability, his detachment from the detail of policy making and his great reliance on his staff has led some to see him as a weak, easily manipulated Chief Executive. This is a mistake. One of the notable features of Reagan's style of leadership was his toughness or resolution: his unwillingness to give way on matters that he deemed especially important. In truth he was an unusually ideological President, who, as we have seen, had vision, or a clear sense of direction, and stuck stubbornly to the paths that he had chosen, even in the face of opposition from Cabinet members and his own staff. Anderson describes Reagan as 'one of the toughest men I have ever known, far tougher, for example, than his predecessors, Carter, Ford and Nixon. Once Reagan has determined what he thinks is right, and what is important to do, then he will pursue that goal relentlessly.'[25]

There is ample evidence to support such a claim. Stockman attributes the big tax cut in 1981 in large part to Reagan's resolution and then bemoans his inability later to overcome the President's stubborn resistance to a tax increase.[26] Hedrick Smith argues that the Tax Reform Act of 1986 would not have become law without Reagan's tenacious insistence on sticking with the bill once he had decided to support it.[27] The Strategic Defense Initiative was at first regarded with scorn within the Reagan administration, but the President insisted and the 'Star Wars' policy was adopted. However that same tenacity came close to wrecking Reagan's Presidency when, against the advice of senior Cabinet members, he stubbornly insisted on exchanging arms for hostages with Iran and funnelling aid to the Contras. Nevertheless, while President Reagan may at times have been passive and disengaged, he was clearly very difficult to shift on matters that he regarded as of central importance. This is not to say that Reagan was incapable of compromise. As a variety of observers have noted, he was at the same time an ideologue and a pragmatist. He conveyed an impression of being firmly committed to certain principles yet recognized the need to settle for half a loaf when the circumstances demanded it.[28]

Finally, to complete this survey of Reagan's style of leadership, we will focus on one of his more evident strengths, his talent as a communicator. It is obvious that the ability to communicate effectively is a necessary requirement in a political leader and it is hardly any less apparent that, in the modern age, that requires a capacity for conveying ideas, selling policies and garnering popular support via television. On the other hand, remarkably few Presidents have been masters of that form of communication, whereas Reagan shared with Kennedy an exceptional ability to come to terms with the demands of television. The former's pre-political training and experience gave him an enormous advantage over other politicians in the age of television. That advantage, it should be emphasized, was invaluable, not only in campaigning for office, but also in statecraft, or governance.

As Reagan sought to impose his priorities on the political system it was crucial to whatever success he enjoyed that he brought with him an inbred willingness to accept direction from media advisers. He recognized the importance of standing in a particular spot and holding himself in the most advantageous way as the cameras rolled. He knew how to read a script, or a speech, for maximum effect and was comfortable with media contrivances such as the teleprompter.

In this century, Presidents seeking to bring about change have often tried to overcome Congressional resistance to their proposals by appealing over the heads of members of Congress to their constituents, by using their office, in other words, as a 'bully pulpit'.[29] Television, for those able to master it, provides a potent channel of communication for such purposes and Reagan exploited the opportunities the medium provided to the full. It was not, however, his command of television alone that made him such a formidable communicator; he also developed over the years an unusual rapport with the American people. Factors helping to make that possible included his humble, middle America origins, his status as a Washington outsider and his talent for speaking to his compatriots in a language that they had no difficulty in understanding. He has been much mocked for his fondness for stories derived from movies, but in talking in this way he evoked myths and shared experiences that many Americans could relate to. Furthermore the well-known ordinariness of his mind, his modesty, his self-deprecating humour and his personal charm all gave him the aura of a political leader in close touch with the hearts and minds of those whom he led.

A great deal of nonsense has been written about Ronald Reagan's style of leadership. This is not to suggest that it was flawless. Even if he was not an 'amiable dunce', he was prone to naïve and simplistic approaches to the problems of governance. Chief Executives must do much more than merely provide overall guidance; they must avoid the perils of being overwhelmed by the detail, yet must display a better grasp of the nitty-gritty of policy making than Reagan felt was necessary. He did fail to recognize the dangers of delegation, such as an undue reliance on staff and the inappropriateness of the strategy in some areas of policy. Nevertheless there were also strengths to set against these weaknesses; however simplistic his 'vision' may have been, it gave his administration a sense of direction that others have lacked. And then his outstanding skill as a communicator was crucial to his greater measure of success in achieving his objectives than most modern Presidents. That is to say, leaving aside any personal preferences we may have as to the desirability of his policies, he was, *relatively speaking*, rather successful in mastering the American political system sufficiently to bring about significant public policy change.

The Bush Presidency

Background and Experience

The portents for a successful Presidency appeared to be mixed when Bush entered the White House in 1989. His margin of victory over Michael Dukakis in the popular vote was close to 8 per cent and he had won nearly 80 per cent of the Electoral College vote. However there had been no 'coat-tail effect', with Bush generally running behind his party's candidates for Congress across the country and the Republicans losing three seats in the House and one in the Senate. As a consequence, the new President would be confronted, from the outset, by a Congress with large Democratic majorities – 85 in the House and ten in the Senate.[30] By contrast, every modern Democratic President has had a national legislature controlled by his own party and even Reagan had the advantage of a Republican majority in the Senate for the first six of his eight years in office. Nevertheless those concerned by the prospect of deadlock between the executive and the legislature could take comfort from the fact that the President was far less ideological than Reagan, had himself been a member of Congress in the 1960s and now spoke warmly of working constructively with his former colleagues.

In a number of other respects Bush's route to the Presidency was quite unlike that of his predecessor. As we saw earlier, Reagan had sprung from a middle American, working-class background and had been educated at an obscure, church-related college. By comparison, Bush's beginnings were marked by wealth and privilege; the son of an investment banker who later became a US Senator, he grew up in Greenwich, Connecticut in a house with three maids and a chauffeur to take him and his brother to preparatory school. Bush received his secondary education at Phillips Academy, the equivalent of an exclusive public school in Britain. Subsequently, after distinguished war service, he attended Yale and began his working life with all the credentials of a member of the Eastern patrician class.[31]

In 1948, Bush moved to Texas to begin work in the oil industry and became active in Republican politics in that state in the 1950s. After an unsuccessful campaign for the US Senate in 1964, Bush won a seat in the US House of Representatives in 1966, serving two terms. Appointed by President Nixon in 1970 to be US Ambassador to the United Nations, Bush later became Chairman of the Republican National Committee. During the Ford administration Bush was first head of the United States Liaison Office in Beijing and then, for one year, he was Director of the Central Intelligence Agency. After being defeated in the contest for the Republican Presidential nomination in 1980, Bush agreed to be Reagan's running mate and held the office of Vice-President from 1981 to 1989.

When campaigning for the Presidency in his own right in 1988, Bush, with some justification, made much of his curriculum vitae. In marked contrast to Jimmy Carter and Ronald Reagan, he was able to offer himself for election as a man with a wide range of experience in national government and an understanding of the way the political system worked. His former service in Congress could be expected to aid his dealings with the legislature, while his work at the UN, in China, as Director of the CIA and then as Vice-President had brought him into contact with many world leaders and given him an invaluable grounding in international affairs. Nevertheless Bush's résumé was not without flaws; most of the positions he had held were dependent on the patronage of others and provided him with little scope for independent leadership. Furthermore, only for 12 months at the CIA had he been responsible for directing a sizeable, administrative operation. In that sense, at least, Reagan, with eight years as Governor of California behind him, was rather better qualified for the Presidency.

Reagan was, of course, dogged throughout his political career by qualms about his intellect, but there were fewer reservations in Bush's case; there seemed little reason to question the intellectual capacity of a man who had graduated from Yale with a Phi Beta Kappa key and a prize in economics. For all that, Bush, was arguably less interested in ideas than Reagan, read less widely and as President became notoriously prone to grotesque syntactical errors when making off-the-cuff remarks.[32] According to Gail Sheehy,

Bush is not fired up by ideas or issues. For all his superior education [he] could not remember a single book that influenced him. ... Nor does he have any of that easy, self-confident mellifluousness common to Ivy Leaguers. He rarely uses words with more than three syllables, scrambles his syntax, and evinces considerable difficulty in completing a sentence.[33]

If Sheehy is correct, it may be that there is less of an intellectual gap between Reagan and Bush than is commonly assumed.

Leadership Style

Likeability has been a major leadership resource for Bush no less than it was for Reagan, although with different ramifications. Those who know Bush well are united in their depiction of him as an unpretentious, civil and witty man of great personal warmth. Despite his legendary affability and charm, Reagan was, in some ways, rather remote; a man close to very few people other than his wife, capable of forgetting the names of Cabinet members and even his own staff. No such mistakes were made by Bush, who throughout his life has carefully cultivated personal relationships, constantly endeavouring to make friends of those with whom he came into contact. He had a 'preternatural tendency to make and keep acquaintances and friends in all the walks of life. ... He built a habit of writing prompt and affectionate notes to people with whom he was dealing.'[34] These compulsive tendencies made possible the networking leadership style that, as we shall shortly see, became Bush's hallmark.

Even though both were conservative Republicans, George Bush held to a world view quite different from that of Reagan. The latter entered politics as an 'outsider' bent on fundamental change, whereas Bush was a Washington 'insider' whose primary motivation appeared to lie in the idea of service. He had grown up in a home where it had been stressed that those born in privileged circumstances incurred a duty to serve. As the President himself put it, 'Our father had a powerful impact on the way we came to look at the world. Dad taught us about duty and service.'[35] Given this background it was not surprising that Bush, on entering the White House, should swiftly distance himself from Reagan's anti-government stance, the position encapsulated by 'government is not the solution to our problem; government is the problem'. During his first week in office Bush addressed a gathering of senior federal bureaucrats and appalled good Reaganites with comments such as, 'You are one of the most important groups I will ever speak to. What we really have in common is that each of us is here to serve the American people. Each of us is here because of a belief in public service as the highest, noblest calling.'[36] Such notions reflected the President's upbringing and his own public service career; it also defined him as a quintes-sential insider, content to work within the system rather than adopting the militant outsider posture of Reagan or his forerunner, Goldwater.

In this sense Bush subscribed to a different, and arguably more orthodox, brand of conservatism. He shared Reagan's faith in individualism and mar-ket forces, but had no time for crusades or for overturning the existing system. As far as possible he sought to preserve the status quo; he was sceptical of innovation, had little faith in the power of government to effect social or economic improvement and believed that as President he was obliged to 'see to it that government intrudes as little as possible in the lives of the people'.[37] This was an approach similar to that of President Eisen-hower, who had also seen himself as a *conservator*, or guardian, wedded to preserving things as they were and to resisting any further extension of the reach of government.[38]

Both Eisenhower and Bush doubted whether legislation could make a useful contribution to that most troubled of domestic policy areas, civil rights. Eisenhower was convinced that legislation 'could not change the hearts of men' and insisted that 'improvements in race relations is one of those things that will be healthy and sound only if it starts locally. I do not believe that prejudices, even palpably unjustified prejudices, will succumb to compulsion'.[39] When he ran for the Senate in 1964, Bush advanced the same argument in his campaign literature. Progress in race relations would only come as a result of moral suasion, 'I believe that the solution to this grave problem lies in the hearts and goodwill of all people and that sweep-ing federal legislation like the Civil Rights Act can never fully succeed.'[40]

Arguments of this nature provide a rationale for inaction on the part of leaders in the face of injustice and suffering and as such are anathema to American liberals and others more optimistic about the possibilities of reform arising from government action. However, Bush, no less than Eisen-hower, is entitled to be judged on his own terms rather than those implicit in the liberal Democratic models of Presidential power so prevalent in the political science literature. To put it another way, Bush in office proved to be no Franklin Roosevelt, but given his view of the world this should have surprised no one.

Criticism of Bush from the liberal Democratic side of the political spec-trum was to be expected; however in the second half of his Presidency many of the most serious complaints against his style of leadership came from within his own party. Unlike Reagan, so it was argued, Bush had no overall vision of where he wanted to take the nation. He possessed no ideology and lacked the beliefs or convictions necessary to provide his administration with a sense of direction: 'Reagan's stated convictions provided a road map for his administration. ... [Unlike] the Bush administration which had no ideals and therefore no sense of direction.'[41] To some extent such complaints were misplaced, reflecting little more than the anguish of frustrated Reaganites unable to come to terms with the approach of a rather different President, one who saw himself, not as a crusader, but as a case-by-case problem solver; in fact, Bush's pragmatism was far more typical of American Presidents than Reagan's taste for ideology. Traditionally there has been little place for ideology in American politics and even great achievers in the White House like Franklin Roosevelt could be said to have lacked vision, to have taken up office without a master plan or blueprint. As Theodore Lowi observes, 'no one knew Roosevelt's specific positions and plans until after he became President in 1933. ... [whereas] Ronald Reagan's program was clear for all to see before the 1980 election'.[42]

It has been pointed out that, while Bush may have not possessed a blueprint, it is not really the case that he is without beliefs. He is unreservedly committed to the American political and economic system: 'I believe in the integrity of the process. I believe our institutions can still cope.'[43] However it is surely the case that belief in the process alone is not enough; a successful President needs to be seen to believe in something beyond mere form. It is insufficient for him to adopt a completely reactive position, responding to problems as they arise and appearing to have no preconceived beliefs on the great issues of the day. The American people may not expect their Presidents to be ideologues, or the leaders of crusades, but the credibility of Chief Executives is likely to suffer if they give the impression that everything is negotiable, that they have no core convictions beyond a belief in the merits of the process.

The allegation that Bush lacked convictions appeared to be dramatically confirmed by his abandonment in office of the 'no new taxes' pledge he had made at the 1988 Republican Convention and which had been the centrepiece of the programme he had laid before the electorate. In early 1990, the President sent a budget to Congress which honoured his tax pledge, but it soon became apparent that the proposed budget, as it stood, would not secure the approval of the legislature. Eventually the administration let it be known that the President might be prepared to agree to a tax increase in order to facilitate an agreement. This news horrified conservative Republicans who regarded the tax pledge as sacrosanct. When a package of increased taxes and expenditure cuts, agreed between the White House and Congressional leaders, came before the House of Representatives it was heavily defeated, with a large majority of the President's party voting against.

This crisis was finally resolved by further negotiation and agreement on a revised package of tax increases and expenditure cuts, but the damage to Bush's standing was considerable, particularly among an important, influential segment of the Republican electoral coalition. Matters were hardly improved by Bush's actions during the 1992 primary season, when the President told a radio interviewer that signing the 1990 tax bill was the 'biggest mistake' he had made in office. This astounding second U-turn might have been more acceptable if Bush has justified it in economic terms. Instead he appeared to be motivated by electoral considerations: 'Listen. If I had to do that over, I wouldn't do it. Look at all the flak it is taking. ... [Republican voters were] just overwhelmed by the fact that I went for a tax increase.'[44]

The political expediency that Bush demonstrated on the tax issue showed itself in a number of other policy areas, as Jefferson Morley has shown with regard to civil rights:

> The George Bush of 1964, 1988 and 1990 campaigned against federal civil rights legislation, evoked the specter of black violence against whites and criticized racial quotas. Between 1966 and 1980, on the other hand, George Bush refused to appeal to the white backlash, supported federal civil rights legislation, and favored using federal power to promote black economic empowerment.[45]

On abortion Bush has been similarly flexible over the years. As a member of Congress he became an enthusiast for family planning, chaired a House of Representatives task force on the issue and supported the liberalization of abortion laws. In the 1980 primary campaign Bush originally opposed the idea of an anti-abortion clause in the Constitution, but abandoned his opposition on becoming Reagan's running mate. During the 1980s Bush threw his weight behind the attempts of those on the right to overturn *Roe* v. *Wade*, the decision of the US Supreme Court legalizing abortion.

It was argued above that resolution was one of the great strengths of Ronald Reagan's style of leadership. To some extent this was a matter of perception. By no means was Reagan above compromise and, after his great tax-cutting coup in 1981, he was, in subsequent years, obliged to accept a series of tax increases. Nevertheless his abhorrence of taxes was never in any doubt, whereas Bush lacked consistency and commitment on this as on other issues, thereby exposing himself to charges of political opportunism, of being prepared to say almost anything for electoral purposes.

The budget crisis of 1990 may have shown Bush's approach to leadership in the worst possible light, while the confrontation in the Persian Gulf that erupted in the same year might be said to have revealed some of its advantages. Over a period of seven fraught and difficult months President Bush provided an impressive display of foreign policy crisis leadership comparable to that of John Kennedy in the Cuban missile crisis.[46] When it came to foreign policy Bush was very much a 'hands on' Chief Executive, but without being excessively so. He struck a sensible balance, it would seem, between, on the one hand, Reagan's sometimes alarming tendency towards disengagement and, on the other, the inclination for micromanagement displayed by Presidents such as Carter and Johnson.[47]

George Bush's propensity for 'networking' was another feature of his style of leadership that proved invaluable during the Gulf crisis. Throughout the various phases of his career he had assiduously cultivated personal relationships with those with whom he came into contact, showering them with thank you notes, telephone calls, Christmas cards and other tokens of his esteem. As President, Bush drew heavily on his large circle of friends in making staff and Cabinet appointments and, in other ways, made use of his multitudinous ties of friendship for leadership purposes, both at home and abroad. For instance, according to one account Bush participated in 190 phone conversations and 135 meetings with world leaders during his first year in office.[48]

In dealing with the crisis brought about by Iraq's invasion of Kuwait, Bush made impressive use of networking. It was essential to his strategy to gain the whole-hearted support of the United Nations and this was convincingly accomplished partly as a consequence of the President's skill in personal diplomacy. By assiduous use of the telephone and drawing on the wide range of friendships with world leaders he had developed over the years, Bush was able to hold together the international coalition required to bring about the defeat of Saddam Hussein. Throughout the crisis crucial resolutions were passed by a unanimous Security Council in support of American policy, in part as a result of Bush's networking skill.[49]

Controversy continues to surround both the circumstances that led to the Gulf War and its aftermath, but leaving those aside it is difficult not to concede that Bush provided impressive leadership during this particular crisis. With the advantage of hindsight it is easy to be critical, to emphasize the elements of luck and to play down the hazards that had to be negotiated and the desperately difficult choices that the President alone had to make. Under fire Bush appears to have remained calm, resolute and decisive. He stated his objective in August – 'this aggression will not stand' – and drove unflinchingly towards it, declining to be deflected by those who looked for compromise, wanted more time for sanctions to work, or shrank from the probability of large-scale bloodshed. On this occasion, at least, Bush's long and varied experience came into its own, even if some have berated him for his failure to place the defeat of Iraq in a wider framework of goals, for his lack of vision.[50]

Leadership from the White House quite obviously requires the ability to communicate effectively, but communication was not the strongest of George Bush's suits. Despite holding many more press conferences and making more speeches in four years than Reagan made in eight, there was never any chance of Bush being dubbed a 'great communicator'.[51] His friendly, informal style had its merits, but his patrician background and his often garbled way of expressing himself stood in the way of his developing the sort of rapport with ordinary Americans that Reagan enjoyed. After he had left office Bush freely admitted that he had limitations as a communicator. In explaining his defeat in 1992 he confessed, 'I wasn't articulate enough to overcome the politically driven, press-driven perception that the economy in 1992 was in deep recession. I just was not a good enough communicator.'[52]

As was noted earlier, in the late twentieth century Presidents unable to master television are badly disadvantaged and Bush undeniably belongs in that category. Unlike Reagan, he was not an adept performer in front of TV cameras and was not amenable to advice from media advisers. While his predecessor's staff constantly sought to get their man on television, those who worked for Bush were far less enthusiastic in seeking such opportunities. During the first 60 days of the Reagan administration the President was the subject of 399 items of major news network coverage, as against 265 such items during Bush's initial 60 days.[53] As one prominent newscaster observed in early 1989, 'This White House doesn't care if the President gets on the evening news or not.'[54]

We may presume that the reluctance of Bush to exploit the opportunities offered by television partly reflected his personal lack of comfort with the medium while also meeting his desire to lower expectations: to be something other than an expansive Chief Executive. Both from the left and the right Bush has been criticized for his failure to use his office as a 'bully pulpit'. By contrast, Reagan has been admired for his willingness to throw his weight behind major initiatives, using television to reach out to the American people over the heads of members of Congress. However Bush's disdain for rhetoric needs to be seen in the context of his view of his office. This was a President who aspired to lead no crusades and exuded respect for the political system. Rather than exciting expectations, as so many other Presidents had done, he remained deeply sceptical of government action as a vehicle of social and economic reform. In other words, Bush's lack of rhetorical flourishes on television, or anywhere else, was all of a piece with his guardianship notions of the way a President should act.

To summarize, George Bush's responses to the problems of statecraft, or governance, differed fundamentally from Ronald Reagan's. After years of public service he took up office as an insider respectful of the governmental process. Broadly content with the political and economic system as it stood, he had no inclination towards great change and was always reluctant to extend the reach of government. President Bush had little taste for the detail of domestic policy making, but when it came to foreign policy he was impressively 'hands on' – a strength that, coupled with his penchant for networking, made possible his success in the 1990–91 Gulf crisis. Finally, while his lack of vision, his reactive style of leadership and his limitations as a communicator would have been grave handicaps in an ambitious reformer in the White House, this was not the model of the Presidency that George Bush subscribed to.

Afterword: The Clinton Presidency

This afterword comments briefly on President Clinton's efforts to deal with the problems of governance. Unlike either Reagan or Bush, Clinton's electoral mandate was decidedly insubstantial: at 43 per cent of the popular vote, the lowest percentage for any President since Woodrow Wilson in 1912, although Richard Nixon in 1968 fared hardly any better with 43.4 per cent. Yet, unlike so many Republican Presidents in the modern era, Clinton enjoyed a victory in 1992 which was flanked by comfortable majorities for his party in both the House and the Senate.[55]

By background and pre-political experience Clinton is almost an amalgam of the two Presidents who preceded him. His origins were as modest as Reagan's, but his education at Georgetown University, Oxford University and Yale Law School was more akin to that of George Bush. Being Governor of Arkansas for five two-year terms imparted useful experience in governing, albeit in a small, poor, one-party state and, while it gave Clinton some claim to outsider status, the formative years spent in Washington, in Britain and at an Ivy League university made him something of a cosmopolitan.

In running for the Presidency Clinton positioned himself as a centrist, as a New Democrat, turning away from liberal nostrums such as the New Deal and its successor the 'Great Society'. Accordingly, Clinton has eschewed interest group liberalism and big government while advocating welfare reform, free trade and a hard line in dealing with crime. 'We must,' Clinton said, 'honor those basic values of opportunity, responsibility and community, of work and family and faith. This is what it means, in my view, to be a New Democrat. I was proud to campaign as one. I am proud to govern as one.'[56] As a New Democrat Clinton has helped to move his party along the political spectrum away from its liberal traditions; nevertheless he clearly rejects the guardianship, minimal government model of the Presidency associated with George Bush. As a fervent advocate of change and an enthusiast for positive government, Clinton has no doubt that governmental action can effect meaningful social and economic improvement.

In the 1992 campaign Clinton displayed almost Reaganesque talents as a communicator, including an impressive mastery of television that enabled him to overcome major weaknesses such as those related to his private life. However, whilst committed to change, it could hardly be said that he had campaigned with a vision, with a clear-cut programme of where he wanted to take the country. He argued in general terms for changes in the welfare system, for reform of health care and the need to reduce the budget deficit, but the specifics of most of his policy objectives are being worked out in office.[57]

It is also the case that Clinton's Presidency has not been marked by a high degree of resolution. In being less than firm in holding to previously ex-pressed positions on the issues, the present incumbent has been closer to George Bush than to Ronald Reagan. Campaign promises such as securing the rights of homosexuals in the armed services and a tax cut for the middle class have not been met. The President has backed away from appointments that have run into difficulties and failed to live up to various foreign policy undertakings, including his expressed determination to take strong action in Bosnia.[58] For all that, Bill Clinton was relatively successful in his first year in getting Congress to accept his policies. His intensely 'hands on' style and his gifts as a communicator allowed him to gain acceptance of his budget deficit plan and to win passage of legislation concerned with matters such as family leave, voter registration, gun control and national service.[59]

And then, in late 1993, Clinton enjoyed his most dazzling legislative success of all, when Congress passed the North American Free Trade Agree-ment. The President's victory in the struggle over NAFTA provided an illuminating illustration of the difficulties that statecraft poses in the United States. The crucial vote on the agreement took place in the US House of Representatives where, it soon became clear, party mechanisms would be of little assistance to the President. Party discipline counted for almost noth-ing, with the second and third most senior party leaders irreconcilably opposed to the plan; several major committee chairmen were also against and in the final vote no less than 60 per cent of Democrats voted no. Also arrayed against the President on this issue were core elements of the Demo-cratic electoral coalition, including blacks, blue-collar workers and organ-ized labour.

To overcome these formidable obstacles, President Clinton, after a falter-ing start, gave a stunning display of executive leadership. Skilfully using his office as a 'bully pulpit', he declined to bow to special interests and made abundantly clear to everyone his complete commitment to the agreement. Gathering together in the White House a clutch of former Presidents to support him, Clinton gave 'an impassioned, extemporaneous' speech on NAFTA of such quality that George Bush was heard to comment ruefully, 'Now I understand why he's on the inside looking out and I'm on the outside looking in.'[60] As the NAFTA vote drew near, Clinton swung into action to bring waverers into line. Dominating the media, exercising his considerable powers of persuasion in face-to-face meetings and via the telephone, striking deals and making compromises, the President finally won through. This ability to place the full weight of his office behind his stance on a deeply controversial issue was a capacity that Clinton shared with Reagan, whereas Bush lacked both the inclination and the skills required. For Clinton, however, the ultimate test of his statecraft was posed by the problems of passing health care reform. Even if it was only couched in general terms, a commitment to reform in this area was entered into during the 1992 campaign and was seen as the key legislative priority of the administration. The failure to persuade the 103rd Congress to act on his proposal was a severe setback for President Clinton.

Notes

1 Statecraft has been defined as 'the capacity of presidents to steer the political system toward outcomes that accord with their goals': Bert Rockman, *The Leadership Question: The Presidency and the American System*, Praeger, 1984, p.12.
2 See Richard Rose, *The Postmodern President: George Bush Meets The World*, Chatham House, 1991, *passim*.
3 Clinton Rossiter, *The American Presidency*, Harcourt, Brace and World, 1956, p.143.
4 The best studies of the Reagan Presidency so far are Lou Cannon, *President Reagan: The Role of a Lifetime*, Simon & Schuster, 1991; Martin Anderson, *Revolution*, Harcourt Brace Jovanovich, 1988; Charles O. Jones, (ed.), *The Reagan Legacy: Promise and Performance*, Chatham House, 1988. See also David Mervin, *Ronald Reagan and the American Presidency*, Longman, 1990.
5 Anne Edwards, *Early Reagan: The Rise of an American Hero*, Hodder & Stoughton, 1987, p.1.
6 See James David Barber, *The Presidential Character: Predicting Performance in the White House*, Prentice-Hall, 1972.
7 Peggy Noonan, *What I Saw At The Revolution: A Political Life in the Reagan Era*, Ivy Books, 1990, pp.187–8.
8 David Stockman, *The Triumph of Politics: How the Reagan Revolution Failed*, Harper & Row, 1986, *passim*.
9 Edwin Meese, *With Reagan: The Inside Story*, Regnery Gateway, 1992, p.14; Caspar Weinberger, *Fighting For Peace: Seven Critical Years in the Pentagon*, Warner Books, 1990, p.11.
10 Anderson, *Revolution*, p.279.
11 Donald Regan, *For the Record: From Wall Street to Washington*, Harcourt Brace Jovanovich 1988, p.250.
12 On Reagan's intelligence, see also Cannon, *President Reagan*, pp.136–40.
13 Hedrick Smith, *The Power Game: How Washington Works*, Random House, 1988, p.426.
14 Lou Cannon, *Reagan*, G.P. Putnam's, 1982, pp.305–6.
15 George Reedy, *The Twilight of the Presidency*, New American Library, 1970, *passim*.
16 Smith, *The Power Game*, p.426.

17   Charles D. Jones, 'A New President, A Different Congress, A Maturing Agenda', in Lester Salamon and Michael Lund (eds), *The Reagan Presidency and the Governing of America*, The Urban Institute, 1984, p.276.
18   Tip O'Neill, *Man of the House*, Random House, 1987, p.335.
19   Jane Mayer and Doyle McManus, *Landslide: The Unmaking of the President 1984–1988*, Houghton Mifflin, 1988, p.21.
20   Stockman, *The Triumph of Politics*, p.88.
21   Regan, *For the Record*, p.142.
22   Anderson, *Revolution*, p.210.
23   Terrel Bell, *The Thirteenth Man: A Reagan Cabinet Memoir*, The Free Press, 1988, p.32.
24   *The Tower Commission Report*, Bantam Books, 1987, p.80.
25   Anderson, *Revolution*, p.288.
26   Stockman, *The Triumph of Politics*, pp.229–30, 373.
27   Smith, *The Power Game*, p.383.
28   Anderson, *Revolution*, p.285.
29   See Jeffery Tulis, *The Rhetorical Presidency*, Princeton University Press, 1987.
30   Howard Stanley and Richard Niemi, *Vital Statistics on American Politics*, Congressional Quarterly Press, 1994, pp.115, 125.
31   On Bush's early life, see Fitzhugh Green, *George Bush: An Intimate Portrait*, Hippocrene Books, 1989. Early studies of the Bush Presidency include Colin Campbell and Bert Rockman (eds), *The Bush Presidency: First Appraisals*, Chatham House, 1991; Michael Duffy and Dan Goodgame, *Marching in Place*, Simon & Schuster, 1992; John Podhoretz, *Hell of a Ride: Backstage at the White House Follies 1989–1993*, Simon & Schuster, 1993; Charles Kolb, *White House Daze: The Unmaking of Domestic Policy in the Bush Years*, The Free Press, 1994.
32   Kolb, *White House Daze*, p.347.
33   Gail Sheehy, *Character: America's Search for Leadership*, Rev. edn, Bantam Books, 1990, p.179.
34   Green, *George Bush*, p.90.
35   Robert Shogan, *The Riddle of Power: Presidential Leadership from Truman to Bush*, Dutton, 1991, p.270.
36   Podhoretz, *Hell of a Ride*, p.153.
37   Rose, *The Postmodern President*, p.355.
38   Ibid., p.50.
39   Robert Ferrell (ed.), *The Eisenhower Diaries*, W.W. Norton, 1981, p.246.
40   Duffy and Goodgame, *Marching in Place*, p.65.
41   Podhoretz, *Hell of a Ride*, p.162.
42   Theodore Lowi, 'Ronald Reagan – Revolutionary', in Salamon and Lund, *The Reagan Presidency*, pp.29–56.
43   Quoted in Aaron Wildavsky, *The Beleaguered Presidency*, Transaction Books, 1991, p.320.
44   Martin Walker and Simon Tisdall, 'Bush Says Sorry for Tax U-turn', *The Guardian*, 4 March 1992, p.1.
45   Jefferson Morley, 'Bush and the Blacks: An Unknown Story', *New York Review of Books*, 16 January 1992, pp.19–26.
46   Dan Balz and Ann Devroy, 'Bush became a leader when it mattered most', *Washington Post National Weekly Edition*, 11–17 March 1991, p.9.
47   Campbell and Rockman, *The Bush Presidency*, p.99.
48   Wildavsky, *The Beleaguered Presidency*, p.315.

49 Dan Goodgame, 'What if we do nothing?', *Time*, 7 January 1991, pp.14–15.
50 See Daniel Pipes, 'What kind of peace?', *National Interest*, Spring 1991, pp.8–12.
51 Podhoretz, *Hell of a Ride*, p.197.
52 Martin Fletcher, 'Bush says Clinton has hurt image of US leadership, *The Times*, 29 January 1994.
53 Ryan Barilleaux and Mary Stuckey (eds), *Leadership and the Bush Presidency*, Praeger, 1992, p.53.
54 Lesley Stahl, quoted in David Ignatius, 'After Reagan the Media Miss Being Manipulated', *Washington Post National Weekly Edition*, 15–21 May 1989, p.23.
55 Stanley and Niemi, *Vital Statistics*, pp.115, 125.
56 Martin Walker, 'Clinton returns to his centrist roots', *The Guardian,* 4 December 1993, p.15.
57 Sidney Blumenthal, 'The Education of a President', *New Yorker*, 24 January 1994, pp.31–44.
58 'The year of loving dangerously', *Economist*, 15 January 1994, pp.23–8.
59 'What Congress Got Done', *New York Times,* 24 November 1993, p.A21.
60 Blumenthal, 'The Education of a President', p.40.

2 Congressional Oversight: The Development of Legislative Review

Peter Falconer

Since the adoption of the Constitution, the history of the governance of the United States has been characterized by pendulum swings of power between the legislative and executive branches of government.[1] Throughout much of the nineteenth century, Congress was the dominant actor in both the formulation and implementation of public policy. However, through the twentieth century, until the end of the 1960s, government power swung to the executive branch of government, with the ever-expanding nature of the federal bureaucracy in the wake of the New Deal and World War II together with the freedom gained by executive agencies as the recipients of broad delegations of authority by Congress.

In the early 1970s, Congress, in response to events surrounding the war in Vietnam, Watergate and the alleged abuses of power on the part of the Nixon administration, sought to reassert the authority of the legislative branch. The War Powers Act of 1973 was passed in an attempt to enhance legislative authority in relation to the commitment of US armed forces overseas, and the Congressional Budget and Impoundment Control Act of 1974 was enacted to restore legislative authority over the power of the purse. In addition, Congress established the Congressional Budget Office and the Office of Technology and Assessment as Congressional support agencies, strengthened the Congressional Research Service and significantly increased the number of Congressional committee and sub-committee staff. Moreover, during the 1970s and into the early 1980s, Congress imposed greater limits on executive discretion across a wide variety of policy areas through the use of legislative veto provisions. In such policy fields as health, environmental protection, consumer safety, transport and foreign aid, the legislative veto was employed to impose detailed and precise requirements on executive agencies' implementation of laws and programmes.

A central concern in the Congressional effort to reassert the authority of the legislative branch was the desire to improve the oversight capacity of Congress, the power of Congressional committees to monitor and investigate the activities and behaviour of executive branch agencies and personnel, including the President. Because Congress has a statutory right to oversee the executive branch, oversight is central to its work and involves virtually every Congressional committee. Over time, Congress has often affirmed its formal commitment to oversight. The Legislative Reorganisation Act of 1946 required all Congressional committees to exercise 'continuous watchfulness' over executive branch agencies within their jurisdiction. The 1970 Legislative Reorganisation Act was more specific: 'Each standing committee shall review and study, on a continuing basis, the application, administration, and execution of those laws, or parts of laws, the subject matter of which is within the jurisdiction of that committee.' The oversight power of Congress was further underscored by House and Senate committee reforms during the 1970s. In 1975, under House Resolution 988, many House committees were required to establish formal oversight sub-committees. Senate reforms in 1977 added the concept of 'comprehensive policy oversight', by which Senate committees were permitted to conduct oversight in areas which extended into the jurisdiction of other Senate committees.

However, despite its growing importance, legislative oversight as a Congressional activity is conventionally viewed as being a 'neglected function' of Congressional committees, taking place in an intermittent and episodic fashion, with what oversight does take place being ineffectual.[2] Indeed Congress has itself been highly critical of its oversight record. In 1973, the House Select Committee on Committees mourned Congress's failure to 'engage in anything like the beginning of an adequate oversight function' and complained of the lack of oversight activity as 'the greatest shortcoming of Congress'.[3] This neglect of oversight has, in the words of McCubbins and Schwartz, 'become a stylized fact; widely and dutifully reported, it is often bemoaned, sometimes explained, but never seriously questioned'.[4]

More recently, however, a growing body of literature has emerged which offers a more positive evaluation of oversight.[5] Indeed, somewhat paradoxically, an increasing body of writing is critical of oversight as being overly effective. In this work, Congress is attacked for its 'micromanagement', by which Congressional committees are viewed as intervening excessively in the details of administration, to the detriment of policy implementation. As Donald Kettl notes, Congress is thus criticized 'both for not overseeing the bureaucracy enough and for overseeing it in obsessive detail'.[6] This debate on the question of whether or not oversight is neglected by members of

Congress is, in large part, definitional, in the sense that evaluations of the conduct of oversight activity are contingent upon the way in which scholars have defined their subject. As such, an analysis of Congressional oversight must consider the fundamental question, what exactly is oversight and what Congressional activities constitute the oversight function?

Perspectives on Oversight

It is an unfortunate characteristic of the oversight literature that no agreement has been reached – or, it would appear, even been looked for – on the matter of definition. Beyond a general consensus that oversight as a legislative activity involves primarily the monitoring of the actions of agencies and personnel of the executive branch and the federal bureaucracy, there is no agreement amongst scholars on the fundamental question – what is oversight? Students of legislative–executive relations have defined oversight in various ways, each reflecting different normative propositions as to what oversight ought to be. Some definitions are very specific, while others are much broader, encompassing a variety of Congressional activities under the oversight rubric. In its narrowest conceptualization, oversight is viewed as a post-legislative activity, concerned primarily with the 'review of the actions of federal departments, agencies and commissions and of the programs and policies they administer'.[7] Advocates of this narrow definition are concerned primarily with oversight as a means by which the legislative branch inquires into the behaviour of executive branch personnel and the way in which policies and programmes are being implemented by executive branch agencies. These inquiries, moreover, are viewed as occurring in response to evidence of alleged misconduct on the part of an executive agency or official. As such, oversight is defined as a reactive Congressional activity, in the sense that it is demand-induced, consisting primarily of Congressional committee investigations.

Conventionally, however, oversight has been defined in a much broader sense, as legislative activity 'which results in an impact, intended or not, on bureaucratic behavior'.[8] Here we are faced with a definition of the oversight function based less on some set of activities which constitutes its conduct and more in the context of a broad set of goals and objectives which it seeks to pursue. Oversight is viewed as Congressional activity designed to monitor and check executive branch behaviour and, *ipso facto*, any Congressional activity which embodies this goal is defined as oversight. The vast majority of research on oversight views it as much more than a post hoc, investigative function, and holds to a perception of oversight as a continuing activity, occurring in a whole range of Congressional duties and responsibilities.

The most striking example of the wide range of Congressional activities commonly regarded as oversight is provided in the *Congressional Oversight Manual* (1984), produced on behalf of the bipartisan Congressional leadership by the Congressional Research Service. In advising members of Congress as to their oversight duties and responsibilities, the manual identifies a wide array of oversight forms by which Congressional committees monitor and review the executive branch. Most of these activities can be grouped into the following broad categories reflecting their goals: legislative; fiscal; investigative; evaluative; interpretative; supervisory; affirmative; prohibitive; and removal.[9]

Legislative Oversight

The legislative process itself, although not concerned primarily with oversight, generates a significant amount of review activity.[10] Committee hearings held to consider proposed legislation often enable a committee to question executive branch personnel concerning the implementation and administration of programmes or the performance of federal agencies and departments. In this way, investigation instigated for legislative purposes can provide valuable oversight evidence. Furthermore views expressed during hearings or in committee reports on bills and resolutions generally provide notice of the 'committee position' on their meaning. This may subsequently have a significant impact on the nature of their implementation.

The classic image of what legislative hearings do states that 'their most important function has been to collect facts so as to enable committee members to make informed judgements regarding legislative proposals'.[11] However the stress upon fact finding and legislation underestimates other functions performed in these sessions. First, hearings serve to heighten a member's interest in a particular issue, focusing attention on specific subjects. Second, assuming that a conditioning factor in stimulating oversight is a member's own assessment of executive branch personnel, hearings can represent an important forum for oversight by providing a 'testing ground' in which agency officials can either damage or enhance their standing with Congressional committees. Thus legislative hearings, though not central to oversight, serve as a potentially valuable oversight resource.

Fiscal Oversight

Fiscal oversight refers to the Congressional review of executive activity through the appropriations and budgetary processes. The strategic position of these processes as regards oversight stems from two main sources: first, the constitutional requirement that 'no money shall be drawn from the Treasury but in consequence of appropriations made by law'; and second, the Congressional power of the purse which provides the appropriations and budget committees of the House and Senate with the opportunity to play a prominent role within the policy process. Basically the oversight function of the appropriations and budget panels derives from their position of responsibility for the examination of budget requests from executive departments as an important element of the annual Congressional budget process.

The significance of the Congressional budget process for oversight lies in the continual review by Congressional committees of executive departments as part of the annual appropriations and budget process. The importance of this review lies in the fact that, for a number of federal agencies, the review of their budget requests is the only significant Congressional monitoring to which they are subjected. Thus the budget process facilitates the close scrutiny of various aspects of executive agency activities through the Congressional review of programme budgets and operations. For example, studies conducted by the budget committees may focus attention on an individual programme as well as on overall prospective revenues and expenditures. The 'interrogation' of official witnesses during both authorization and appropriations hearings can serve as a useful source of oversight information and may influence the direction of spending priorities. Furthermore the consideration of departmental programme requests provides the appropriations panels with an excellent opportunity to monitor the pattern of public expenditure. Finally specific directives or limitations incorporated through committee initiatives in appropriations measures can be used, not only to circumscribe executive discretion, but also to expand committee opportunities for the review of agency behaviour.

Investigative Oversight

The power of Congress to conduct investigations, the United States Supreme Court noted in 1957, 'comprehends probes into departments of the Federal Government to expose corruption, inefficiency and waste'.[12] Committee investigation exists as the most traditional and publicly visible method of exercising the Congressional oversight function, and its incidence has intensified significantly since the establishment of oversight sub-committees in Congress in the mid-1970s. Several diverse investigative procedures can normally be employed by committees in the pursuit of investigative oversight. Congressional staff – or organizations outside Congress – may be assigned to monitor particular problems or situations. Congressional support agencies – the Congressional Research Service, General Accounting Office and Congressional Budget Office – may be called upon to provide research and analysis of various aspects of executive activity pertinent to an investigation.

Investigation into the activities of executive agencies or departments is commonly initiated by a committee or sub-committee in response to a perceived problem, complaint or impropriety brought to the attention of members by staff, constituents, interest groups, the media or by executive personnel themselves (sometimes referred to as 'whistle-blowers'). Once it is decided to commence with an investigation, a variety of techniques are available to the investigating panel to enable it to secure information and uncover any evidence of maladministration on the part of an executive agency. For instance, the agency under investigation may be directed to provide information in writing; agency personnel may be required to meet Congressional investigators; or agency documents may be subpoenaed by Congress. The most visible element of the oversight inquiry is the actual committee investigation, which usually consists of a series of hearings following which its findings are made public. Normally these hearings are conducted in public although, in certain cases (usually on grounds of security), some part of the hearings may take place in private session.

The authority of Congressional committees to conduct oversight investigations is reinforced by two important concomitant powers: reporting requirements and resolutions of inquiry. The use of reporting requirements has escalated over time as a corollary to the increased concern with oversight on the part of Congressional committees. Almost every piece of legislation enacted carries with it requirements for federal managers to report to Congress on the status of a programme, a research project, or some other executive branch activity, in addition to the programme and budgetary information that each agency must compile and present to Congress at least once a year as part of the appropriations process. Reporting requirements represent a major impelling force which compels executive agencies under review to supply information required by investigating committees. High-ranking bureaucrats, particularly those appointed by the President, quickly get used to the fact that, regardless of party affiliation, much of their time in Washington is going to be spent responding to demands from Congress for information to be supplied through written reports and/or through personal appearances at Congressional hearings. The significance of these requirements for oversight is enhanced by the power invested in committees to issue subpoenas for the presentation of files and documents desired by their members pursuant to an investigation.

A further aid, not dissimilar to reporting requirements, to the conduct of investigative oversight by House committees is provided by resolutions of inquiry by which the investigative power of the House is sharpened. These resolutions, which can be introduced by an individual member, authorize a

House committee to request information from the heads of executive departments. The responsibility for providing an answer to resolutions of inquiry falls to departmental officials, either directly or through the President. As with reporting requirements, in cases where the executive branch resists a request for certain documents or information, committees may issue subpoenas for the required materials or compel executive branch officials to appear before a Congressional hearing. There are, of course, restrictions on the investigative powers of Congressional committees. Citizens are protected by a number of constitutional rights: First Amendment rights of free speech and association; Fourth Amendment rights to freedom from unreasonable searches and seizure; Fifth Amendment rights protecting against self-incrimination; and certain Sixth Amendment rights of due process. However these restrictions generally protect private citizens rather than agency officials.

Evaluative Oversight

According to the *Congressional Oversight Manual*, evaluative procedures 'are related closely to and may even duplicate certain aspects of items in other categories. Nevertheless, their importance justifies special emphasis.'[13] Without careful analysis and assessment, information gathered by Congressional committees about policy implementation and administration and executive behaviour may have only limited oversight value. Consequently Congressional committees have an important evaluative duty by which information is distilled into a more usable form, comparing and contrasting varying points of view, resolving meaningful conflicts, noting important gaps or discrepancies, attempting to measure accomplishments according to acceptable norms and determining whether Congressional purposes and goals have been complied with, altered or ignored.

Interpretative Oversight

In the conduct of its generally accepted role as the interpreter of, and spokesman for, questions concerning the purpose, meaning or scope of policies and programmes within its jurisdiction, a Congressional committee is often able to influence the way in which such policies and programmes are administered. In this way, according to the *Oversight Manual*, the oversight function is augmented, although it is conceded that the impact of these activities is difficult to evaluate.

Supervisory Oversight

When Congressional oversight authority is employed to help guide the implementation of a particular policy, the committee's approach may become more supervisory than interpretative in character, and may result in far greater committee influence than usual in the shaping of administrative decisions and actions. Clearly a large number of factors will determine the nature of the directive force which a Congressional committee is able to exert. Statutory powers, standing rules, precedents, mutual respect among Congressional and executive personnel, shared confidence and individual relationships can each enhance or diminish a committee's potential supervisory role. The *Oversight Manual* advises:

> effective stewardship over management activities seems to be more contingent upon vigilant use by a committee of all appropriate means of scrutiny, inquiry and appraisal than anything else. Significant agency reports and publications ought to be thoroughly analysed. Close liaison with agency personnel should be maintained. Proposed rules and regulations should be monitored and assessed. Major administrative problems and alleged wrongdoing should be investigated. Program evaluation efforts should be critically examined. Regular oversight hearings should be held.[14]

In short, every element of administrative performance should be subjected to constant surveillance and evaluation.

Affirmative Oversight

Affirmative oversight opportunities, although limited in number, stem from the Senate's unique powers of confirmation over major Presidential appointments. During the confirmation process, a Senate committee has the opportunity to subject a Presidential nominee to extensive questioning, seek assurances on future policy implementation strategies and propose that confirmation is contingent upon certain specific conditions. In some cases, the Senate may put pressure on a President to adjust his policy stance on particular issues by refusing to confirm a nominee for executive office until they receive certain assurances from the President.

In their 1988 study, *The Imperial Congress*,[15] Jones and Marini argue that the Senate's power of confirmation has pulled the pendulum of power too far towards Congress, granting to Congress an allegedly excessive level of influence over the executive, to the extent that the President is in danger of losing control over his appointment power. Recent Presidential experience with nominations, such as Reagan's nomination of Robert Bork to the

Supreme Court and Bush's nominations of John Tower and William Lucas as Secretary of Defense and Assistant Attorney General, respectively, demonstrates the willingness of the Senate to block senior Presidential appointees. The central question raised by Jones and Marini concerns whether the power of 'advice and consent' has become the power to decide. As Senator Howell Heflin stated in announcing his support for the Tower nomination on 6 March 1989, 'It's called the President's cabinet, not the Congress's cabinet.' Congress does have a legitimate role to play in the Presidential appointments process, but, *The Imperial Congress* argues, the sort of unrestrained inquisition which accompanied the Senate's deliberations in the above cases and which have come more and more to characterize the confirmation process threatens to transform that process into something of a 'show trial' of Presidential nominees, and places an unreasonable burden on the President in his selection of nominees for senior posts in his administration.

Prohibitive Oversight

From the standpoint of Congress, the oversight forms described so far suffer from two limitations. In the first place, they do not prevent instances of maladministration. As Sundquist states, 'oversight occurs usually after the fact; by the time the oversight hearing takes place, the administrative action has been taken'.[16] Second, with the exception that it may give rise at some later stage to new legislation, oversight produces advice and does not impose mandatory directives upon administrators. It is these twin shortcomings of oversight – too late and too weak – which impelled Congress in its period of resurgence to develop the use of a more timely and authoritative means of intervention in the administrative process, the legislative veto.

Emerging in the early 1930s as a technique of reconciling the President's wish for greater discretionary authority to pass to the executive branch with the Congressional desire to control that authority without having to pass additional public laws, the legislative veto was employed most extensively during the 1970s as Congress acted to reassert its authority over the executive branch. Legislative vetoes are statutory provisions which authorize Congress, or its committees, to approve, disapprove or defer the implementation of actions proposed by the executive branch in connection with the implementation of these laws.

> By reviewing resolutions of approval or disapproval introduced under such acts and by recommending action for the Senate or House to take thereon, a Congressional committee often could be instrumental in determining whether a 'legislative veto' should or should not be invoked in particular cases. During the

process of considering and evaluating resolutions of this type, a committee would have opportunity to exercise effective oversight.[17]

According to Rosen, the legislative veto served as the 'sharpest and most far-reaching (Congressional) reaction to limit executive agency discretion'[18] and, as such, represented an important means of ensuring continuing oversight of policy administration. A common component of most legislative veto provisions was a requirement that the executive agency responsible for implementing a particular piece of legislation notify the appropriate committees of Congress before taking action to implement policies pursuant to the legislation. Two main forms of legislative veto can be identified. First, either or both houses of Congress may adopt a resolution of disapproval which prevents the implementation of executive proposals concerning the administration of a particular programme or policy. Second, proposed executive actions can be 'vetoed' by the requirement that a concurrent resolution of approval is passed by both House and Senate authorizing these actions.

By the end of the 1970s, the legislative veto had become an important expression of Congressional resurgence, and gave rise to serious conflict between Congress and the White House over the legitimate scope of the legislative veto. According to President Carter, 'such intrusive devices infringe on the Executive's constitutional duty to faithfully execute the laws. They also authorise Congressional action that has the effect of legislation while denying the President the opportunity to exercise his veto.'[19] In opposition, the House of Representatives appeared ready to apply the veto universally in relation to a series of executive activities such as agency rule making, expenditure of appropriated funds and the deployment of military forces.

The legislative veto had been the subject of a series of lawsuits in which these polar positions had been refined and embellished. For example, when the Court of Claims upheld a one-house veto in the Federal Salary Act of 1967,[20] the Supreme Court refused the opportunity to review that decision on appeal. However, in another case, Associate Justice Byron R. White offered a dictum affirming the constitutionality of the legislative veto 'in light of history and modern reality ... at least where the President has agreed to legislation establishing the disapproval procedure or the legislation has been passed over his veto.'[21] While Justice White's statement gives little clue as to where the Supreme Court might stand on the issue, that stance became clear in 1983 when, in *The Immigration and Naturalisation Service* v. *Chadha*, the Supreme Court held that statutory provisions authorizing a one-house or two-house veto, and by implication a committee veto as well, were unconstitutional because they violated two constitutional principles. The one-house veto was deemed to contravene the principle of bicameralism, while the two-house veto violated the Presentation Clause, which requires that every order, resolution or vote 'to which the Concurrence of the Senate and House of Representatives may be necessary (except on a question of adjournment)' shall be passed to the President. In the words of Louis Fisher, 'the sweeping nature of this decision appeared to invalidate every type of legislative veto'.[22]

Removal

Congressional committees may become involved in oversight activity in the context of the constitutional provision vesting the Senate with the power of impeachment over 'all civil officers'. While impeachment is an uncommon event, its very existence, states the *Congressional Oversight Manual*,

> constitutes a potential oversight weapon tending to restrain improper or illegal activities. To the extent that any committee might be assigned the task of investigating or evaluating charges that could lead to the forced removal from office and future disqualification of an official of the United States, it would be engaged in an oversight function of great significance.[23]

This list of oversight forms and mechanisms illustrates the broad canvas covered by those Congressional activities commonly classified as oversight. Not only are Congressional investigations defined as oversight, but virtually every other Congressional function is viewed as involving or facilitating oversight to some extent. The legislative and budgetary processes; the way in which Congressional committees evaluate how policies and programmes are administered; the way in which Congress 'supervises' the executive branch through its statutory powers, standing rules, precedents and individual relationships; the Senate's power of confirmation over Presidential appointments; the Congressional power of impeachment – all these activities are identified by the *Congressional Oversight Manual* as constituting the oversight responsibilities of Congressional committees.

In terms of evaluating oversight, it is this wide conceptualization that has been adopted by much of the oversight literature and which has contributed to the common conclusion that Congress has failed in its duty to oversee effectively the administration of laws and policies by executive agencies. However, given the level of expectation contained within the broad definition of oversight, it is perhaps not surprising that conclusions predicated upon it are negative and pessimistic. Scholars of oversight have tended to accept the 'fact' that Congress neglects its oversight responsibilities and offer reasons for this neglect. Ogul provides a much-quoted statement on this matter:

No amount of Congressional dedication and energy, no conceivable increase in the size of committee staffs, and no extraordinary boost in committee budgets will enable Congress to carry out its oversight obligations in a comprehensive and systematic manner. The job is too large for any combination of members and staff to master completely.[24]

Lambro is equally forthright:

Congress as the legislative branch of our government has to a large extent abdicated its role and its responsibilities for monitoring and controlling the vast bureaucracy it has so painstakingly created. Not only does Congress lack the time, the interest or the desire to regularly conduct its myriad oversight functions, but there is a serious question of whether, with all its resources, it has the capacity to survey and control everything under its vast legislative domain.[25]

McCubbins and Schwartz reject this approach to the evaluation of oversight. They reject the 'fact' that oversight is neglected and offer an explanation for its persistence. They identify oversight as having been classified in two different ways: as what they refer to as 'police patrol' and 'fire alarm' oversight. Analogous to the use of real police patrols, Congress maintains a continuous vigilance over executive branch activities 'with the aim of detecting and remedying any violation of legislative goals'.[26] Conversely, fire alarm oversight involves

less active and direct intervention than police patrol oversight; instead of looking for violations of legislative goals, Congress established a system of rules, procedures and informal practices that enable individual citizens and organised interest groups to charge executive agencies with violating legislative goals, and to seek remedies from agencies, courts, and Congress itself.[27]

Thus, with police patrol oversight, Congress initiates oversight proceedings, conducting continuous reviews of executive branch behaviour to ascertain whether any instances of maladministration are taking place. With fire alarm oversight, oversight occurs in response to complaints concerning alleged executive wrongdoing to which Congress will respond. For McCubbins and Schwartz,

scholars who decry the neglect of oversight have focused on a single form of oversight (police patrol), ignoring the fire alarm alternative – and therewith the major part of actual oversight activity. ... The perception that Congress has neglected its oversight responsibility is a widespread mistake. ...What has appeared to be a neglect of oversight is really a preference for fire alarm oversight.[28]

The value of this contribution to the oversight debate lies in the identification of oversight as having been defined in two distinct ways: as an ongoing Congressional activity and as a demand-induced, investigative activity. Given that much oversight is reactive in nature, it is not surprising that those researchers looking for 'continuing watchfulness' are disappointed and forced to conclude that oversight is neglected. Yet studies which view oversight activity as essentially reactive conclude that Congressional interest in oversight has intensified over time, particularly in the post-Watergate period, and that what was once regarded as Congress's neglected function is now a high priority.[29] Sundquist points to the 'excesses' of executive power perpetrated by the Nixon administration as a watershed in the fortunes of oversight, with the escalation of Congressional concern with reasserting Congressional authority in response to what was perceived to be executive branch encroachment into the legislative preserve. Oversight came to be viewed more and more as a means by which imbalances of power between Congress and the executive could be redressed and as a way of reversing the loss of Congressional authority.[30]

Clearly the way in which oversight is defined has serious implications for its study. Ogul makes the simple but important point that 'assessment of oversight is conditioned by one's perception of what oversight is'.[31] The association between definition, expectation and assessment illustrates the major deficiency in research on oversight. In the words of Allen Schick, 'consideration of oversight has been hobbled by disagreement over its meaning'.[32] The study of oversight has in fact embodied the study of two distinct phenomena: first, the process by which Congressional committees conduct investigations in response to alleged wrongdoing on the part of executive agencies or the President; and second, a whole range of legislative duties and responsibilities which involve Congressional committees in exerting a degree of influence or control over executive branch behaviour. The former is more clearly identifiable as a distinct legislative activity, whereas the latter constitutes a more nebulous phenomenon, diffused throughout a myriad of Congressional activities. In its application, oversight pervades all legislative branch behaviour. It involves Congressional committees in virtually every area of executive branch activity, from the implementation of policy on the part of agencies of the federal bureaucracy to the behaviour of the President and his Cabinet. In Kettl's words,

> oversight occurs in a multifaceted policy world where competing issues are always struggling for a place on the agenda and where only a few of them will make it. ... Oversight [involves] questions of which issues will surface when, with whose support and opposition.[33]

As such, oversight will occur as members of Congress see issues which offer an opportunity for influencing public policy in accordance with their own policy preferences. Moreover members will weigh these opportunities in relation to the likely prestige that will accrue and the impact upon their reputation, both within Congress and their constituencies. Overall, oversight is inextricably linked with the politics of legislative–executive relations. It is 'one ingredient in a soup, constantly bubbling with new ingredients and continually stirred by complex political forces'.[34] So what sort of oversight behaviour has emerged from this policy 'soup'?

The Swing Towards Micromanagement

As stated above, Congress has over time intensified its interest in exerting control over the executive branch. George Bush and Ronald Reagan entered the White House more encumbered by legal constraints than did Jimmy Carter and facing the suspicious eyes of a Democratic Congress. Jimmy Carter was more limited than Gerald Ford, who was significantly more constrained by Congress than Richard Nixon. Since the 1983 Supreme Court decision on the legislative veto, the oversight pendulum has swung to a new extreme as Congressional committees have sharpened their oversight focus to the extent that they are now 'micromanaging'; that is, applying their oversight responsibilities much more rigorously and specifically, intervening in the day-to-day details of policy implementation and administration:[35]

> Congress has strayed from its historic role of helping to set the overall direction of the nation. Instead, in the name of oversight, it too often busies itself with 'micromanagement' – mucking with the petty details of policy execution. The agencies won't ever function well until Congress gets off their backs.[36]

Micromanagement can be seen in both the prohibitive oversight mechanisms which Congressional committees build into legislation and the legislative and post-legislative scrutiny to which executive agencies are subjected. In the prohibitive field, the removal of the legislative veto from the Congressional arsenal encouraged Congress to look to other prohibitive measures to enhance its oversight powers. As Fisher states, 'the conditions that spawned the legislative veto [did] not disappear' with the Supreme Court's ruling.[37] Executive agencies still desire a substantial degree of latitude in the administration of policy, while legislators still insist on the right to exercise a significant degree of control without having to pass further laws. Indeed the practicalities of legislative–executive relations 'underscore the gap between the Court's decision and the operational realities of government'.[38]

Indeed both the House and Senate regularly employ 'alternative' measures in their conduct of prohibitive oversight. For example, Congress retains the right to insert language within appropriations bills to deny funds for certain agency activities. Moreover members of both houses may attach legislative riders to appropriations bills. Since a President, without the luxury of a line item veto, is unlikely to veto an entire appropriations bill because it contains a rider with which he disagrees, the practical effect of such riders is similar to that of the legislative veto. In practice, therefore, the legislative veto did not vanish. The Supreme Court simply drove underground a set of prohibitive mechanisms which previously had been employed openly by Congress.

In the legislative and post-legislative sphere, many observers, both inside and outside government, criticize a 'myopic legislature', a 'micromanaging legislature', that places an abundance of restrictions on the operations of the executive agencies of government.[39] According to these views, the introduction of multiple control systems imposed by Congress on executive agencies, budgetary restrictions, personnel ceilings, legislatively mandated reports from agencies, the time spent by top agency managers repeating the same testimony to different committees and sub-committees, and a large number of other administrative requirements have significantly reduced the ability of administrative agencies to operate effectively.[40] Of course the idea of micromanagement is not new. It may be a relatively new term, but it describes an old complaint. According to James Q. Wilson,

> Congress is commonly criticised for micromanaging government agencies; it does and it always has. Because of its right to authorize programs, appropriate funds, confirm presidential appointees, and conduct investigations, Congress can convert any bureaucratic decision into a policy choice. What is new is that the form of this micromanagement seems to have changed. Congress is somewhat less likely today than formerly to make administrative decisions and more likely to enforce Congressional constraints on how those decisions are made.[41]

Whether it is characterized as micromanagement or vigilant oversight, one thing is clear: there is still a high degree of disagreement about the effectiveness of Congress's review power. One person's micromanagement is another's proper and effective direction which ensures administrative compliance with legislative intent. What for one person is the proper capacity of the executive branch to exercise discretion in the administration of policy is another's unaccountable bureaucracy. Yet, in its application, oversight effectiveness is too complex to be explained simply in terms of slogans about micromanagement or deficiencies in review activity. Rather than make statements about Congressional 'meddling' in the details of administration, it is more instructive to consider what Congress does in the way of oversight and why it does it. Why do members of Congress engage in oversight? Why are they driven to micromanage? The answer must be understood as part of a reciprocal process located within the balance of powers between the legislative and executive branches of government.

Referring back to the categorization of oversight as comprising 'fire alarm' and 'police patrol' characteristics, the prevailing tendency is for oversight to be reactive in the first instance. For oversight to occur, a problem in the administrative process must be perceived within Congress and must be viewed as serious enough to warrant Congressional action. Oversight is merely one of a large number of duties and responsibilities which make demands on a legislator's time. Consequently administrative problems must be significantly serious to trigger oversight activity on the part of members who will pursue oversight only where it is deemed politically profitable to do so. Moreover members will not actively seek out instances of maladministration. Rather oversight is demand-induced. Congress serves as a focus of complaint for the complex issue networks that operate within and outside Washington DC and from which allegations of misconduct on the part of executive branch officials emanate. Interest groups, the media, Congressional staff, constituency groups and even members of the executive branch itself will make Congress aware of instances of alleged wrongdoing within the administrative apparatus. Members of Congress will then make a political judgement about whether or not to engage in oversight activity. Thus, given that much oversight behaviour involves a response to specific details of maladministration, it is inevitable that, in pursing oversight, Congressional committees will be drawn into micromanagement, whereby the intensity with which executive agencies are subjected to Congressional scrutiny is significantly heightened through the variety of micromanaging constraints which Congress can bring to bear. Moreover, since 'control of administration means control of government',[42] it is not surprising that members of Congress, engaged in the struggle between the legislative and executive branches over political power, should find themselves driven to investigate the details of administrative activity. The swing to micromanagement highlights the fact that oversight, initially reactive in nature, may in certain cases assume a more proactive 'police-patrol' posture. Depending upon the severity of the problem or the degree of executive misconduct uncovered by a Congressional investigation, the executive agency in question may find itself the subject of more continuous oversight, as Congressional committees micromanage its behaviour to ensure that no such instances of maladministration will occur in the future.

Oversight and Divided Government

A commonly held assumption concerning oversight is that members of Congress are more likely to engage in oversight activity when divided government exists. Divided government – where the Congress is controlled by one party and the Presidency is occupied by the other – has become the norm in post-World War II American politics. From 1897 to 1954, divided government occurred only 14 per cent of the time. However, from 1955 to 1992, divided party control of the federal government has occurred 67 per cent of the time and 80 per cent of the time since 1969.

In what has become a common situation – Republican control of the White House and Democratic control of Congress – partisanship and policy disagreement between the branches serve as important determinants of oversight behaviour. This point has been well made by Morris Ogul:

> Sharp disagreement by congressmen with a new executive policy or with a substantial change to an existing policy provides a strong stimuli to oversight, even on subjects where scrutiny was modest previously. The more the legislator agrees with the program being implemented, the less likely he is to want to oversee; policy disagreement is a major stimulus to oversight.[43]

According to Aberbach, split partisan control gives the majority in Congress an incentive to harass and embarrass the President and the executive branch for partisan gain. Although members of Congress tend to view oversight as a less important concern than securing re-election or legislative activity, divided party control of the federal government heightens members' interests in the actions of the President and the agencies of the executive branch. Consequently members will be more zealous in initiating oversight inquiries into alleged executive branch wrongdoing. Hearings during the 101st Congress on the administrative practices of the Department of Housing and Urban Development are a case in point. Members of Congress who saw no significant electoral gain in monitoring the quality of national housing policies did perceive a large political pay-off in the media coverage given to legislators who uncover instances of bureaucratic misconduct.

Similarly, in cases where Presidents have acted improperly, Congress provides a highly visible institutional counter. Indeed the most publicly visible instances of oversight have been those cases in which a Democratic Congress has acted to confront Republican Presidents. The Congressional investigation of the Watergate affair; the impeachment hearings during the Nixon administration; the Congressional inquiry into maladministration at the Environmental Protection Agency (EPA) in the 1980s; and the Iran Contra hearings of 1987 – all these examples serve to illustrate the willingness of the Democratic Congress to employ its oversight powers to attack Presidents who are deemed to have acted improperly or illegally. The tactics and effects of this oversight are demonstrated clearly in the two most recent cases cited above.

Oversight of EPA

During 1982 and 1983, scandals at EPA uncovered by Congressional committee investigations resulted in the departure of 13 senior officials in seven weeks, five of them in one day. EPA administrator Anne Burford resigned and Rita Lavelle, assistant administrator for solid waste and emergency response, was fired. Congressional investigators generated a media barrage which helped to provoke a serious political crisis for the Reagan administration.

Ronald Reagan entered the White House in 1981 committed to shifting the responsibility for environmental policy management away from the federal government to the state and local level. Moreover the strong deregulatory posture of the Reagan policy agenda was aimed at reversing much of the environmental policy development of earlier years and returning the administration of environmental matters to an earlier time in which private interests largely had their way. Consequently the federal government would no longer have a major role in managing environmental policy. Reagan 'loaded' EPA with ideologically loyal personnel, many of whom had little, if any, experience in environmental affairs. Anne Burford, according to critics of the Reagan agenda, was given the position of EPA administrator in order to 'keep things quiet while she shut off the agency'.[44] As a consequence, EPA's capacity and willingness to implement environmental laws in accordance with legislative intent quickly declined.

The response of the Democratic House was swift. In what could be characterized as 'pack oversight', five House panels launched a major oversight investigation of EPA.[45] The Senate initially did not involve itself in the investigation. At this time the Senate was under Republican control, and the Republican majority in the Senate was reluctant to initiate oversight proceedings against a Republican administration. As the House investigation proceeded, the actions of the Reagan administration further fuelled the growing confrontation. Claiming executive privilege, a claim it would later drop, the administration refused to release documents subpoenaed by investigating committees. Moreover, when administrator Burford refused to comply with a subpoena issued by the House Public Works Committee's oversight sub-committee, the full committee and then the entire House voted her in contempt of Congress. This was oversight at its most assertive and, by the spring of 1983, Reagan's management team at EPA had gone and had been replaced by former administrator William Ruckelshaus, whose appointment marked the demise of the Reagan 'anti-environmental agenda'.

The oversight conducted in the EPA case was clearly influenced by partisan concerns. An analysis of the hearings held by House committees demonstrates a significant difference in focus among Democratic and Republican members. While Democratic members subjected witnesses to rigorous questioning concerning EPA activities, Republican members were more reticent, reluctant to uncover evidence of administrative misconduct. Moreover Republican involvement tended to focus on specific instances of wrongdoing, whereas Democrats were motivated by the wider goal of using the EPA issue to discredit the President and his administration. For example, following the resignation of administrator Burford, House Democrats were quick to state that she had not been their primary target. Burford, they argued, was a lightning-rod that had drawn attention away from the real source of wrongdoing, namely the President. John Dingell (D – Michigan), chair of the House Energy Committee and its oversight sub-committee, made the point that to blame Burford for the EPA scandal was wrong, since 'what has happened here has been a result of her simply carrying out the policies of the administration'.[46]

The partisan nature of the EPA investigation is further illustrated by the posture of the Senate Committee on Environment and Public Works, the Senate panel with principal jurisdiction over environmental policy issues. As stated above, when the EPA scandal surfaced, the Senate was under Republican control and the Environment Committee took no part in the investigation. However, as the extent of maladministration at EPA became clear, the Republican Senate, pressed by minority Democratic members, was eventually compelled to become involved. Nevertheless it was not until the Democrats regained control of the Senate in the midterm Congressional elections that the Senate Environment Committee became really active in EPA oversight, setting up an investigative sub-committee for the first time, something which, according to a senior committee staff member, would not have happened had the Republicans kept control of the Senate.

The Iran Contra Investigation

It was no surprise that the announcement made by Attorney General Edwin Meese on 25 November 1986 that profits from the secret sale of arms to Iran had been diverted to the Nicaraguan Contras triggered the most intensive legislative inquiry into administrative activity since Watergate. The administration's policy of funding the Contras through what Congress perceived to be illegal means led to Congress launching a major oversight investigation in which two select committees spent almost a year in open conflict with the Reagan administration. Hundreds of thousands of documents, many of which were top secret, were examined by Congressional investigators. Confidential messages between National Security Council staff were released to Congress and even made available to the public. Cabinet members such as Secretary of State George Schultz and Secretary of Defense Caspar Weinberger testified before the investigating committees. Even parts of President Reagan's own diary were released to the Congressional investigators.

In early 1987, Vice-President Bush objected to Congress's taking 'an increasingly influential role in the micromanagement of foreign policy' and stated that the Constitution did not intend that 'foreign policy should be conducted and reviewed by grand juries'.[47] So why did such intensive oversight occur? Fisher suggests two main reasons. First, President Reagan had failed to see that laws were faithfully executed, since he had failed to maintain control over his subordinates. As Fisher states, 'either he knew of the operations and authorized them, or he was unaware of what was happening in his own administration'.[48] It is not surprising, given this situation, that the Democratic Congress should become concerned. Second, even when the issue became public in 1986, the President failed to respond adequately. Indeed it was the Tower Commission which had to advise the President on what he had done: that he had traded arms for hostages. As Reagan stated in his address to the nation: 'A few months ago I told the American people I did not trade arms for hostages. My heart and my best intentions still tell me that's true, but the facts and evidence tell me it is not.'[49] As Fisher concludes, 'A President who wants to avoid Congressional intrusion has to exercise better control than that'.[50]

As to the nature of oversight itself, the Iran Contra investigation represents Congressional intervention in administration at the highest level. Moreover, as with the EPA case, the inquiry was characterized by a high degree of partisanship. Despite the serious nature of the issue, Republican members of the select committees were again much less rigorous in their questioning and deliberations. Indeed, when the investigating panels produced their final report, the minority Republican membership produced a minority report dissenting from the official Congressional conclusions on the case.[51]

These two cases of oversight illustrate that, under conditions of divided government, partisanship has come to the fore in legislative–executive relations. With different parties occupying the White House and the Congress, ideological differences, policy disagreements and distrust have intensified the propensity for legislative oversight to occur. During the Reagan and Bush administrations there was a sentiment expressed repeatedly by White House partisans to the effect that *no* legislation would be more desirable than any legislation enacted by a Democratic Congress. Such a stance, especially when countered by a similarly partisan Congressional posture towards the Republican White House, mitigates against productive, cooperative dialogue between the legislative and executive branches and significantly strengthens the willingness to engage in oversight on the part of Congress.

Beyond Divided Government: Oversight into the 1990s

When Bill Clinton entered the White House in January 1993, the Presidency and the Congress were both controlled by the Democratic Party. Given that the divided party control which had characterized legislative–executive relations during the previous 12 years had gone, would a new cooperative spirit emerge between a Democratic Congress and a Democratic President? Would a Democratic Congress be less willing to engage in oversight of a Democratic administration? During the Reagan–Bush years, the Democratic Congress initiated more than 25 oversight investigations into various allegations of executive branch misconduct. To what degree of scrutiny would the Clinton administration be subjected?

With specific regard to oversight, the most direct and visible means of holding Republican administrations accountable under conditions of divided government has been the Congressional use of investigative power. Recently, the issue of 'Whitewater' has emerged as an interesting test of whether or not Congressional Democrats are prepared to exercise these powers against President Clinton with the same degree of rigour as they demonstrated against Republican Presidents in the past. The Whitewater affair revolves around a highly complex and, to a large extent, incomprehensible real estate transaction and an unsuccessful land development company, the Whitewater Development Corporation, that was half-owned by Bill Clinton and his wife when Clinton was Governor of Arkansas. Their partner, James McDougall, ran a savings and loan business, Madison Guaranty, which collapsed in 1989, costing American taxpayers in the region of $50 million. At issue is the flow of money between the savings bank and the land development company, whether any of it found its way into Clinton's political funds, and whether or not the President has subsequently attempted to 'muddy the water' for investigators. In addition, a *Money Magazine* study of the Clintons' tax returns suggested that they could owe the Internal Revenue Service as much as $45 000 in respect of Whitewater dealings.

After Whitewater became public it escalated into a major political issue. In January 1994, President Clinton reluctantly agreed to the appointment of a special independent counsel on Whitewater in the hope that an independent investigation would alleviate Congressional concerns about the alleged wrongdoing on his part. However, by April 1994, President Clinton and his White House staff were facing the prospect of a major Congressional oversight inquiry in addition to the independent investigation. Why has the Whitewater issue exploded on to the oversight agenda in this way?

Part of the explanation can be traced to the White House's inability to manage the situation. The increasing Congressional attention to the Whitewater affair has resulted from activities occurring within the White House which gave every indication that there was indeed something to hide. When questions first arose about Whitewater during the 1992 election campaign, the Clintons stated simply that they had lost $69 000 in the real estate deal and declined to provide any further information. However questions continued to be asked when Clinton became President. The Resolution Trust Corporation asked the Justice Department to investigate the savings and loan concern owned by Clinton's partner, James McDougall. In that referral the Clintons were named as potential beneficiaries of the Madison Guaranty Savings and Loan improprieties, though they were not accused of any wrongdoing. However the White House's refusal to provide information only served to fuel the growing belief that Whitewater represented something that the President wanted to keep quiet. The growing tension was further exacerbated by the suicide of Vincent Foster, the deputy White House Counsel, in July 1993.

The first major flare-up came with the disclosure – four months after the fact – that Whitewater documents had been found in the office of Vincent Foster when he committed suicide. Had this been admitted immediately, it probably would have led to no more than questions about the appropriateness of Foster's handling the personal legal work of the President, but the four-month delay in releasing this information appeared as an attempt to conceal the presence of the President's personal papers in Foster's office and served only to seriously wound the White House. Moreover, when Justice Department lawyers investigating Madison Guaranty asked to see these papers, the White House again delayed in turning them over.

Further White House resistance to review of Whitewater revolved around the appointment of the independent counsel on Whitewater, Robert Fiske. President Clinton agreed to his appointment in January 1994 only after Congressional Democrats had joined their Republican colleagues in calling for an independent inquiry. If the President and Congressional Democrats believed that an independent investigation would prevent the need for Congressional hearings on Whitewater, they were to be proved wrong.

Following his appointment, Robert Fiske adopted a highly vigorous strategy in his approach to the investigation and, by March 1994, the White House found itself in a difficult situation. It faced an independent counsel who had taken the very bold step of summoning much of the White House hierarchy before a grand jury. Fiske's tactic of quickly employing his sub-poena power was a surprise to the White House. Fiske could have chosen a less public and less extreme strategy of interviewing White House officials, much in the same way as Lawrence Walsh, the independent counsel who conducted the investigation into the Iran Contra affair, had approached his task. However critics of the administration argued that Fiske was correct to proceed quickly, given the delays which has already occurred in the case and the allegations surfacing to the effect that documents had already been destroyed.

The nature of Fiske's approach to the independent investigation again reinforced the view that Whitewater was indeed a serious issue. Congressional Republicans, who had been the first to call for an independent inquiry, continued to argue for Congressional hearings as well. A leading figure in the call for Congressional oversight was Republican Representative Jim Leach, who argued strongly that the role of the opposition party is to 'kick up a fuss' when the party in power appears to act in improper or illegal ways. He made the direct point that Congressional Democrats had never been slow to subject Republican Presidents to oversight, so why should Republicans in Congress not demand that a Democratic President receive similar treatment? Making references back to Watergate and the Iran Contra affair, Republicans in Congress heightened their calls for a Congressional oversight investigation into the Whitewater affair.

Congressional Democrats suddenly found themselves pulled in different directions. On the one hand, they were keen to provide continued strong support for an administration that had helped to restore the popularity of the Democratic party. On the other, however, they did not wish to be seen as being less concerned with accountable and proper government, or appear unwilling to respond to allegations of executive misconduct. In short, Democrats did not wish to open themselves to attack for being unwilling to subject President Clinton to the same degree of oversight 'enjoyed' by his Republican predecessors. An additional pressure on Democrats to accept the need for Congressional hearings on Whitewater was the fact that public opinion was gradually moving in that direction. By March 1994, polls indicated that some 49 per cent of people believed that Congress should investigate the Whitewater affair. Congressional Democrats were not idle on Whitewater. Many leading Democrats urged the President to make changes to his White House staff through the dismissal of those who had so badly managed the Whitewater issue. Clearly Democrats were growing increasingly dismayed at the inept behaviour of the President's White House aides.

With regard to Congressional oversight, the first senior Democrat to join the Republican call for Congressional hearings on Whitewater was Representative Lee Hamilton, who had been a leading Congressional figure on the

Iran Contra investigating panel. Following Hamilton's 'defection', Congressional Democrats were gradually pulled into the pro-oversight camp, to some extent through deliberate choice and to some extent through miscalculation. For example, when Jim Leach threatened to question witnesses about Whitewater at a routine Banking Committee hearing in March 1994, the committee chair, Henry Gonzalez, rather than allowing the Republican member to pose his questions, cancelled the hearing on the grounds that he did not want Republican members to use such a forum to conduct a 'witch-hunt' against the President. Unfortunately for Gonzalez, the cancellation of the hearing appeared as a deliberate attempt to cover up Whitewater on the part of Democrats, and the Democratic leadership was compelled to commit itself to a full Congressional oversight investigation of the Whitewater issue.

Thus, President Clinton was experiencing a full Congressional inquiry into his involvement in the Whitewater affair. As regards the likely nature of this oversight, we can say at this stage that the affair is unlikely to attain Watergate or Iran Contra-type proportions. For one thing, the Democratic Congress could not be expected to pursue the investigation with the same degree of zeal it reserved for oversight of Republican Presidents. Moreover, it would be mistaken to liken Whitewater to either Watergate or the Iran Contra affair. These two famous cases of oversight involved serious abuses of executive power in Washington DC. The 'original sins' of Whitewater, if indeed they are sins, were committed long before Bill Clinton became President, and the Whitewater damage-control exercise pursued by the Clinton White House, inept as it was, was not, from anything we know at this time, an attempt at a cover-up. However, it seems certain that the Republicans with majorities in both houses of the 104th Congress will pursue a more vigorous investigation into Whitewater than has taken place so far.

Notes

1 See J.L. Sundquist, *The Decline and Resurgence of Congress*, Brookings, 1981.
2 See J.B. Pearson, 'Oversight: a Vital Yet Neglected Congressional Function', *University of Kansas Law Review*, **23**, 1975, pp.277–88; M.S. Ogul, *Congress Oversees the Bureaucracy: Studies in Legislative Supervision*, University of Pittsburgh Press, 1976; L.C. Dodd and R.L. Schott, *Congress and the Administrative State*, Wiley, 1979; D. Lambro, 'Congressional Oversights', *Policy Review*, **16**, 1981, pp.115–28.
3 U.S. House of Representatives, Select Committee on Committees, *Committee Reform Amendments of 1974, Report to Accompany H. Res. 988*, 93rd Congress, 2nd Session, H. Rept. 93–916. The committee reforms of the 1970s and their implications for oversight have been documented in a wide variety of sources. For an excellent discussion, see R.H. Davidson and W.J. Oleszek, *Congress Against Itself*, Indiana University Press, 1977.
4 M.D. McCubbins and T. Schwartz, 'Congressional Oversight Overlooked: Police Patrols and Fire Alarms' *American Journal of Political Science*, **28**, (1), 1984, p.165.
5 See J. Minsky, 'An Integrative Theory on Oversight' *Michigan Journal of Political Science*, **1**, (2), 1981, pp.29–56; M.E. Ethridge, *Legislative Participation in Implementation: Policy Through Politics*, Praeger, 1985; C.H. Foreman, *Signals from the Hill: Congressional Oversight and the Challenge of Social Regulation*, Yale University Press, 1988; J.D. Aberbach, *Keeping a Watchful Eye: the Politics of Congressional Oversight*, Brookings, 1990.
6 D.F. Kettl, 'Micromanagement: Congressional Control and Bureaucratic Risk', in P.W. Ingraham and D.F. Kettl (eds), *Agenda for Excellence: Public Service in America*, Chatham House, 1992, p.94.
7 Aberbach, *Keeping a Watchful Eye*, p.218.
8 Ogul, *Congress*, p.11.
9 *Congressional Oversight Manual*, Congressional Research Service, 1984, p.113.
10 See Ogul, *Congress*, pp.153–80. Ogul refers to oversight arising as part of the legislative process as 'latent oversight', occurring as a by-product of Congressional activities which have ostensible purposes other than oversight.
11 G.B. Galloway, *History of the House of Representatives*, Thomas Y. Cromwell, 1951, p.9.
12 *Watkins v. United States*, 354, U.S. 178 (1957),
13 *Congressional Oversight Manual*, p.114.
14 Ibid., pp.115–16.
15 G.S. Jones and J.A. Marini (eds), *The Imperial Congress: Crisis in the Separation of Powers*, Pharos Books, 1988.
16 Sundquist, *Decline and Resurgence*, p.344.
17 *Congressional Oversight Manual*, pp.118–19.
18 B. Rosen, *Holding Government Bureaucracies Accountable*, Praeger, 1989, p.62.
19 'Legislative Vetoes, June 21st 1978', *Public papers of the Presidents: Jimmy Carter*, Government Printing Office, 1979, pp.1146–9.
20 *Atkins v. United States*, 556 F. 2d 1028 (ct. Cl. 1977). The court divided four to three on the issue.
21 Separate opinion in *Buckley v. Valeo*, 424 U.S. 1, (1976). The case concerned the Federal Election Campaign Act. The court as a whole did not confront the legislative veto issue, and its finding that certain provisions of the law were unconstitutional was based on other grounds.
22 L. Fisher, *The Politics of Shared Power*, Congressional Quarterly Press, 1987, p.100;

see also pp.100–104. For an interesting discussion on the question of the constitutionality of the legislative veto and the *INS* v. *Chadha* decision, see also L. Fisher, 'Judicial Misjudgments About the Lawmaking Process: the Legislative Veto Case', *Public Administration Review*, **45**, 1985, pp.705–11.

23   *Congressional Oversight Manual*, p.119.
24   Ogul, *Congress*, p.5.
25   Lambro, 'Congressional Oversights', p.118.
26   McCubbins and Schwartz, 'Congressional Oversight Overlooked', p.166.
27   Ibid., p.166.
28   Ibid., pp.170, 176.
29   See Aberbach, *Keeping a Watchful Eye*; Minsky, 'An Integrative Theory', p.31.
30   Sundquist, *Decline and Resurgence*, pp.315–43.
31   Ogul, *Congress*, p.6.
32   A. Schick, 'Politics Through Law: Congressional Limitations on Executive Discretion', in A. King, (ed.), *Both Ends of the Avenue*, American Enterprise Institute, 1983, p.164.
33   Kettl, 'Micromanagement', p.96.
34   Ibid., p.96.
35   For a critical overview of the micromanaging Congress, see R. Fitzgerald and G. Lipson, *Porkbarrel: The Unexpurgated Grace Commission Story of Congressional Profligacy*, Cato Institute, 1984; E. Felten, *The Ruling Class: Inside the Imperial Congress*, Heritage Foundation, 1993.
36   D. Kirkpatrick, 'It's Simply Not Working', *Fortune*, 19 November 1990, p.181.
37   Fisher, *Politics*, p.102.
38   Ibid., p.102.
39   M.L. Goldstein, 'Our Myopic Legislature', *Government Executive*, January 1991, pp.10–15; 'Hollow Government', *Government Executive*, October 1989, pp.12–22.
40   See, for example, National Academy of Public Administration (NAPA), *Senior Policy Makers on Congress and Public Management*, NAPA, 1989; P. Fessler, 'Complaints Are Stacking Up as Hill Piles on Reports', *Congressional Quarterly Weekly Report*, 7 September 1991, pp.2562–6; L.G. Crovitz and J.A., Rabkin (eds), *The Fettered Presidency: Legal Constraints on the Executive Branch*, American Enterprise Institute, 1989.
41   J.Q. Wilson, *Bureaucracy: What Government Agencies Do and Why They Do It*, Basic Books, 1989, pp.241–2.
42   A. Schick, 'Congress and the Details of Administration', *Public Administration Review*, **36**, 1976, p.516.
43   Ogul, *Congress*, p.22.
44   Quoted in R. Brownstein and N. Easton, *Reagan's Ruling Class*, Pantheon Books, 1983, p.208.
45   These House panels were the Energy and Commerce Sub-committee on Oversight and Investigations, the Public Works and Transportation Sub-committee on Investigations and Oversight, the Government Operations Sub-committee on Environment, Energy and Natural Resources, the Energy and Commerce Sub-committee on Commerce, Transportation and Tourism, and the Science and Technology Sub-committee on Natural Resources, Agriculture Research and Environment.
46   Quoted in *Congressional Quarterly Weekly Report*, 12 March 1983, p.495.
47   *Washington Post*, 31 January 1987, p.A16; quoted in L. Fisher, 'Micromanagement by Congress: Reality and Mythology', in L.G. Crovitz and J.A. Rabkin (eds), *The Fettered Presidency*, p.150.

48   Ibid., p.150.
49   *Weekly Compilation of Presidential Documents*, vol. 23, 4 March 1987, p.220.
50   Fisher, 'Micromanagement by Congress', p.150.
51   For the most comprehensive analysis of the Iran Contra investigation, see *The Iran-Contra Puzzle*, Congressional Quarterly Press, 1987.

3 The Budget Process and Deficit Politics

Tim Hames

In the last decade Washington politics have in many respects been dominated by the phenomenon of a federal deficit of record levels. The President and the Congress have struggled to resolve budgetary issues and the sheer size and growth of the deficit have created an environment in which, in contrast to past decades, reviewing and limiting existing programmes has had to take priority over establishing new ones with additional spending commitments. The purposes of this chapter are to examine how the federal budget is produced and to address the following issues: how the United States has come in recent years to run very high deficits, with spending far exceeding revenues; what the political impact of these deficits has been and continues to be; and why a significant number of attempts to eliminate the problem have thus far run into the sands and not achieved their objectives.

The Making of the American Budget

The procedure by which the United States comes to acquire its budget each year is a magnificent representation in miniature of the complexity and the inter-institutional and intra-institutional struggles that so characterize contemporary American politics and policy formulation. It involves a familiar cast of characters: the Constitution, the President, Congress and even on rare occasions the Supreme Court. Despite the importance of the budget in a country where the federal government currently spends around $1.5 trillion dollars (or 20 per cent of gross domestic product) virtually everyone concerned with the budgetary system expresses dissatisfaction with the process and the consequences of that process. Nevertheless, despite this condemnation, the system survives and seems likely to continue.

The explanation for this apparent disarray starts with the Constitution, which makes budgetary matters the domain of Congress. This is outlined in Article I, Section 8 which states that the Congress shall have power to 'lay and collect taxes, duties, imposts and excises, to pay the debts and provide for the common defense and general welfare of the United States'. Section 9 of the same Article further states that 'No money shall be drawn from the Treasury, but in consequence of appropriations made by law; and a regular statement and account of the receipts and expenditures of all public money shall be published from time to time.' The latter half of this sentence represents the constitutional obligation to produce a budget.

The Founding Fathers provided one further obligation by asserting, in Article I, Section 7, that 'All bills for raising revenue shall originate in the House of Representatives.' By tradition bills for spending have also followed this constitutional dictum. The important item to note here is the absence of one key figure, namely the President, which might seem ironic given the commonplace usage of such terms as 'the President's budget' in the media and elsewhere.

For most of American history the activities of the federal government were normally so small and inexpensive that budgetary matters were not an important part of political life. In the first half of the nineteenth century all such matters were dealt with by a specialist committee – in both cases called the Appropriations Committee – in the House of Representatives and Senate. In the aftermath of the American Civil War, with the rapid increase in spending and, especially, government debt, Congress decided to divide budgetary decisions into two sections. In the House of Representatives the Ways and Means Committee was instituted to deal with all revenue (taxation) items, whilst the Appropriations Committee continued to tackle spending. In the Senate the Finance Committee now dealt with revenue, while Appropriations managed spending.

The Sixteenth Amendment to the Constitution, passed in 1913, which legalized a national income tax for the first time, and the increase in national spending and debt caused by World War I led to a major reassessment of the way the nation's finances should be organized. In response to the perceived inadequacies of existing practices the Budget and Accounting Act of 1921 was passed. This for the first time brought the President into the process by mandating him to present an annual budget for Congress to consider. To achieve this the Bureau of the Budget (since 1970 the Office of Management and Budget) was created inside the Treasury (since 1939 within the White House itself) to draw up the annual document.

In the 50 years after that Act the President seemed to take on an ever-expanding responsibility for the budget and increasingly appeared to shape its final outcome, although Congress invariably altered thousands of precise details. The White House achieved this position as a result of three factors: first, because Congress dealt with taxing and spending separately, only the President could claim to be dealing with national finances in a unified strategic manner; second, as the President controlled the Bureau of the Budget, and Congress had no equivalent, only the executive had specialist economic advice; finally, where Presidents did not like the spending decisions made by Congress they increasingly resorted to impoundment (ordering the relevant government department not to spend the money Congress wanted spent).

It was unlikely that Congress would tolerate this declining status forever. President Nixon (1969–74) had infuriated the Democratic party in Congress by impounding record levels of spending and the political void created by the Watergate scandal which led to Nixon's ultimate resignation provided the perfect political setting for Congress to reassert its powers. This it did through the landmark Budget and Impoundment Control Act of 1974. This act made impoundment without Congressional approval illegal[1] and established the Congressional Budget Office as the legislature's own economic think-tank to rival the Office of Management and Budget inside the White House. It also established a new timetable for the budgetary process and Budget Committees in both branches of Congress to oversee that schedule.

The 1974 Act largely established the budgeting system that the United States uses today and which will be outlined here. Some changes have taken place in the 1980s which will be referred to later in this section. In January or February each year the President offers his proposed budget which should take effect from 1 October of that year. The modern budget is an enormous item stretching to literally thousands of pages and containing nearly 200 000 individual accounts. On the taxing side it consists of one large bill containing all the administration's proposals for that year; on the spending side it consists of 13 separate spending bills. This document is drawn up by the Office of Management and Budget after extensive consultation and not a little confrontation between all the various departments and agencies that want funding. At best the President can hope that Congress will use it as a broad baseline for their own deliberations; at worst legislators may completely ignore it, which has often happened, and it may be 'dead on arrival' in Congress.

Regardless of the spirit with which Congress receives this enormous document it first has to produce a budget resolution. This is a non-binding guideline to the broad totals of tax, spending and debt that Congress wants to achieve. These totals are deliberated separately in the House and Senate Budget Committees and what they approve then has to be voted on by their respective chambers. If the two bodies approve different totals (which they usually do) representatives of the two Budget Committees meet in conference at which they hammer out an agreed compromise. That bargain then has to win majority support on the floor of both chambers before being accepted. If either branch rejects it then the Budget Committees have to try again. Why all this effort goes into producing advisory targets that are invariably ignored for the remainder of the budget-making process is in itself a worthwhile question.

Congress then goes on to decide the details, and hence the real totals, of taxing and spending. Taxation is a relatively simple affair. In each case one committee (Ways and Means in the House, Finance in the Senate) deliberates in its sub-committees and full committee proposed measures. They make recommendations to the full floor of their respective chambers who, it is hoped, will accept them; otherwise the committees will have to try again. If the two chambers have backed different tax bills (which they usually have) the two committees will hold a conference and agree a compromise and offer it again to their whole membership. Assuming this compromise is accepted, it then goes to the President. He could, of course, veto the entire package so, unless two-thirds of both houses vote to override his veto, the whole process has to start again, until something emerges that satisfies the Ways and Means Committee, the Finance Committee, the House of Representatives, the Senate and the White House.

The taxing side of the budgetary process is relatively straightforward compared with the complexities involved in establishing expenditure totals. This is because there are 13 different bills and each has to go through a process of authorization and appropriation. Authorization refers to the first stage, where the standing committees in both chambers make recommendations about how much should be spent and on what. These proposals go to the Appropriations Committee which actually makes the ultimate recommendations to the floor. This second phase is called the appropriations process. The two chambers can (and usually do) come up with different budgets which at a later stage will have to be moulded into one in each of these 13 cases.

To display the complexity involved, one example, the Foreign Aid budget, will be outlined. The President's proposals on Foreign Aid will go the relevant House of Representatives authorizing committee, in this case the Foreign Affairs Committee. They will send the detailed parts to their various sub-committees (currently seven) who will decide if they want to accept the Presidential figures or (more usually) to alter them. Their recommendations then have to be backed by a majority on the full committee. Once agreement is reached here, this authorization measure has to be supported by a majority on the House floor. Assuming this happens, their recommendation then goes to the Appropriations Committee which will send it to one of their 13 sub-committees, in this example the Foreign Operations sub-committee. That body will re-examine the numbers and usually cut them back somewhat from the invariably inflated bid that the authorizing committee has submitted. The sub-committee's recommendation then has to be voted on by the full committee. Assuming this new budget emerges from the Appropriations Committee, it then goes back for a final vote of the full House of Representatives where, it is hoped, it will be passed; otherwise Appropriations will have to try again.

In fact it is unlikely to be a final vote because in the meantime the Senate is also considering the Foreign Aid budget. In this case it goes first to the authorizing committee, Foreign Relations, where the components are voted on by its sub-committees (currently seven). What they pass then goes back to the full committee for approval and from there the backing of the full Senate has to be achieved. The proposals then go to the Senate Appropriations Committee which sends it to the relevant one of its 13 sub-committees, in this case Foreign Operations. They will reconsider the budget and usually cut it back somewhat.[2] Their recommendations have to be approved by the full Appropriations Committee. If they are, the full Senate must decide if it likes the outcome of the appropriations process. It can either reject it whole or (more probably) make amendments of its own.

The chances of the Senate and House now having approved absolutely identical Foreign Aid budgets are virtually nil. So members of the two Appropriations Committees, especially the pertinent sub-committees, will have to meet in conference committee and argue out an agreed proposal. This will have to be resubmitted to both Appropriations sub-committees, then both full Appropriations Committees and both full sets of membership. If both the House and Senate now vote through an identical Foreign Aid budget, it becomes law. Unless, of course, the President vetoes it. If there are not two-thirds in each chamber willing to override that veto, members of the two Appropriations Committees will have to reconfer, while discussing the issue with administration officials.[3] They will have to find a compromise that will satisfy the Appropriations sub-committees, Appropriations Committees, full House of Representatives, full Senate and the White House or, alternatively, at least two-thirds of both Senate and House so that a second Presidential veto can be overturned if necessary. It should be remembered that this is one example of a spending process that involves 13 separate bills, all of which have to endure the same political obstacle course.

Some attempts are of course made to impose discipline upon this process. Theoretically the task belongs to the Budget Committees established by the 1974 Act. In practice such centralization as does exist comes from the party leadership in the House and Senate. Their ability to persuade members to grant them some authority in this area has been helped by the sense of budgetary crisis that has gripped Congress for a decade. Years of divided party control of the executive and legislative branches has provided incentives for Democratic members to give their leaders greater powers, for fear that Republican Presidents, Reagan and Bush, might otherwise be able to impose their budgetary priorities through a 'divide and rule' strategy. However it is important to note that the inducements that leaders can offer members to obtain support for their proposals is strictly limited and discipline in Congress continues to be weak. Even when the leadership of both parties in both chambers are agreed on a course of action they may find themselves ignored. This happened most spectacularly in 1990, when a draft budget agreement supported by President Bush and almost all the Congressional leadership (House Minority Whip Newt Gingrich being the most notable exception) was unceremoniously thrown out by the House of Representatives. Coordination of the budget process from the top continues to be extremely difficult.

Given this procedure, which allows virtually all individual members of Congress to at least try and write the national accounts, it might seem amazing that the United States gets an annual budget at all. It does, but at the expense of coherence, as the separate parts are all dealt with so microscopically that the institution cannot keep much control over the big totals of taxing, spending and deficit (or, theoretically, surplus). The widespread criticism, therefore, is that the budget is not a carefully considered accounting document but just the final result of lots of different taxing and spending decisions that, when finally made, are just glued together and described, very kindly, as a budget. This criticism seems difficult to counter.

The Rise of Deficit Politics

As Table 3.1 illustrates, for most of the last two decades the American political system has worked against a background of significant budget deficits. If the reality of ever-present high deficit numbers is widely accepted, exactly what has caused them is much more politically contentious. There are a number of legitimate candidates worthy of study.

The fiscal position of the United States first began to show signs of strain in the late 1960s. In part this was because the very high rates of economic growth that had marked the 1950s, when most of America's economic partners and rivals remained crippled by the impact of World War II, began to slow as those other countries recovered. High economic growth increases government tax revenues, helping to keep the budget in order. President Johnson (1963–9) attempted to fight an expensive war in Vietnam while also embarking on a host of generous social welfare programmes. The most

Table 3.1 Fiscal years and budget deficits (billion dollars)

1976	66.4	1981	57.9	1986	220.7	1991	268.7
1977	44.9	1982	110.6	1987	149.7	1992	290.2
1978	48.8	1983	195.4	1988	155.0	1993	327.3
1979	27.7	1984	185.3	1989	153.4	1994	255.0*
1980	59.6	1985	212.2	1990	220.4	1995	176.1*

* Figures for fiscal years 1994 and 1995 are projections.

significant of these were the so-called 'entitlement schemes' of Medicaid and Medicare. Medicaid is a joint national and state government plan of health care assistance for the poor and disabled, while Medicare is a similar national plan for 'senior citizens'. They are called entitlements because by law any American who meets the qualifications (that is, poor, disabled or old) automatically gets the benefits every year and this must be paid for out of the budget. Since their introduction the number of claimants for both programmes – but especially with an aging population the Medicare component – has risen, forcing up government spending, with a knock-on effect for the deficit.

The 1970s saw the introduction of the Budget and Impoundment Control Act 1974 and the internal reforms designed to help control government spending and debt, through budget resolutions[5] and Budget Committees, have signally failed to match that task. As we have seen, the complex American budget process is hardly designed for tight coordinated control over spending policy but instead more closely resembles a bazaar where politicians bid on behalf of their favourite spending projects.

What rescued the system from endemic massive deficits before the 1980s was a phenomenon known as 'bracket creep'. Before 1981 the various tax bands (the levels of income at which the next rate of tax had to be paid) were not raised to take account of inflation levels (index-linked) but stayed the same each year. During an era of high inflation (which the United States had from approximately 1967 to 1982) nominal salaries and wages would increase to meet the inflation rate. So, for example, someone on $20 000 p.a. under 10 per cent inflation needed to see their income rise to $22 000 just to keep pace with prices. If in doing this they went over the next tax band (say, at $21 000 the tax rate becomes 35 per cent not 30 per cent) they would pay an extra amount of tax, even though they were not really any better off. Hence every year the federal government saw its tax coffers increase without having to pass a politically unpopular tax increase because inflation was doing their dirty work for them. By this underhand route the overall budget numbers looked tolerable even though government spending was being pushed up by entitlements.

Such a process was highly corrupting, in that it gave governments an incentive not to do anything effective to prevent inflation. It also provoked the great revolt against taxes by American voters which drove Ronald Reagan into the White House in 1980 and which is still enormously powerful today.[6] Once elected, President Reagan fulfilled his promise to end 'bracket creep' through a 1981 law that tied tax bands to the rate of inflation with effect from 1985. Meanwhile a combination of the Reagan administration, the Federal Reserve Board (which controls American interest rates) and a recession in 1981/2 all conspired to drive down the inflation rates from the double-digit levels of the 1970s to under 5 per cent by 1983, and it has stayed there virtually continuously since. This was good news, in that it produced lower prices and taxpayers stopped being cheated into paying annual tax increases. However it did remove one vital prop that had prevented the slide into budgetary chaos.

That slide grew much more dramatic as a consequence of the policies of the Reagan administration. Reagan entered office committed to a massive reduction in American taxation, a major boost in national defence spending to counter a Soviet Union that had just invaded Afghanistan and was threatening Poland, cutting 'wasteful' domestic spending but not entitlements, and producing a balanced budget by 1982. It was always over-optimistic of the administration to argue that the achievement concurrently of all these objectives was realistic. Nevertheless Ronald Reagan persuaded Congress to enact his economic priorities. His Economic Recovery Tax Act 1981 reduced tax revenues by some $160 billion in their first full year and by an estimated $750 billion over five years. Defence spending leapt by 17 per cent in 12 months and continued to rise until the middle of the decade. Cuts in domestic spending were modest and more difficult to achieve because of political opposition within Congress, and these totalled $37 billion. The Reagan administration, operating under the theory of 'supply-side economics', hoped that the massive tax cuts would so stimulate the American economy that the consequent boom would bring in much higher total tax revenues despite a lower tax rate. This it did to some extent, but not nearly enough to offset the overall reduction in government income and rise in defence outgoings. Hence the deficit, as Table 3.1 highlights, jumped from approximately $60 billion in 1981 to nearly $200 billion by 1983.

Essentially, despite a number of attempted cures set out below, the budget deficit has continued to average around $200 billion ever since. In years of stronger economic growth such as the late 1980s it has fallen towards $150 billion; in years of recession such as the early 1990s it has ballooned towards $300 billion. On present estimates it is likely to continue in this range until the end of the century, after which current forecasts suggest it will increase again. The impact of this sudden change in the United States' economic position has been profound for the nation as a whole and for the political system specifically. Whilst academics and analysts often disagree as to exactly why large budget deficits are detrimental to the economy's longer-run health, there are few who dispute that they are. Debt has to be repaid eventually and the United States has gone from being the largest creditor nation on the planet to the largest debtor in little over a decade. Repayments on the total national debt (some $4 trillion and rising) are now the second largest item of government spending after social security. Large deficits are also believed to have an adverse affect on long-run inflation and interest rates. They also undermine a nation's currency. Furthermore large deficits make tackling recessions harder because the ordinary response to an economic slowdown – higher government spending and deficit to boost the economy – is hardly practical or wise if the nation is already in heavy debt.

In terms of domestic politics the impact has been enormous. With such large deficits, and with an electorate that has consistently displayed its hatred of tax increases and willingness to throw out politicians who support them, there has simply been little or no extra government money available for spending in areas such as education, housing, inner city regeneration or a host of other proposals. This has been especially frustrating to the Democratic party which generally supports higher government expenditure on projects it believes are socially worthwhile. Indeed, by the end of his term of office, some Democrats began to believe in a conspiracy theory whereby Ronald Reagan had deliberately engineered high deficits through low taxation as a way of forever blocking liberal proposals to increase social expenditure. The continued deficit has been seen by many voters as condemnation of the operation of the entire political system and was a major factor in explaining the 19 per cent Presidential election vote of maverick independent candidate Ross Perot in 1992.

In foreign policy also the impact has been stark. The United States welcomed the fall of totalitarian regimes around the world as a victory for its long-standing belief in freedom. Nonetheless the huge deficit has meant that American financial support to help establish democracies and market economies has been pathetically inadequate. As George Bush rather sadly admitted in his 1989 inauguration address, 'We have more will than wallet.' The gloss certainly has been taken off victory in the Cold War and this was displayed by the conflict in the Gulf, where the United States had to ask its allies to pay towards the cost of liberating Kuwait. The most pessimistic view argues that the last stages of the superpower struggle saw not only the USSR but the United States fight itself to exhaustion and near-bankruptcy, although this is almost certainly an exaggeration. What clearly is true is that the budget deficit massively reduces the ability of the United States to use its economic influence and shape the post-Cold War world. Without full American participation, the process of developing democracy and market economies in formerly totalitarian states is put in jeopardy.

Given that the impact of ten years and more of high budget deficits has been so profound at home and abroad, one might have anticipated earnest attempts to eradicate it. There have actually been a large number of genuine attempts to tackle this fiscal problem. Between 1982 and 1993 there were no less than six efforts. These were the Tax Equity and Fiscal Responsibility Act 1982; the Deficit Reduction Act 1984; the Balanced Budget and Emergency Deficit Control Act 1985 (popularly known as Gramm-Rudman); the 1987 rewriting of that Act after the Supreme Court made certain objections in *Bowsher* v. *Synar 1986* (popularly known as Gramm-Rudman II); the 1990 budget agreement negotiated between President Bush and Congress coupled with the Budget Enforcement Act to implement it; and the 1993 deficit reduction pact passed by President Clinton and Congress. None of these measures has succeeded in eradicating the problem, although it is perhaps too early to judge how much of an impact the Clinton proposal will make. These attempts divided between those that aimed at a straightforward political solution by increasing tax revenues, reducing government expenditures or both, and those that sought a more complicated institutional solution by writing new rules into the budget-making procedure.

The Tax Equity and Fiscal Responsibility Act 1982 and the Deficit Reduction Act of 1984 were both political, in that they relied, in the former, on a major increase in federal revenues via a crackdown on prominent loopholes and, in the latter, on a modest mix of tax increases and spending cuts to bring down the deficit. Neither piece of legislation could prevent the deficit increasing to nearly $221 billion by 1986, although they may well have been responsible for keeping that figure below $300 billion.

Both Gramm-Rudman I and II were institutional reforms. Each created a set of deficit targets to be met over a five-year period until a federal balanced budget was achieved. They relied on a process of automatic cuts (called sequestration) to achieve those objectives: if the normal budgetary process could not meet the targets then the General Accounting Office (the Office of Management and Budget in the 1987 version) would order cuts to come equally from defence and non-exempted domestic spending until the required limits were reached. Many of Gramm-Rudman's backers supported it with a great deal of reluctance. It was widely viewed as 'a bad idea whose time has come'. Legislators voted for it anyway, partly to display to the public that politicians were serious about deficit reduction and partly in the belief that the proposed cuts were just so crude that the threat of them would force the President and Congress to come together and find an alternative, compromise means of reaching the deficit targets.

There was real hope that there now might be steady progress towards a balanced budget. Unfortunately for the Bush administration, falling economic activity in 1989/90 with rapidly rising estimates of the deficits (predictions for 1991 increased from $100 billion to $300 billion in a matter of months) rendered the Gramm-Rudman targets redundant. These disastrous projections led George Bush to abandon his 1988 'Read my lips, no new taxes' promise and negotiate a five-year $500 billion deficit reduction package with the Democratic Congressional leadership that contained some small tax increases. These were too large, however, for Republicans in the House of Representatives (especially) and the Senate, who revolted and voted the accord down. They then sat out the second round of discussions between their isolated President and Congressional Democrats, who altered the details and produced a final package that passed. The 1990 budget accord was an interesting mixture of the political and institutional approaches. The core of the deal – $492 billion deficit reduction over five years – was political. It relied on increased personal taxation on the wealthy, closing tax loopholes, a 5 cent federal gas tax increase, enhanced defence cuts, reductions in the growth of certain entitlements such as Medicaid and Medicare, and some smaller cuts in domestic spending. It thus represented the political priorities of the majority Democratic party in Congress.

To police the agreement the Budget Enforcement Act was passed. For three years this would divide spending into three sections (defence, domestic and international); for the remaining two years these sections would be merged. The law set out a set of spending caps which could only be broken for agreed emergencies. It required that any proposed rise in spending in one section be offset by another cut in that section (the 'pay-as-you-go' principle) and that money could not be moved between sections (the 'firewall' principle). It also set out non-binding deficit targets that would see the deficit fall to $83 billion by 1995. This golden scenario of endless deficit reduction never happened. The promised $492 billion reduction was wiped out by a $655 billion increase in the deficit by mid-1992. This turnabout was caused by a little emergency spending (3 per cent) and over-optimistic forecasts of economic growth (33 per cent), but mostly by a massive underestimate of the rising costs of Medicaid and Medicare (64 per cent). These terrible projections were increased further by the Bush administration just before it left office in January 1993.

The Clinton Administration thus came to office facing an awesome set of deficit statistics. This forced it to dilute drastically its initial hopes of reviving the American economy by a very large injection of government spending especially geared towards infrastructure programmes and high-technology innovations. These plans were to be watered down even further when Congress came to consider Clinton's proposals. His package, offered in February 1993, had to take account of the accelerating budget deficit crisis. For the current year he proposed an economic stimulus of only $30 billion (drastically down from earlier promises) divided between government works and an investment tax credit. For the next four years he proposed an overall gross deficit reduction of $493 billion divided equally (it was claimed) between tax increases and spending cuts. This was to be achieved by significant tax increases on the wealthy, an attack on certain tax loopholes, much higher defence cuts (an extra $76 billion), cuts in Medicare and other entitlements mostly aimed at rich recipients ($91 billion) and assorted domestic spending reductions ($54 billion). He also added one truly original touch, a new broad-based energy tax based on heat content (British thermal units) with an estimated revenue gain of some $74 billion.

This gross reduction of $493 billion would be reduced to a net gain of $324 billion by a $169 billion investment package consisting of $109 billion worth of new federal spending and $60 billion of new tax incentives. All this would have the overall effect of reducing the anticipated deficit by 38 per cent over four years. The Democratic majority in Congress wanted to pass a deficit reduction programme but was not wildly enthusiastic about the President's preferences. They refused to pass his public works plans for 1993 and dropped his investment tax credit. They then set to work on his long-term solution. They were happy to keep his tax increases on the 'super-rich' (earning more than $200 000 a year) and even happier that he suggested it, not them. His proposals on tax loopholes were welcomed, as was his significant increase in defence cuts.

The other elements were less popular. Congress scaled back the proposed cuts in Medicaid, Medicare and other domestic spending programmes. These were simply too difficult to accept for liberal members who wanted to spend more money on social schemes, not less. The proposed British thermal units energy tax proved unpopular with voters and key legislators and was dumped in favour of a small increase in the federal gasoline tax of 4.3 cents. It is a reflection of the strength of anti-tax feeling amongst voters that this tiny increase just survived elimination on the Senate floor in a 50–48 vote, despite the fact that it would cost the average motorist only $27.60 annually in a country with among the cheapest petrol prices in the world and at a time when American gasoline prices are at their lowest in inflation-adjusted terms since 1945. To make up for these changes, Congress voted to reduce the new spending the President had proposed from $169 billion to $53 billion and introduce a slightly gimmicky one-year freeze on all discretionary domestic spending. They also changed it from a four-year to five-year timescale. At the end of all this, Congress managed to pass a budget (by 218 to 216 in the House of Representatives and with Vice-President Gore's casting vote in the Senate) that planned to cut the deficit by a total of $496 billion over five years.

Both the overall totals and the individual elements of the final 1993 deficit reduction agreed by Clinton and Congress look very similar to the $492 billion five-year deal agreed by Bush and Congress. Both relied on tax increases on the rich, a small rise in the gasoline tax, defence cuts, modest entitlements reform and some domestic cuts. The main impact of having a Democrat in the Oval Office was that taxation on the wealthy and defence cuts were a little higher and genuine domestic spending reduction a little lower than was the case with President Bush. This combination of very limited tax increases and selective spending reductions appears to be the maximum politically feasible in present-day America. Of course the Bush proposals were blown off course because of lower than expected economic growth and higher entitlements payments. It is perfectly possible that the 1993 version will suffer a similar fate. Even if all its economic assumptions were to prove valid, the Clinton plan only expects deficits to fall to the $150 billion range by the end of this century at which point the increasing costs of providing health benefits to the elderly will drive them up again.

So it seems likely that the overall influence of the 1993 budget will be modest. It will reduce the net increase in national debt over its period from $1.6 trillion to $1.1 trillion, but that still suggests a total debt of over $5 trillion by the year 2000. Without very high economic growth or effective containment of health care costs it cannot be expected to better this. Like its predecessors, the Tax Equity and Fiscal Responsibility Act 1982, the Deficit Reduction Act of 1984, the various Gramm-Rudman notions and the 1990 Bush/Congress pact, the best than can probably be said of it, and it is not without value, is that it prevented a rather bad situation getting truly terrible; but the continuing straitjacket of the deficit on domestic politics, policy making and foreign policy seems unlikely to be eased.

Future Policy Initiatives

Given that the best the conventional political process appears able to produce is periodic – and unpopular – deals that at most moderate the seemingly ceaseless rise in the budget deficit, and given that there is virtually unanimous support for the view that this is a highly unsatisfactory outcome, it seems likely that pressure will grow for substantial institutional change. Whilst most legislators would strongly support the principles upon which the Budget and Impoundment Control Act 1974 was based, that is that Congress should be, as the Constitution states, the engine of the fiscal process, few would argue that the actual mechanics of the Act work well and suit modern times. However getting beyond the consensus that the present system does not work well towards an agreed alternative is much more difficult. At least five ideas outlined below have received widespread discussion. As will become apparent, none commands political consensus and all have their drawbacks. The first three suggestions here focus predominantly on internal changes in the way that Congress organizes the budget-making process; the final two are much more radical and would require amendment of the Constitution itself.

As we have seen in the first part of this chapter, the way that Congress organizes its spending with decisions made by both authorising committees and the Appropriations Committees via a host of sub-committees is hardly a streamlined model of efficiency. It involves so many individual Congressmen who invariably want to spend money on their own district or pet project (most frequently their own pet project in their own district) that maintaining control of spending is very difficult. One suggestion for reform, therefore, is to increase massively the power of the Appropriations Committees and consequently reduce the role of authorizing committees. One widely canvassed version of this would put all budgetary decisions solely in the hands of Appropriations, allowing present authorizing committees merely to fill in the precise details of where and on what the money would be spent. A truly draconian approach would not even allow them that power. Were this enacted, the Budget Committees introduced by the 1974 Act would be largely irrelevant and could be scrapped.

Supporters of this approach believe that by having a smaller number of politicians involved in the process (60 House members sit on Appropriations, twenty-nine in the Senate) the process would be made much more coherent. This would be further strengthened if the informal rule of 40 years ago[7] – that members did not sit on Appropriations sub-committees where the interests of their own districts were involved – could be revived. They also point to previous times in Congressional history where control over the purse-strings did lie more squarely with the Appropriations Committees and spending seemed to be much more tightly monitored.

On the face of it, this sounds quite sensible, but it has many critics. Many liberal Democrats argue that it tackles the deficit problem from the wrong direction. The problem, they would claim, is not that the United States spends too much (rather the opposite, many liberals believe) but that it refuses to raise enough taxes to pay for generally valuable expenditure. What is needed then is institutional reform or, more probably, political will to increase the tax base. The same people would also point out that the so-called halcyon days of Appropriations Committee control and fiscal prudence were the result of the committee being dominated by conservative

Southern Democrats. Recreating centralized control in the modern era, when the Democratic party has changed so much, would not produce the same political outcome.

Finally there is the blatantly political assessment. Just how likely is it that Congress will vote to end the present system whereby nearly all members (certainly all majority party members) have the chance to influence spending decisions and to institute a world in which control is passed to a minority of their membership? The cynic, who generally gets a good return from Congressional politics, would say 'fat chance', and probably be right.

A second suggestion focuses on a different problem in the present system. At the moment the only chances Congress gets to contemplate the overall levels of total spending, taxing and deficit are right at the beginning of the process, through the opening budget resolution, and right at the end, when it votes on the final figures. Because the budget resolution is only advisory it is habitually ignored afterwards and, by the time that the final vote comes, it is rather late in the day to discover that the process has produced an unsatisfactory result. Some reformers would make the budget resolution a legally compulsory instruction to Congress to produce a budget within those targets. The tougher version of this idea would let the President veto a resolution he thought too soft on debt.

Through this means the system of authorizing and appropriating so loved by politicians could continue, but would centre on the details of previously agreed overall numbers. This, it is asserted, would make policy much more coherent. This proposal also has drawbacks, although most of them are political rather than practical. It is unclear why Congress should be any more likely to vote for tax increases or spending cuts with this formula. The present situation that has months of political argument following a non-binding budget resolution may simply be replaced by one that has months of argument in advance of a binding resolution. The possibility of utter stalemate between the President and Congress completely paralysing the whole system would be enhanced. Further, as control over the budget resolution currently lies primarily with the 37-member Budget Committee and with the party leaderships, the idea may not appeal to other members.

The third and final internal scheme is concerned with the fact that so many important budgetary decisions are rushed into a relatively small amount of Congressional time. In an ideal world the merits of each individual spending proposal should be contemplated and an analysis made of its real worth. In reality the frenzy to make a budget somewhere close to the deadline overcomes all that. It has therefore been suggested that a two-year rather than annual budget cycle be adopted to allow much more time for these decisions and to permit a greater degree of strategic planning. This idea has been strongly backed by Vice-President Albert Gore Jr. in his

National Performance Review (or 'reinventing government' exercise). Although the proposal has certain merits, it has its drawbacks as well. It is not entirely certain that, of all the many problems with the way that the budget is currently assembled, the time factor is the most important. Critics charge that in practice it is difficult to plan a budget so far ahead and Congress would always be voting to change parts of it as it became obvious that circumstances had changed. It is not axiomatic that giving politicians longer to think about decisions ensures that they will make much better ones. Nor is it certain why the adoption of this formula will lead to much lower budget deficits.

That leaves two much more radical possibilities, a line item veto for the White House, or a Balanced Budget Amendment to the Constitution. At present the President, unlike 43 state Governors,[8] has to accept or reject budgetary measures in their entirety, even if he thinks that certain items within them are good value while others are extravagant. In most states Governors can veto individual items they object to (subject to legislative override) and keep other elements. Supporters of this line item veto believe it exercises a strong control over wasteful, politically inspired expenditure. Hence the proposal's backers, which include Ronald Reagan, George Bush and (more quietly) Bill Clinton, believe that giving the White House constitutional authority to strike out individual details of spending would lead to much lower deficits.

Once again this proposition has its opponents. Liberals would again argue that the problem is not too much spending but too little tax. Others would point out that by far the biggest sections of government spending are entitlements which must be paid to qualified citizens each year by law and which would therefore be beyond the scope of the line item veto. Others would dispute the amount of money which has been saved in the states by its deployment. Critics claim that, rather than reducing expenditure, the line item veto would simply replace Congressional spending priorities with those of the President. In this respect the change would have truly fundamental consequences for the separation of powers principle.

This leaves the possibility of a Balanced Budget Amendment to the Constitution. This is again based on the provision in state constitutions that government expenditures must be matched by revenues.[9] This is the ultimate 'big fix' in that it would require that Congress always set a balanced budget except in certain emergency situations where an extraordinary majority in the legislature could vote to bypass the rule. The latest attempt (March 1994) to force it through Congress failed to reach the necessary two-thirds level by just four votes in the Senate and 12 in the House of Representatives. Significantly virtually all members of the Republican party supported it and the party supported the proposal in the 1994 elections.

Backers of the idea claim it would force Congress to actually solve the deficit problem and stop putting off hard decisions.

There are large numbers of opponents. They claim that many states find ways of effectively avoiding their obligations and Washington would do the same. They question whether it is really good public policy to have a balanced budget every year anyway, pointing out that most nations run modest deficits. Some purists object to using the Constitution to force politicians to do what as responsible representatives they should do anyway. The most powerful argument notes that such an amendment would do nothing to explain how the United States would reach a balanced budget; which taxes would be raised and which programmes would be cut? The states look at the whole notion nervously, suspecting, correctly, that the easiest way for Congress to get a balanced budget would be by transferring large numbers of expensive programmes currently run by the centre back to the states and getting them to make the difficult decisions over how to fund them.

Although the implications of a Balanced Budget Amendment are really immense, it is nevertheless a bold and radical move that commands very strong support amongst the voters. How the same electorate would feel when some of the measures it would oblige actually happened is likely to be another story. Its passage would allow Congress to say that it has 'fixed' the deficit and leave untouched the internal procedures of authorizing and appropriating, just adding the final obligation that the ultimate numbers broadly balance. It gives the impression that the political system has finally turned the tide of debt. Although it is in many ways a deeply dubious idea, if Bill Clinton's 1993 deficit reduction package proves no more successful than George Bush's effort of 1990 then the Amendment has a real chance of being accepted by Congress. It would then go to the state legislatures for consideration. They would be trapped between their own suspicions of its impact and the strong public support that opinion polls consistently show the measure has. The final result could be very close indeed.

This chapter has examined how the American budget is made, why there has been a strong trend towards large budget deficits, the impact those deficits have had, why solutions have not thus far been found and what the possible future options are.[10] One matter does seem near certain. The budget process and deficit politics have been absolutely central to an understanding of American politics during the presidencies of Ronald Reagan and George Bush. This is likely to prove true for Bill Clinton and at least his immediate successor as well.

Notes

1   The 1974 Act allowed permanent impoundment (rescissions) only if both branches of Congress agreed and temporary impoundment (deferrals) if at least one branch assented.

2   Because authorizing committees usually consist of members whose districts' interests coincide with the committee's subject matter, they usually want maximum spending. Hence Appropriations sees part of its role as eliminating the worst of this special pleading.

3   In many years the 13 bills are late and actually go to the President together as one enormous continuing resolution, thousands of pages long, which the President cannot veto without bringing the entire Federal Government to a halt.

4   American fiscal years run from 1 October to 30 September. Hence fiscal year 1995 starts on 1 October 1994 and runs to 30 September 1995.

5   The 1974 Act also had a second budget resolution meant to conclude the procedure. However this rapidly became just a rubber stamp for whatever the inter-branch conference had agreed, and it was abandoned in 1985.

6   The extent of anti-tax sentiment can still be seen in the public distaste for President Clinton's 1993 budget, even though it contained minimal tax increases for most citizens, and in the 1993 defeat of Governor James Florio, Democrat of New Jersey who significantly increased taxes.

7   This was known as the Cannon–Taber norm, after its chief Congressional sponsors.

8   This includes the Governor of Maryland, who has only limited line item veto powers.

9   Only Vermont operates without any kind of budget constraint.

10   For further reading on federal budgetary issues see John Marini, *The Politics of Budget Control*, Crane Russat, 1992; Howard Shuman, *Politics and the Budget*, Prentice Hall, 1992; Marvin Kostes, *Fiscal Politics and the Budget Enforcement Act*, American Enterprise Institute, 1992; Allen Schick, *The Capacity to Budget*, Urban Institute Press, 1990.

4 Legislative Careerism and the Term Limitation Movement

Alan Grant

As the 103rd Congress assembled in Washington DC in January 1993, talk among the members was not only about their recent campaigns and the election of the first Democratic President since 1976, but also about a new, and to some disturbing, phenomenon that had made its mark on the political landscape. A third of the members arriving on Capitol Hill were doing so with the voters of their states having imposed legal restrictions on the number of years they could serve in office. Many other Congressmen could also expect that this populist brushfire would sweep across the country in the coming years and affect them as well. In November 1992, electors in 14 states, 12 of them with overwhelming majorities, had voted through the initiative process to introduce term limits for federal legislators, thus joining Colorado, which had led the way in 1990. In addition many state law-makers and members in local government, including big cities such as New York and Los Angeles, were also served notice by the voters that their legislative and council careers would be foreshortened.

The passage of term limitations initiatives in the early 1990s was a clear reflection of the fact that Congress had sunk to a new low point in public esteem. Voters were angry and cynical, questioning the integrity and effectiveness of the national legislature. In July 1992 a CBS News/*New York Times* poll indicated that 71 per cent of respondents disapproved of the way Congress was doing its job, while approximately one-third said that they would almost never trust Congress to do the right thing. When one examines the recent history of Congress and the problems facing the nation it is easy to see why the electorate had become frustrated with 'politics as usual'. A long list of scandals had hit the national headlines, many of them involving some of the most senior and powerful leaders in Congress, and members had granted themselves large pay increases while at the same time apparent deadlock in government meant a failure to deal effectively with the nation's most urgent and important problems.

In June 1989, two of the top party leaders in Congress, House Speaker Jim Wright and Democratic Majority Whip Tony Coelho, were forced to resign following unrelated cases where they had abused their positions or broken House rules for personal gain. In 1991, five US Senators were severely criticized by the Senate Ethics Committee for their improper inter-vention with federal regulators on behalf of Charles Keating, the head of a savings and loan empire and a major contributor to their re-election cam-paign funds. Two other Senators were also accused of the misuse of public money or trying to use their influence to benefit relatives or campaign contributors. In May 1994, the Chairman of the powerful House Ways and Means Committee, Dan Rostenkowski, was indicted by a federal grand jury on 17 corruption charges, including the embezzlement of funds at the House post office. What all these individuals had in common was that they were prime examples of career politicians with many years' seniority who had demonstrated an arrogance that can come from long periods in power, usually without effective challenge.

In 1991, it was revealed that 325 current and former members of the House of Representatives had abused the privilege of having their own bank on Capitol Hill by routinely floating bad cheques and maintaining over-drafts without incurring any bank charges, a story that infuriated the public, who saw this as an example of legislators being prepared to play by differ-ent and more favourable rules from those that the rest of the community has to operate by. What is more, following the resignation of Speaker Wright, Congressmen voted themselves a large pay increase in return for giving up the right to receive honoraria for making speeches to or attending seminars arranged by outside organizations.[1] Public anger at this move led to the passage in 1992 of the Twenty-Seventh Amendment to the Constitution (first mooted over 200 years ago) that delays the implementation of any new increase in Congressional salaries until after an election has been held. As Christopher Bailey has pointed out, while scandals affecting Congress are nothing new, the spate of recent allegations has served to focus concern on the performance of Congress as an institution while, in an increasingly partisan climate, discussion about substantive issues and problems has often taken second place to debates about ethics.[2]

Failure of politicians to deal with the spiralling federal deficit and the pain of economic recession served to create a mood of disenchantment among the voters which Ross Perot skilfully exploited in his 1992 Presiden-tial election campaign, when he obtained 19 per cent of the nationwide popular vote. When the public did watch their legislators at work on tele-vision, all too often it was not an edifying spectacle. The hearings held by the Senate Judiciary Committee into the nomination of Clarence Thomas for a place on the US Supreme Court and the interrogation of law professor Anita Hill by the all-male committee members were described as an 'ugly circus' and created a public outcry.[3]

Many people came to believe that legislative failures were identified with Congressional careerism; that the system produced legislators who were so busy protecting their own jobs and looking after their own personal interests that they were neglecting to do what was in the public interest. While American voters have often had a low opinion of Congress as an institution, they have usually held their own individual legislators in high regard. This apparent paradox explains why previously detected 'anti-incumbent' moods in the country have not been reflected in Congressional elections, when voters have overwhelmingly returned their sitting members. The term limitation movement offered a simple, alternative answer: to restrict all members' service in office so that even popular incumbents were forced to retire, thus changing Congress as an institution in the process. Supporters of term limits pointed to the re-election rates of Congressmen and the advantages of incumbency that made the positions of challengers in most elections difficult or well-nigh impossible. In 1988, for example, 97.5 per cent of those House members who sought re-election were successful and only six out of 408 were defeated in the November elections. In the same year only 38 members won with less than 55 per cent of the vote and 88 per cent were re-elected with over 60 per cent of the vote in their districts. Nearly one-fifth – 81 members – actually had no major party opposition at all in the November elections.

In 1990, despite what appeared to be widespread voter discontent with politicians, 95 per cent of House incumbents were returned. Senators, who have larger and more diverse constituencies, generally have more competitive elections than House members, but there is also usually a high re-election rate among incumbents.

In 1992, in the wake of the House banking scandal and the redrawing of constituency boundaries to take account of the 1990 census, which meant that some states lost seats, a record number of 53 House members, as well as eight Senators, decided not to seek re-election. A total of 19 House members and one Senator lost in primaries and a further 24 House members and four Senators were defeated in November. The percentage of House incumbents re-elected fell to 88.3 per cent and the 103rd Congress had 110 new members, the largest freshmen class in the House for 44 years, while the Senate had 11 newcomers. There was also increased competitiveness in House elections: 111 members won with 55 per cent or less of the vote and those facing no major party opponent dropped to 34.[4] Therefore, as the term limit movement gathered momentum, there was a simultaneous trend, with members by their own decision standing down or electors forcing early retirement on some incumbents, which had its own impact on the composition of Congress.

The advantages of incumbency are, of course, formidable and weight the odds at election time heavily in favour of sitting members and against challengers, real or potential. Congressmen start with much better name recognition among the electorate, enhanced over the years by media coverage and the use of the franking privilege which allows members to mail their constituents, free of charge, regular newsletters outlining their activities and achievements. In 1990, franked mail is estimated to have cost the US taxpayer $114 million. In fighting elections incumbents usually have a huge financial advantage over challengers. It is easier for them to raise money from both individuals and pressure groups, many of whom have interests in their constituencies or in issues coming before the committees and sub-committees they serve on. In 1990, 80 per cent of PAC contributions went to incumbents and the large war chests built up by members from funds unspent in previous elections often act as deterrents to challengers, either at the primary stage or in the general election. (See Chapter 8 in the present volume.) Over the years state legislatures, which have the responsibility for drawing electoral boundaries for the House of Representatives, have tended to create districts with partisan factors in mind, so that seats are 'safe' for one or other party. However some observers have argued that the main factor in the decline of competition in House elections has been the increasing emphasis members have placed upon providing an effective constituency service to their electors. Concern for their own re-election, it is argued, has tended to make Congressmen cautious about taking stands on controversial issues or making bold decisions that might be necessary in the national interest. Instead members concentrate on non-controversial work in their districts, using their Congressional staff, based both in Washington and in their constituencies, to help electors with their problems and trying to gain advantages in the distribution of public funds, government projects, contracts and jobs for their own areas. This form of 'pork barrel politics' has been extended by the growth of 'big government'; the bureaucracy which has been created makes members more indispensable in helping their constituents find their way around it.[5] Conservative commentator George F. Will cites Senator Robert Byrd of West Virginia, a former Senate Majority Leader, as an example of the career politician par excellence. Byrd became a professional legislator over 45 years ago and has done no other job.

> His career has become a caricature of a particularly crass and cynical theory of representation. The theory is that election to Congress is tantamount to being despatched to Washington D.C. on a looting raid for the enrichment of your state or district, and no other ethic need inhibit the feeding frenzy.[6]

Similar concerns about careerism, re-election rates and the occasional scandal sparked moves to limit the terms of state legislators, with Oklahoma and California joining Colorado in 1990 in imposing such restrictions. The early 1990s were therefore clearly a time that was ripe for such constitutional developments but the concept of term limitation, with the ideal of a 'citizen legislature' made up of people who were not interested in becoming career politicians, is not a new one; indeed, its origins lie in the early history of the nation.

Historical and Philosophical Background

Term limits are a reflection of the anti-authority political culture of the United States and the two major themes in American political thought that are related to that culture. The concept of popular sovereignty, with the belief that ultimate power belongs to the people, and the idea of limited government with constitutional safeguards placing constraints on those in authority, came together in the movement to ensure the rotation of elected office-holders.

The principle of rotation in office has its roots in classical republican political thought and can be traced to the emergence of democratic theory in ancient Greece and Rome and its development through the influential writings of seventeenth- and eighteenth-century thinkers. Dutch colonists introduced it to American shores and the practice was also developed in colonial New England. After the Declaration of Independence in 1776, several states passed limitations on the terms of both legislative and executive officials. The Articles of Confederation in 1781 limited legislators to serving three years in any period of six years, with annual appointment of delegates to the national legislature.

Despite criticisms that rotation in office had forced the retirement of effective and popular officials, the principle was still sufficiently influential to be included in the proposals presented to the Philadelphia Constitutional Convention of 1787 by Edmund Randolph as the Virginia Plan. However, after a brief discussion, the provision was dropped, with most delegates believing that frequent elections for the House of Representatives, the separation of powers and other constitutional safeguards, along with the fact that most state legislators practised rotation on a voluntary basis, made mandatory restrictions unnecessary. During the ratification process for the new constitution a passionate debate did take place between the anti-Federalists, who were suspicious of a newly strengthened central government and who wanted term limits, and the Federalists who argued that such restrictions were an unnecessary constraint on those holding public office.

George Washington's voluntary retirement after two terms as President set an important precedent, while Jefferson advocated the rotation principle be extended from elective to appointive officials to prevent the development of a permanent bureaucracy. President Andrew Jackson believed not only that rotation in office opened up opportunities for citizens to become involved in government but that all men were capable of holding public office. Jackson's extension of the principle to the administration of government may have been in tune with the democratic spirit of the time but the subsequent creation of a spoils system distributing patronage to supporters and which was seen as bolstering the position of the party in power ultimately led to rotation in office being discredited as it came under sharp attack in the second half of the nineteenth century. However the breaking of the two-term convention by President Franklin D. Roosevelt, who went on to his fourth election victory in 1944, revived the issue. Republicans in Congress introduced what was to become the Twenty-Second Amendment to the Constitution. Despite its partisan origins there was widespread support for the argument that, as the two-term convention had been violated, it needed to be formally included as part of the Constitution, and the amendment was ratified in 1951. Suspicion of the possible development of a too-powerful executive and fear that the balance of power between the branches of government was endangered were key factors in the passage of a term limit for the Presidency, although members of Congress firmly and overwhelmingly rejected any idea that such a limit should apply to legislators as well.[7]

Limitations on gubernatorial terms based upon the same fear of excessive executive power have always been fundamental to the design of state governments' constitutional arrangements. As Thad L. Beyle has pointed out, these limits have followed two general patterns – they have either imposed very short terms of office with frequent elections but no limit on the number of terms a person might serve or they have provided for longer periods in office but limits on the number of terms served or a requirement of a break in service.[8] In recent times constitutional changes in the states have tended to permit longer tenure in office, with more states adopting four-year rather than two-year terms and some dropping restrictions on the number of terms served. Consequently fewer people are serving as Governor now than at any time in the past and, once elected, Governors tend to stay in office for a longer period of time.

As far as Congress is concerned, there was a high turnover rate of membership in both the House and Senate during much of the nineteenth century. In the first half of the century it was rare for the percentage of first-term members in the House to be less than 40–45 per cent and House members rarely served more than two terms. After the Civil War the establishment of

Congressional committees made seniority more important, and between 1860 and 1920 the average length of service doubled to eight years. By the turn of the century, for the first time, less than 30 per cent of members were freshmen.[9] The 101st Congress, elected in 1988, had fewer than 8 per cent of its members newly elected. The seniority system as the determining factor in committee assignments and the appointment of committee chairmen put a premium on members staying alive and getting re-elected. Long service in the legislature became the key to obtaining positions of power and influence and resulted in the creation of the committee 'barons'. After the 1910 revolt against Speaker Joseph Cannon, power in the House became more decentralized to committees and the seniority principle became all but inviolate. Even after the reforms of the 1970s, seniority is still significant and members can argue at election time that the district or state would lose out if it was to replace the incumbent with a freshman who would have to work his or her way up from the bottom.[10]

In the nineteenth century it was therefore possible to become a leader in the House after a relatively short period. As Nelson Polsby has shown, the seven Speakers who were elected between 1870 and 1894 had between three and seven terms' experience in the chamber on taking the office.[11] Jim Wright, who became Speaker in 1987, had to wait until his seventeenth term, while his successor, Thomas Foley, who was elected in 1989, served 13 terms, before taking over the leadership. Until 60 years ago Congress usually only met for a few months a year and legislators spent most of the time in their districts, often working in other jobs. The growth of government has now made serving in Congress a full-time job and members are forced to give up any other career; indeed ethics legislation has severely curtailed their ability to receive income from outside sources, thus making them full-time salaried politicians. Not surprisingly, legislators have sought to make their positions more secure and to make sure they were adequately remunerated to cover the high cost of living in Washington and the restrictions on their earning power. Congressmen have also provided themselves with increased staffing to help them deal with large legislative workloads and the rising demands of their constituents. By 1989, there were 17 306 staff working for individual legislators and committees as well as many thousands of officials who provide support through bodies such as the Congressional Research Service, the Congressional Budget Office and the General Accounting Office.

Similar trends towards careerism, longer tenure in office and professionalization of legislatures have been experienced in the states since the 1960s. Until that time low pay and poor working conditions contributed to a high turnover of legislators, resulting in membership instability. Excessive amateurism was criticized as having a negative effect on both the legislative process and the policy outputs. As late as the 1960s two out of five state legislators were newcomers. The underlying premise of those who advocated the reform of state governments was that inexperienced members are less effective in legislative terms than career professionals who have mastered the process and developed expertise in understanding policy technicalities. From the 1960s on, the modernizers promoted reforms throughout American state legislatures, with the provision of professional staff, legislative offices and secretarial support, higher salaries and legislative pensions. By 1988, there were 33 000 staff working in state legislatures, with 40 per cent of them full-time professionals, and by 1990 all but seven states met in annual sessions. Research indicates that turnover of legislators declined and, although varying from state to state quite widely, averaged about 20 per cent in 1988.[12] Ironically the reforms may have made the states more effective but they also brought about the very conditions that bred the current clamour for term limits to be introduced for state legislators.

Term Limitation: The Arguments For and Against

The major arguments in the debate about term limits for legislators at national or state level are in many respects echoes of the cases made for and against the idea of rotation in office going back to the earliest days of the Republic. They have been revived and updated to take account of the experience of the way American legislatures have developed, particularly in the twentieth century.

Proponents of term limits argue that the reform would reinvigorate democracy by substantially increasing the number of competitive elections. It would give voters real choice with more open seats becoming available where the advantages incumbents hold over challengers would not apply. They anticipate more interest in elections and higher turnouts as contests would not be foregone conclusions. George Will argues: 'Limits are required to institute healthy competition in the political market just as antitrust intervention in economic markets can serve the values of a basically free market economy.'[13] Supporters claim that a better quality of legislator would also be elected. At present the seniority system means that members have to spend many years in office before gaining positions of real influence, which can be a deterrent to many talented people. It is argued that, rather than professional politicians who often have little or no recent experience of the 'real world' outside government, term limits would produce a 'citizen legislature' of civic-minded individuals who would be prepared to take a break in their careers to serve their communities but who would then be content to go back home to resume their normal lives. Such people would only wish to serve if they could get things achieved as a matter of urgency rather than letting things slide, as current legislators are accused of complacently doing. Without long service as the key to power and influence, chairmanships and other leadership positions could be awarded on the basis of talent and ability.

Term limits would also prevent professionalism and careerism, which some argue is the antithesis of proper representative government, as well as countering the 'culture of the ruling'. The creeping corruption that insidiously comes from people being in power for too long means that politicians become a class apart from the people they are supposed to be representing. George Will also argues that a new, healthier relationship would develop between the people and Congress; the electorate would be purged of its cynicism and suspicion about politicians' motives; voters would show a greater willingness to trust government to spend their money prudently and this would result in a diminution of the 'taxophobia' we have witnessed in recent times.[14]

Advocates of term limits also argue that in the new environment the cosy relationships that have developed between legislators, bureaucrats and special interests would be broken. Members would be less likely to support spending programmes favoured by such interests, that have led to spiralling public expenditure and federal deficits. Pork barrel politics and the buying of present benefits and votes at the cost of burdening future voters with the bill, which it is argued is the mark of legislative careerism, would no longer be so attractive for members. What is more, former Congressmen who lobbied on behalf of interest groups would inevitably find that their value would be diminished as there would be fewer and fewer former colleagues in the legislature with whom they could ingratiate themselves.

Opponents, however, have argued that term limits are a simplistic solution proposed to solve complex problems and that they would almost certainly have unintended consequences. They believe that other reforms, such as those on election campaign finance and the registration of lobbyists, are better ways of dealing with some of the maladies identified by supporters of term limits. Opponents argue that such restrictions actually limit the electorate under the guise of limiting politicians. By preventing people from voting for popular legislators who have served their constituents well, term limits are fundamentally undemocratic. As one opponent put it: 'We already have term limits. They're called elections.'[15] Critics also believe that by compulsorily retiring members after a set period the legislature, whether Congress or state, would be robbed of the experience and expertise that has been built up over the years and which is essential for an effective law-making body. With the complexities of modern government it is naïve to believe that 'amateur' legislators could quickly master the technicalities of the issues and the legislative process. They argue that term limits would therefore inevitably weaken the legislature as an institution, giving more power to the executive branch and the bureaucracy, while making legislators more dependent on their staff and more vulnerable to pressure group influence.

Some opponents have claimed that a 'citizen legislature' would not in practice result from the imposition of term limits. They believe that few talented people would be prepared to give up their careers and professions for a short period of public service; in fact it is more likely to be a deterrent to attracting able people to serve in the legislature. It is probable that similar types of individuals to those who now seek office would be candidates – with possibly fewer people from less well-to-do backgrounds who would be more concerned about the increased insecurity of the position – and that professional politicians would move around to different posts within the political system. It has been argued that some special interests would find it worthwhile to promote their own candidates for office, being prepared to take them back on their payrolls when they had completed their terms. Opponents have argued that legislators would be distracted from serving the public as they would be looking for new positions as they came to their last terms. At worst corruption or the threat of corruption could be increased as some members sought to exploit their positions while they could or 'make hay while the sun shines'. The argument that pork barrel politics would be reduced is also challenged. Members would still be eligible for re-election a certain number of times and, for those legislators, the same incentive structure to provide an effective constituency service, with the associated spending projects for their own areas, would still be in place.

Constitutional Issues

Quite apart from the political arguments submitted by supporters and opponents of term limits, lawyers for the two sides have also been putting forward their cases on the constitutional issues involved. Term limitations have passed through the initiative process in many states which would apply separately to members of the US Congress and to state legislators, and the constitutionality of both forms of restrictions has been challenged in the courts.

Proponents argue that states may set term limits for Congress under Article I, Section 4 of the US Constitution, which establishes their power to regulate 'the time, places and manner' of federal elections. They claim that the US Supreme Court has long upheld the right of states to regulate elections, including the electoral procedures related to the candidacies of persons seeking federal office. In various decisions the Court has denied candidates' challenges to specific state laws which kept them from the ballot. For this reason many of the term limit initiatives have been formulated as 'ballot access' provisions which prevent the names of incumbents from appearing on the ballot paper but technically allow them to compete as 'write-in' candidates.

Opponents argue that the Founding Fathers explicitly considered and rejected the idea of legislative term limits. Their introduction would add to the constitutional qualifications for office established in Article I, Sections 2 and 3, namely age, citizenship and residency. They suggest that precedents have established that neither Congress nor the states may add to these qualifications and the Court has prohibited, for example, limitations against former felons and against service by people residing outside a Congressional district. They cite the case of *Powell* v. *McCormack* when the Supreme Court ruled against the House of Representatives' attempting to add a further qualification for membership, in this case by excluding a duly elected member on the basis of prior ethical transgressions. The relevance of the Powell case is disputed because the supporters of term limits argue that the Court's ruling dealt with the House's attempt to prevent a *duly elected* member taking his seat, rather than with the issue of a state's authority to set requirements for the election.

Authorities on constitutional law have found the term limits question to be a thorny legal issue. A.E. Dick Howard of the University of Virginia Law School concluded that term limits are probably unconstitutional on the grounds that Congress is a national representative body, not just a collection of members from various states. He argues that, with the entire country having a stake in Congress and its composition, states should not be allowed to impose irrational or discriminatory limits on members.[16]

Separate legal debates are involved in the question of whether voters can directly impose term limits on their state legislators. Each state has its own constitution and court system and, as the actual conditions laid down in term limitation resolutions vary widely, it is to be expected that legal challenges will be mounted in individual states. State supreme courts will reach their conclusions on the constitutionality of term limits for state legislatures, having regard to their own constitutions and particular circumstances.

In California, one of the first states to introduce such restrictions, the state supreme court found in the case of *California Legislature* v. *March Fong Eu* (October 1991) that the 1990 term limits provision of Proposition 140 was constitutional and did not violate the First and Fourteenth Amendments to the federal Constitution, as claimed by opponents. The Court concluded that, on balance, the interests of the state in incumbency reform outweighed any injury to incumbent office-holders and those who would vote for them. It argued that the enlargement of the franchise by guaranteeing competitive primary and general elections, when weighed against the 'incidental disenfranchisement' of some voters, furthered rather than frustrated the policy of the Fourteenth Amendment.

What, then, is the strategy of the supporters of term limits for the national legislature and how do they see this being achieved?

> Term limit advocates are convinced that a Congress filled with members whose terms are not limited will never vote to place limits on themselves. Therefore, advocates have decided to use state ballot initiatives to put limits on the service of individual state delegations, one at a time. Over time, as an increasing number of members are forced to live with limits for themselves, advocates expect that these members will be willing to vote to impose similar limits on their colleagues.[17]

Seventeen state constitutions include provisions for electors to petition to have proposals placed on the ballot papers that can then be determined by statewide popular voters. The direct initiative process effectively bypasses the state legislature in making decisions, on constitutional amendments and a range of other measures. A further four states provide for indirect initiatives where the measure must be first submitted to the legislature for consideration before it can be placed on the ballot and two states' constitutions allow both direct and indirect initiatives. Influenced by the populist movement of the early twentieth century, many of the states using this process are in the West and it is here that the term limitations movement has particularly flourished. Voters have been able to take the decision themselves, rather than having to persuade state legislators to impose limits on themselves and their Congressional colleagues. By November 1994 all the initiative states, with the exception of Mississippi, had voted on the issue.

Advocates hope to build on the momentum achieved in these states in the early 1990s and, with the support of Congressmen serving under term limit provisions and those who backed the idea in their 1994 election campaigns, persuade Congress to introduce a Constitutional Amendment on the issue. They would argue that having a nationally laid down standard limit would be necessary on the grounds of fairness, otherwise the seniority system would be tilted in favour of law-makers from states without term limits. Supporters also believe that Congressmen from states where voters do not have the opportunity to impose term limits themselves would nevertheless be under great pressure in 1994 and subsequent elections to declare their support for such an Amendment. Republican gains in the 1994 Congressional elections would help maintain the momentum. If Congress were to back a proposal by the necessary two-thirds majority, proponents believe state legislatures, many serving under their own term limits, would quickly ratify the reform, which would unclog the system and open up higher offices to competition, particularly as many state legislators would have their own eyes on some of the newly available Congressional seats. If the US Supreme Court were to declare that state limits on Congressional terms were constitutional before Congress itself acted, then the pressure on the national legislature to agree to a national standard in order to achieve an even playing-field would be intense.

Critics of term limits remain confident that the US Supreme Court would declare state limits unconstitutional and they believed that Congress itself would not support a proposal for a Constitutional Amendment, even if it was to find its way to a floor vote. Opponents also felt that popular support for the idea would eventually run out of steam, particularly if the deadlock in Washington was broken by the new Clinton administration being able to work effectively with Congress: if voters saw that government can actually work again, much of the anger and frustration that has prompted the term limitation movement would be dissipated. In a number of states opponents have challenged the legality of the measures supported by the electorate and, in July 1993, an Arkansas state circuit court became the first judicial body to rule that a term limitation proposition passed by voters was unconstitutional. In March 1994, the Arkansas supreme court supported this view on the basis that the measure passed by the voters, in requiring incumbents to run only as 'write-in' candidates whose names did not appear on the ballot paper, was in effect establishing a fourth qualification for office and was thus unconstitutional. In June 1994, the US Supreme Court agreed to review *US Term Limits* v. *Thornton*. In February 1994, US federal District Judge William L. Dwyer ruled that Washington's 1992 term limit law for national legislators was unconstitutional: not only did it set qualifications for office beyond Article I, Sections 2 and 3 but also violated the First Amendment (by constraining members' freedom of association) and the Fourteenth Amendment (by imposing undue restrictions on ballot access for 'one disfavored group of candidates'). Again the ruling is due to be appealed to US Court of Appeals and eventually the US Supreme Court.[18]

Term Limitation Campaigns in the States

Oklahoma became the first state to pass a term limit proposal for its state legislature on 18 September 1990 by 67 per cent–33 per cent, imposing a 12-year restriction on future service for both its legislative chambers. None of the current state legislators will be affected until the year 2003. In November of that year voters in California passed by 52 per cent–48 per cent a proposition with much tougher limits on their state government. Members of the assembly were restricted to three two-year terms, while holders of all other state offices, executive officials as well as state senators, were limited to two four-year terms in any one office. The limit was to be a lifetime ban. Proposition 140 also reduced the California legislative budget by nearly 40 per cent, which led to a considerable reduction in staffing, and eliminated the legislators' pension scheme, a condition that was later declared unconstitutional. Under California's staggered term system, incumbent state senators re-elected in 1992 will have to retire in 1996. In Colorado voters decided by 71 per cent–29 per cent to restrict their state legislators to eight years in office, but also imposed a limit of 12 years on their Congressional delegation. However Colorado did not impose a lifetime ban but required a four-year break for elected officials. It is important therefore to recognize that a wide range of alternative constraints on legislative service have been included in successful term limitation resolutions, which are likely to have variable effects over the coming years.

In 1991, Washington became the first state to have rejected a term limitation initiative proposal when voters turned down 54 per cent – 46 per cent a measure that would have imposed very strict limits on both state and federal office-holders. The limits, which for US Senators were to be for 12 years and for members of the House of Representatives six years, would have come into effect immediately and been retroactive. House Speaker Foley and seven of his colleagues, for example, could have sought and served only one more term before leaving office in 1994. In 1992, the term limitation movement, having learned the lessons of the setback in Washington a year earlier, avoided proposals that were retroactive and gained momentum, with 14 states, including Washington, passing term limits for members of Congress (see Table 4.1). In 1994 voters in six more states supported term limits for Congress. Only Utah rejected an initiative which complicated the issue by combining term limits with an unpopular proposal for run-off elections.[19]

In many states campaigns on the issue have been fairly low-key, with attention focused in 1992 principally on the Presidential election and legislators concentrating on their own re-election within their districts rather than taking part in statewide debates about term limits. However, in some states, large amounts of money were spent in hard-fought contests. Advertising has principally been through press and radio campaigns, although in a few states, such as California, extensive use has been made of television commercials. The supporters of term limits have generally been better organized than their opponents and have been highly motivated in their efforts, firstly to secure sufficient signatures on a petition to get the issue on the ballot and then to win public support in the referendum. Opponents were slow to recognize the threat in the first states voting in 1990 and, with the exception of Washington in 1991, have found it difficult to hold back the tide of public opinion in favour of term limits.

Table 4.1   State limits on Congressional terms

Date	State	Senate (years)	House (years)	Percentage for/against
1990	Colorado	12	12	71–29
1991	Washington	12	6	46–54
1992	Arizona	12	6	74–26
1992	Arkansas	12	6	60–40
1992	California	12	6	63–37
1992	Florida	12	8	77–23
1992	Michigan	12	6	59–41
1992	Missouri	12	8	74–26
1992	Montana	12	6	67–33
1992	Nebraska	12	8	68–32
1992	North Dakota	12	12	55–45
1992	Ohio	12	8	66–34
1992	Oregon	12	6	69–31
1992	South Dakota	12	12	63–37
1992	Washington	12	6	52–48
1992	Wyoming	12	6	77–23
1994	Alaska	12	6	63–37
1994	Colorado	12	6	51–49
1994	Idaho	12	6	59–41
1994	Maine	12	6	63–37
1994	Massachusetts	12	6	51–49
1994	Nebraska	12	8	68–32
1994	Nevada	12	6	70–30
1994	Oklahoma	12	6	67–33
1994	Utah	12	6	35–65

The arguments put forward by both sides in the campaign have tended to reflect the general cases which were examined earlier in this chapter, with adaptations to take account of the particular circumstances of individual states. Agenda setting and defining the terms of the debate have proved to be very important. Supporters of term limits have sought to exploit public frustration and anger at politicians by focusing on the attractions of a simple solution to end legislative careerism. Opponents have attempted to redefine the issue, concentrating on the complexities of particular proposals and their effects. In Washington in 1991, for example, the successful opposition campaign emphasized the benefits the state had gained as a result of having many of its legislators in senior positions in Congress and the impact on the state's fortunes that might result from losing the services of such powerful leaders as Tom Foley. They also pointed to the unfairness that would be created if states such as neighbouring California, already seen as exerting too much power in Congress because of the size of its delegation, did not have such limits on its Congressmen. Until then opponents had seemed to be merely self-serving vested interests or to be advocating abstract constitutional arguments; in Washington they managed to persuade voters that the state's political clout and their own interests would be harmed if term limits were to be introduced unilaterally.

The movement for term limitation has been one of grassroots activism which has over the last few years become organized into a national as well as state-level campaign. The national organizations have offered guidance to state groups on issues such as gaining access to the ballot and the most effective wording of proposals. They have provided expertise on legal and constitutional questions, logistical support and, in some cases, finance to help local campaigns. They have also acted as national spokesmen on the issue, providing information to the media and the Washington political community. For example, in 1994, following the indictment of House Ways and Means Chairman Dan Rostenkowski on corruption charges, one group (US Term Limits) distributed 100 000 copies of a poster featuring 'Rosty-the Postman' on a mock postage stamp to news organizations nation-wide. State groups have overseen strategy and day-to-day operations in their own states, while retaining a large degree of autonomy and separate organizational identities. The major national bodies have been Americans to Limit Congressional Terms (ALCT), Citizens for Congressional Reform, which became US Term Limits (USTL) in 1992, and Americans Back in Charge (ABIC) which evolved from Coloradoans Back in Charge (CBIC), the movement that had promoted the successful state campaign in 1990. In 1993, the term limits movement suffered from adverse publicity as factional in-fighting came to the surface. ALCT filed for bankruptcy and was subject to what was described as the equivalent of a hostile takeover by USTL.[20]

Support for term limits has been drawn from a wide coalition of true believers across the ideological spectrum. Although it is often perceived as being principally a conservative movement, with the backing of former President Bush, ex-Vice-President Quayle and many Republicans inside and outside Congress, it has also been supported by people such as consumer advocate, Ralph Nader, and liberal Democrats frustrated by what they see as a system that has been hijacked by entrenched incumbents and supported by special interests. In Washington, for example, prime movers in the LIMIT campaign were left-wing Democrats who had supported losing candidates in the Democratic primary campaigns of 1990. United We Stand America, the grassroots movement formed by supporters of Ross Perot in 1992, has also backed term limits as part of its campaign to reform the political process.

Opponents of term limits have accused the national organizations of pouring money into particular states, an argument that damaged the pro-initiative campaign in Washington. Allegations that wealthy and mysterious backers, such as billionaire brothers David and Charles Koch, who are known for their support of right-wing causes, were secretly financing the term limits campaign were made in Washington and resurfaced in California in 1992, charges that were strenuously denied by supporters of the movement. Some critics have also argued that support among conservative Republicans has been motivated not so much by a desire to see limits placed on government, as they claim, as by their frustration at their failure until the 1994 elections to win control of the House of Representatives under the normal rules; by clearing out incumbents, the majority of whom are Democrats, the party would, it is argued, have a better chance of forming a majority in Congress.

Those resisting term limits have not developed an effective national organization, but they have been helped by bodies such as the American Federation of State, County and Municipal Employees (AFSCME), the AFL-CIO and the League of Women Voters, which have provided staff support and acted as clearing-houses for information. Opposition has been strongest from incumbent legislators, particularly Democrats, organized labour and a range of corporate and professional interests, as well as academics and political scientists in particular. While the vested interest of sitting members is obvious and pressure groups that do well out of the existing system can be expected to resist change, the opposition of most political scientists has been based on what they see as the negative impact term limits would have on the stability, professionalism and effectiveness of legislative bodies as institutions.

The Impact of Term Limits

As we have seen, supporters and opponents of term limitation agree that such a constitutional change, whether at state or national level, would have significant effects on individual legislators, on legislative bodies as institutions and on the relationship between legislatures and other actors in the political system, but they generally disagree on what the consequences would be and whether they would be desirable or not. While it is possible to hypothesize as to what some of the effects of term limits might be, it is also likely that there will be unintended and unpredictable consequences as well.

What is more, as the full impact of proposals will not be felt for many years, it is inevitable that there is a great deal of speculation and conjecture but very little empirical evidence from which conclusions can be drawn. However, we can safely say that the different types of term limit proposals that have been approved in the states are likely to have different consequences. As Gerald Benjamin and Michael J. Malbin have pointed out, the key variations include:

- the length of the limits;
- whether limits last a lifetime or require a break (or discontinuity) in service;
- the length of the break, if a break is required;
- whether service in the legislature is governed by a single aggregate limit or by limits that apply separately to different legislative bodies;
- whether limits apply to service at national level;
- whether the length of the service to be limited is counted from the date of the proposal's adoption or retroactively.[21]

With regard to the length of the limits, we can see from Table 4.1 that those imposed on members of Congress so far range from six to 12 years. Given the low turnover in recent times among Congressional incumbents, it is clear that such restrictions would over time have a major impact on the composition of the national legislature. On the other hand, Oklahoma's 12-year limit for its state legislature would not affect most of the legislators sitting when it was passed in 1990, because relatively few Oklahoma legislators normally serve 12 years in office and turnover has traditionally been high. It is possible that the new limit may, paradoxically, have the effect of increasing average length of service by making 12 years the norm and encouraging legislators to serve 'to the limit'. Research by David H. Everson indicates that, with the exception of California, those states that allow initiative and referendum decisions by the voters tend to be less likely to have large numbers of long-serving state legislators; in other words, term limits for state legislators are most likely to be imposed in places where they would have the least impact.[22] Term limits are likely to have their greatest impact where states have developed highly professionalized legislatures and turnover has traditionally been low.

One of the most fundamental differences in the proposals passed by voters is between a simple limitation and lifetime limits. The former restricts the length of continuous service in one office without placing any constraints, other than re-election, on what the office-holder may do after that term has ended, so that incumbents can maintain an active political career by seeking another office. The less common lifetime limits would place a cap on the number of years a person could serve in a lifetime and thus legally ban political careerism. A simple limitation may therefore open up more offices to competitive elections but may lead to professional politicians seeking to move from one position to another as their terms end. Lifetime bans are more likely to create a wider pool of people seeking and achieving legislative office and more closely approximate the 'citizen legislature' concept favoured by supporters of term limits.

The impact of a break in service is likely to depend on how long the period out of office actually is. Experience of state Governors who have been forced to stand down for a term or indeed have been defeated (such as Michael Dukakis and Bill Clinton) suggests that it is quite possible to be out of office for a term and then resume one's political career. On the other hand, if the break was for a longer period, its impact might well be similar to that of a lifetime ban.

Term limits may well have major consequences for the organization and operation of American legislatures. The greatest impact is likely to be felt by those who have attained leadership positions, whether as party leaders or committee chairmen. In some state legislatures, relatively few politicians have stayed in office for a long time and they have taken important leadership roles, while the majority of the membership have exhibited a high turnover in office; in those states term limits will remove what may have been entrenched elites and open up the leadership to newcomers. There is likely to be less value placed on seniority, with members seeking leadership positions earlier and possibly more aggressively. It is probable that no one will be allowed to stay in leadership positions for very long and some sort of rotation of offices may develop, with power being dispersed more widely. Legislatures will lose the services of a minority of very senior, well-respected elder statesmen who have provided the 'institutional memory' and been important in the transmission of legislative norms and values. Term limits will also reduce the incentives for members to adopt a long-term strategy for increasing their own influence within the legislature. Members may be less willing to take on the less glamorous and more routine legislative chores by which members in the past have served their apprenticeships and earned respect and support amongst their colleagues. Legislatures may well become more individualistic, with members attempting to achieve their own agendas more quickly, seeking more media attention and, where they are able, to obtain new positions when their terms end, keeping an eye on future offices they may seek.

Many commentators have suggested that legislative term limits will affect the balance between the branches of government in the separation of powers system and increase the influence of the executive at the expense of the legislature. One important factor here is whether the executive officials are also serving under term limits. As we have seen, the Twenty-Second Amendment limits the President to two four-year terms and, although the trend until recently was for the less restrictive conditions to apply to most state Governors, it is worth noting that some of the most recent term limit reforms, such as in California, apply to the Governor as well as to other executive officials. It may also be the case that, by weakening the legislative branch, one does not necessarily see a strengthening of the executive. It is possible that with a lack of strong leadership in the legislature it is more difficult for Governors to build and maintain the coalitions of support necessary for executive policy making.

Morris Fiorina has shown that one of the consequences of the professionalization of state legislatures since the 1960s has been the increasing control of these bodies by the Democratic party. He argues that higher salaries and more regular sessions have made legislative service more attractive to Democratic candidates and less attractive to Republican candidates. This is because fulltime legislative service is incompatible with another career and Democrats, on average, have less lucrative career opportunities than Republicans. He believes that term limits on service in themselves will make little impact on partisan composition; in 'amateur' legislatures term limits would bind few members and in 'professionalized' legislatures eight to 12 years in office should be sufficiently long lead time that even the most risk-averse Democrat would not be discouraged. However, where term limitation initiatives also significantly restrict the number of days-in-session, legislative salaries and perks, such measures should make legislatures more amateur and, quite likely, more Republican.[23]

Finally we may hypothesize that term limits will affect the relationship between pressure groups and lobbyists and the legislature they are seeking to influence. Despite the fact that most organized interests have been opposed to term limits because of their potentially disruptive impact on the relationships they have nurtured with existing members, particularly leaders and committee chairmen, it is possible that the overall effect will be to increase the influence of these bodies. Interest groups will find their task more difficult and time-consuming as they have to educate greater numbers of freshmen and inexperienced legislators, but they may find them more susceptible to persuasion. There are, after all, no term limits for lobbyists. As Gary W. Copeland has written: 'In short, lobbyists see the task of influencing legislators becoming less efficient but more effective under term limits.'[24]

The 1994 Congressional elections were the first when term limits became a significant issue in the campaign. Over 90 per cent of incumbents won re-election but the defeat of prominent Democratic opponents such as Speaker Tom Foley and House Judiciary Committee Chairman Jack Brooks and the election of many Republicans pledged to support term limits was a major boost to the movement. House Republicans included term limits as a key proposal in their campaign 'Contract with America' and promised the first floor vote on the issue within the first hundred days of the 104th Congress in which 182 House members and 44 Senators would be covered by state-imposed limits.

Notes

1   Alan Grant, *The American Political Process*, 5th edn, Dartmouth, 1994, pp.32–3.
2   Christopher J. Bailey, 'Ethics as Politics: Congress in the 1990s', in Philip John Davies and Frederic A. Waldstein (eds), *Political Issues in America*, Manchester University Press, 1991, p.146.
3   *Time*, 21 October 1991.
4   *Congressional Quarterly Weekly Report*, 10 April 1993, pp.965–8.
5   Charles R. Kester, 'Bad Housekeeping: The Case Against Congressional Term Limits', *Policy Review,* Summer 1990, The Heritage Foundation.
6   George F. Will, *Restoration: Congress, Term Limits and the Recovery of Deliberative Democracy*, The Free Press, 1992, p.31.
7   John H. Fund, 'Term Limitation: An Idea Whose Time Has Come', *Policy Analysis No. 141*, October 1990, The Cato Institute.
8   Thad L. Beyle, 'Term Limits in the State Executive Branch', in Gerald Benjamin and Michael J. Malbin (eds), *Limiting Legislative Terms*, Congressional Quarterly Press, 1992, p.159.
9   Fund, 'Term Limitation'.
10 Grant, *The American Political Process*, pp.48–52.
11 Nelson Polsby, *The Congressional Career*, Random House, 1971, p.23.
12 David H. Everson, 'The Impact of Term Limitations on the States: Cutting the Underbrush or Chopping Down the Tall Timber?', in Benjamin and Malbin (eds), *Limiting Legislative Terms*, pp.191–5.
13 Will, *Restoration*, p.180.
14 Ibid., p.183.
15 *National Journal*, 12 September 1992, p.2053.
16 Ibid., p.2056.
17 Gerald Benjamin and Michael J. Malbin, 'Term Limits for Lawmakers: How to Start thinking about a Proposal in Process', in Benjamin and Malbin (eds), *Limiting Legislative Terms*, p.9.
18 *Congressional Quarterly Weekly Report*, 12 February 1994, p.342; 12 March 1994, p.622.
19 In addition Colorado voters supported a tougher limitation than that passed in 1990 and Nebraska held a fresh ballot after judicial objections to the 1992 vote. Opponents of term limits have often made legal challenges to either prevent the initiative appearing on the ballot paper or challenging its validity after passage by the electorate.
20 *National Journal*, 26 June 1993, pp.1646–8.
21 Benjamin and Malbin (eds), *Limiting Legislative Terms*, p.9.
22 David H. Everson, quoted in ibid., p.12.
23 Morris P. Fiorina, 'Divided Government in the American States: A By-product of Legislative Professionalism?' *American Political Science Review* **88** (2), June 1994, p.313.
24 Gary W. Copeland, 'Term Limitations and Political Careers in Oklahoma: In, Out, Up or Down', in ibid., p.154.

5   The Supreme Court Nominations of Presidents Reagan and Bush

Richard Hodder-Williams

The Context of Nominations

Less than two weeks after his election, Ronald Reagan received a lengthy communication from Richard Nixon in which the former President wrote that 'the most lasting legacy will be your impact on the Supreme Court'.[1] Three arguments underpinned this view. First, since Justices leave the Court only as a result of 'an act of God or of will',[2] as a simple matter of fact Justices remain on the Court long after their nominators have left the White House. Second, several of the Justices were well advanced in years and Reagan could expect, therefore, to make an unusually large number of nominations. On 1 January 1981, Brennan was 74, Powell 73, Burger 73, Marshall 72 and Blackmun 72.

The third argument, however, was the critical one. The Supreme Court, by virtue of its position as court of last resort, determines the application of federal statutes and the meaning of the Constitution. These authoritative judgements may not in practice be final (for political responses which moderate them are often generated by them),[3] but they are, in the short term and often in the long term, decisive and important. Since the early 1950s, the Court had outlawed the racially segregated schools of the South, found the saying of prayers or reading of the Bible in state schools unconstitutional, set down a detailed list of suspects' rights which had to be met before evidence could be used in a trial, instructed the states to ensure that the districts for all elections were drawn in such a way that each individual vote had an equal value, permitted courts to make educational authorities bus children in order to desegregate a school system, and created a right for women to have an abortion at least in the first three months of pregnancy.[4] These were just some of the decisions which, in other countries, would have been taken by legislatures.

The power of the Supreme Court was well known. Many of those who strongly supported Reagan shared his belief that the Court had over-extended its authority and needed to be reined in. It had, in the shorthand language of public debate, been too 'activist' and needed to become more strictly 'constructionist'. Imprecise though the concept of strict constructionism is, it nevertheless was presumed at least to espouse the view that Justices should be less ready to expand the sparse words of the Constitution to areas which it did not specifically cover (such as abortion or busing) and more willing to defer to the decisions of elected bodies and officials. Since Reagan and his supporters disliked what the Court had done, Nixon's reminder that nominations to the Supreme Court could transform those aspects of American life fell on receptive ears.

This chapter examines the Supreme Court nominations of Ronald Reagan and George Bush and attempts to evaluate how successful they have been in producing different policy outcomes. First, however, the wider context in which the nominations take place needs to be sketched in. Without a conception of the way the Supreme Court relates to the rest of the judicial branch or a feel for the political forces at work when nominations are made, it is impossible to evaluate the success of the two most recent Republican Presidents.

At first sight the Constitution is clear about the status and provenance of Supreme Court Justices. To ensure their independence, federal judges can only be removed through the very cumbersome procedure of impeachment and their salaries cannot be diminished during their period of office.[5] There are no qualificatory requirements and no hierarchy of promotion from a lower level to a higher level in the Court system. Appointment is accounted for in a deceptively simple clause in Article II, Section 2: '[The President] shall nominate, and by and with the advice and consent of the Senate, shall appoint ... judges of the Supreme Court'. There has been much argument over how this should be applied, especially the extent to which – and the criteria on which – Senators ought to be involved. What is clear, however, is that only the President can nominate and no appointment can succeed without out the consent of the Senate. All nominations are made within these two contexts, which may be called the White House context and the Washington context, respectively.

The White House context is created exclusively by the Presidents themselves. They establish the structures through which nominees have to be filtered; they set the goals and strategies to be achieved through nominating particular individuals; they set the administration's priorities. It is hard to argue that Harry Truman had a *strategy* for his nominations, but he had a clear notion of how he would use the opportunities offered to him by vacancies on the Court; they would, to put it crudely, allow him to reward friends.[6] He created nonetheless by himself the critical context in which his nominations took place; another President would have had different goals, different priorities and different procedures. Both Ronald Reagan and George Bush used this Presidential autonomy to establish their own policy goals and the appropriate structures within which choices would be made.

The Washington context, although theoretically subject to a skilled President's influence, is essentially outside the control of Presidents. Presidents cannot alter the party strengths or the ideological preferences of the Senate, without whose consent no nomination can be successful. An able President can minimize the limitations imposed (for example, by a Senate controlled by a different party or dominated by a different ideology) but such factors cannot be ignored. Additionally Presidents represent parties which are internally divided – for both American parties are coalitions of diverse interests – and they are often constrained by the need to satisfy part of the coalition through whose help and activities they reached the White House. Thus the 'law of anticipated reactions' may prevent a President from nominating his ideal choice since ignoring those likely reactions may ensure that a nomination fails. In short, deciding which name to put forward is often affected by a careful calculation of the political realities of Washington politics.[7]

The Process and Politics of Nominations

The first opportunity to influence the Supreme Court directly came early in the Reagan Presidency, but from a quarter which had not been anticipated.[8] In March 1981, within the first 100 days, Justice Potter Stewart confided to his old Yale friend, Vice-President George Bush, that he would retire at the end of the term. He also informed Attorney-General William French Smith of his intention. The President was not told, however, until later in April, when he had recovered from the attempt on his life. Stewart, an Eisenhower appointee, was only 64, but he knew that he was not well; indeed he died in 1985, at which time all his colleagues were still alive and active on the Court.

During the 1980 Presidential campaign, when Reagan was under some pressure from women's movements because of his alleged unconcern for women's issues (he was known to be opposed to the Equal Rights Amendment), he addressed the issue in a Los Angeles statement on 14 October: 'I am announcing today that one of the first Supreme Court vacancies in my administration will be filled by the most qualified woman I can find, one who meets the high standards I will demand for all my appointments.'[9] Although this was not a commitment that *the* first nomination would be a woman, the political reality was that he had boxed himself into precisely that position. Attorney-General Smith accepted that Reagan was happy to stand by this commitment and he, as did the White House, began to produce a list of possible candidates. This was not an easy task.

Over the previous 50 years a series of important changes in attitudes had taken place in the United States, without which the nomination of a woman would have been impossible.[10] Women would not have been thought eligible for a Supreme Court judgeship in the 1930s, but gradually the informal opposition broke down, among the public at large, in Presidential eyes (both Richard Nixon and Gerald Ford had considered women for Court vacancies), in the minds of the American Bar Association's Committee on the Federal Judiciary and, perhaps finally, in the view of the Justices themselves. Finding a well qualified woman was difficult for, as President Carter had discovered and had attempted to remedy, discrimination against women over many years had inevitably left the pool of those with extensive experience in the practice of law, litigating and judging very small. The growth in the number of female judges in the late 1970s was essentially a Democratic party growth, since Carter's nominations were overwhelmingly Democrats, and the Republican pool was limited. However on both the White House and Justice Department lists was the name of Sandra Day O'Connor.

O'Connor had grown up on a Texan ranch and gone to Stanford University as a 16-year-old. She majored in economics, graduated magna cum laude, and went straight into law school at Stanford, from which she graduated in 1952, third in her class and a member of the *Law Review* editorial team. Despite those qualifications, Los Angeles law firms refused to hire her except as a legal secretary and it was not until she settled in Phoenix, Arizona, that her career began to pick up. She joined the state Attorney-General's staff and became active in Republican politics. In 1969, the Maricopa County Board of Supervisors appointed her to fill a vacancy in the state senate, to which she was elected in 1970 and 1972, when she became majority leader. In 1975, however, she moved from the legislative to the judicial branch, being elected to the Maricopa County Superior Court, from where Democrat Governor Bruce Babbitt appointed her to the state court of appeals in 1979.

O'Connor was not the only woman to be considered, but the more the administration thought about the matter, the better she seemed. It was helpful to have influential backers like Senator Barry Goldwater and Justice William Rehnquist (who had graduated first in O'Connor's year at law school), both of whom had been political friends in Phoenix. She interviewed well. And she had a varied and apposite experience for a Justice. As one Presidential aide is supposed to have observed, she 'really made it easy. She was the right age, had the right philosophy, the right combination of experience, the right political affiliation, the right backing. She just stood out among the women.'[11] Although some of the conservative groups, such as Rev. Jerry Falwell's Moral Majority, were worried about an apparently pro-abortion vote she had cast in the Arizona Senate, the general view was enthusiastically positive. On 21 September 1981 the Senate confirmed her 99–0.

This was the only opportunity to nominate a Justice to the Supreme Court in Reagan's first administration. Many Reagan supporters had interpreted the 1980 election as a landslide and as providing the President with a mandate for change, and the 1984 election provided an even more spectacular victory. But the liberals on the Supreme Court stayed on and showed little intention of retiring. At Reagan's second inauguration, Brennan was approaching 79, Powell and Burger were both 77, and Marshall and Blackmun both 76. Of these, Burger had proved the nearest to Reagan's ideal, while Powell, although normally safe on law and order issues, had cast the critical fifth vote in a variety of cases (covering affirmative action, the separation of church and state, abortion rights) with which the President's supporters strongly disagreed.[12]

As the Reagan Presidency extended into its seventh year, conservative court watchers became more dispirited. For all their ailments (and neither Powell nor Marshall was fully fit), the elderly Justices seemed determined, perversely determined perhaps, to soldier on. There was a feeling in 1986 that the Democrats would do well in the coming November's Senatorial elections and might gain control of the Senate. With a Judiciary Committee chaired by a liberal Democrat like Senator Joe Biden or Senator Edward Kennedy, the prospects for radical conservatives turning their favourite nominations into appointments were poor. Already the Senate, even with a Republican majority, had shown it was prepared to fight, and occasionally prevail, against Reagan nominations. Edwin Meese had managed, after a bruising set of hearings lasting 13 months, to be confirmed as Attorney-General, but the 62–32 vote represented the greatest number of negative votes cast against any confirmed Cabinet nominee in recent years; the Judiciary Committee had voted down the elevation of Bradford Reynolds to the third highest position in the Justice Department; there had been close votes on Court of Appeal judges Alex Kozinski (54–43), Sidney Fitzwater (52–42) and Daniel Manion (48–46), while one district judge nominee, William Sessions, had actually lost his confirmation battle.

'Time may almost have run out,' said Daniel Popeo, general counsel to the conservative Washington Legal Foundation.[13] Patrick McGuigan, the director of the Judicial Reform Project at the Free Congress Foundation's

Institute for Government and Politics, was equally resigned: 'Nature has taken its course,' he commented. 'It's a combination, I guess, of God's will and their will, but it's obvious that if it's up to them they're going to stay.' James Gattuso, from the Heritage Foundation, observed: 'All I know is that in 1980 everyone was saying that Reagan was going to have all these court picks. The way things are going, I won't be surprised if they're still saying it in 1988.'

It was within this gloomy context that a retirement from the Court did take place, but, from the conservative perspective, it was not the ideal one. According to Donald Regan, then the President's Chief of Staff, Chief Justice Warren Burger's decision came as a surprise.[14] The public reason was Burger's wish to devote himself fully to the chairmanship of the Commission on the Bicentennial, a task he could not possibly do in addition to both the administrative and judicial roles of the Chief Justiceship. His decision remained secret.[15] Within the administration, however, the process of selecting a successor, who had in Regan's view to be a judge rather than a politician, was quickly put in hand. Meese was the most significant player, but his right-hand man in the Justice Department, Charles Cooper, contributed decisively. For several years, those involved in judicial appointments had been preparing a list of possible replacements for retiring Justices, but they had not focused on the position of Chief Justice. Cooper could see many advantages in a double play, promoting Associate Justice William Rehnquist, for whom he had clerked, and then filling his vacancy with the top person on that list of potential nominees. It made good sense. In administrative terms, the Supreme Court's workload was such that an outsider would have particular difficulties in managing the responsibilities that fall to any Chief Justice. Furthermore Rehnquist had intellect and, despite the extremely conservative reputation he enjoyed on jurisprudential matters, personal warmth, both of which Burger had lacked. To the extent that a Chief Justice can lead a Court, Rehnquist offered the ideal solution for conservatives. In personal terms, too, the chance of advancement would help to alleviate Rehnquist's growing disenchantment with the Associate Justice's role. Illness, familiarity and the passage of time were making him restless. The administration could not afford to lose him.

The next question concerned his replacement. Although several names were on the original list of possibilities, the choice was almost immediately reduced to two, Robert Bork and Antonin Scalia, both ex-professors, ex-members of the Nixon administration, public speakers concerned to challenge the liberal jurisprudence associated with the Warren and Burger courts, and currently judges on the DC Circuit Court of Appeals. Conservative activists rated them both highly but Bork was their particular hero, their most articulate and well placed spokesman; indeed there was still some unhappiness that he had not been nominated to replace Potter Stewart. The White House was divided. Bork had perhaps the higher claim, but he was older and, together with Rehnquist, would ensure a bitter confirmation battle; perhaps it would be safer to nominate Scalia first and hold Bork over to the next vacancy. But that, others argued, would be risky since the prospects for the Democrats regaining control of the Senate were high and Scalia was more likely to be confirmed under those circumstances than Bork. Ultimately another consideration persuaded Ronald Reagan; Scalia would be the first Italian–American ever to sit on the Court and this appealed to his political instincts. Thus Scalia received the nod.

As predicted, the promotion of William Rehnquist did not go smoothly. Liberal interest groups collected considerable evidence to embarrass him: a memorandum he had written when clerk to Justice Robert Jackson making a defence of the 'separate but equal' doctrine, claims of behaviour in Phoenix to limit blacks' access to the ballot, purchasing properties with restricted covenants, advice when in the Justice Department that seemed antithetical to First Amendment rights, a long line of speeches and judgements which supported positions opposed by most women's, African–American and liberal groups. Considerable energy and publicity were put into the effort to derail Rehnquist's nomination. It failed. The Senate confirmed him by 65 votes to 33, the largest number of negative votes ever cast against a nominee for the post of Chief Justice. Scalia skipped through virtually unchallenged.

The double appointment in 1986 did not do much to shift the Court's ideology in the conservative direction sought by the Reagan administration. Rehnquist was the same Rehnquist; Scalia was younger, brighter, more ebullient than Burger, but his votes were likely to be very similar. Scalia took his seat on the Court at the beginning of the 1986 term. Within a few weeks, elections in the United States had returned to the Senate a Democrat majority and the Judiciary Committee's chairmanship passed from the conservative Strom Thurmond to the liberal Joseph Biden. It was within this changed context that Lewis Powell took Washington by surprise in July 1987 by announcing his retirement.[16] Powell, appointed by Nixon in 1972, was a cautious conservative whose votes had increasingly become pivotal; his fifth vote had ensured the continuation of *Roe* v. *Wade* as good law, had approved the principle of affirmative action, had kept a strict separation between church and state and had supported the principle of busing. Now Reagan had a golden opportunity to make an appointment which could decisively alter the Court's jurisprudence. And there was no doubt who that nominee would be. With Edwin Meese as Attorney-General and the movement conservatives pressing hard for 'one of them', Robert Bork at last had his chance.[17]

The following three months witnessed some of the most extraordinary politics ever seen in Washington. At first sight, Bork was an ideal candidate.

An intellectual and scholar, he had been Solicitor-General in the Nixon administration, a lawyer in private practice, a professor and, for several years, a judge on the DC Circuit Court of Appeals. But he was a lightning-rod in the battle between liberals and conservatives for the soul of the Constitution. The debate got off to a hyperbolic and mischievous start. Senator Edward Kennedy was ready with a powerful statement opposing the nomination:

> Robert Bork's America is a land in which women would be forced into back alley abortions, blacks would sit at segregated lunch counters, rogue police could break down citizen's doors in midnight raids, writers and artists could be censored at the whim of the government, and the doors of the federal courts would be shut on the fingers of millions of citizens.[18]

On the right, the Heritage Foundation had fired off an opposite salvo a week earlier:

> The Rehnquist Court believes the Constitution should be interpreted in light of the Founders' intent. The Brennan Court thinks the framers had no purpose (that they were, in effect, *non compos mentis* when they drafted our national charter). Or, if they did mean something, why should enlightened jurists follow the whims of a bunch of slave-owning, 18th-century yokels? The Rehnquist Court holds both society and victims have rights in criminal cases. If the Brennan Court had its way, police and prosecutors not only would be handcuffed, but simultaneously blindfolded, gagged and hog-tied. The Rehnquist Court believes in equality before the law, as does the Brennan Court, unless – of course – you happen to be a white male or an unborn child.[19]

Such passion fuelled interest groups on both sides of the political divide. Masterminded by the Leadership Conference on Civil Rights, an umbrella organization of nearly 200 groups, and building on the campaign against Rehnquist's nomination, Bork's opponents raised millions of dollars, launched a public campaign in the media, activated grassroots branches and orchestrated with great skill a multi-faceted campaign to derail the nomination. Remarkably they were joined by many groups not normally associated with the civil rights lobby (such as the Sierra Club Legal Defence Fund, the Association for Retarded Citizens and the National Mental Health Association) and they managed to galvanize popular opinion sufficiently to impress several wavering Senators, especially the critical Southern Senators who had been elected in 1986 largely by the votes of blacks. Suddenly a single event, the nomination of Judge Robert Bork, crystallized the opposition to Reagan and provided the opportunity to translate that antagonism into a triumph. With the Democrats back as the majority party in Senate, the Iran

Contra scandal fresh in their minds, concerns over Meese as Attorney-General still alive and fears over what Bork might do to many programmes close to their hearts, the momentum against confirmation built up.

The passion on Bork's side, though real enough, was insufficient to offset the liberal campaign. It was less well funded, less organized, less widely based. Judicial restraint did not raise dollars; conservative groups had already invested heavily in Reagan; the White House seemed too little committed to the nomination and then decided to package Bork as a moderate in Powell's mould (thus appearing disingenuous to many and wrong-headed to conservatives); and Bork himself, righteous and bearded, did his cause little good during the hearings which, unfortunately from his point of view, were more about symbols than constitutional law. When the Senate voted, 58 cast their votes against the nominee, thus providing the most decisive defeat for any candidate this century.

With the Bork nomination doomed, the President needed a new candidate. Because Bork had been the unquestioned choice that July, there was no runner-up ready to be promoted in his place.[20] In the White House, Chief of Staff Howard Baker wanted a readily confirmable candidate and he had a dozen possibilities which had been mentioned over the past years checked out. One seemed ideal and discussions on Capitol Hill strengthened his view that the Californian Anthony Kennedy, then a judge on the Ninth Circuit of Appeal, would be the right choice.

The Justice Department had other ideas. Bradford Reynolds and Charles Cooper favoured a younger man, very newly placed on the DC Circuit Court of Appeals. They knew him personally from the time when he worked in the anti-trust division of the department, they had witnessed him in action, and they were certain that his values were right. Douglas Ginsberg was 'one of us'. Fortified by an endorsement from Bork himself, Meese went to the White House with Ginsberg's name, determined not to be pressurized by fear of what the Senate might do into nominating only a second best choice.

Reagan was forced to arbitrate between the two positions. Losing the Bork nomination had hurt him, perhaps because he felt that he could and should have done more. When speaking extempore in New Jersey soon after the Senate vote, Reagan told his enthusiastically conservative audience that he would choose a nominee whom the Democrats would 'object to just as much as the last one'.[21] Ginsberg gave him a chance to do exactly that; additionally, he was ten years younger than Kennedy and could be expected to carry the Reagan legacy longer into the twenty-first century; above all, he was Meese's choice and the President was much closer in personal terms to Meese than to Baker.

The response to the nomination was very different from that which followed the announcement of Bork's name. No Edward Kennedy came forward to denounce him; the conservative interest groups immediately moved into supportive action, while the liberal groups bided their time. The following seven days proved almost farcical. Each day some new story broke in the media: Ginsberg had failed to acknowledge a conflict of interest when acting for the government; Ginsberg's wife had once performed two abortions; Ginsberg had been somewhat economical with the truth when cataloguing his forensic experience for the Senate Judiciary Committee; and Ginsberg had smoked marijuana when a young professor at Harvard University. None of these, even the last, would have been critical in a strong candidate, but the truth of the matter was that the virtue of youth masked the weakness of inexperience.

Liberals had wondered how to challenge Reagan's nomination. They did not have the sort of evidence, in speeches and writings and judgements, which they had manipulated so successfully in Bork's case. They did not need it. The conservatives themselves split. Given the First Lady's highly publicized crusade against drugs, given Meese's recent decision to initiate a mandatory urinalysis to test white-collar Justice Department employees, given the Religious Right's antipathy to the drug culture of the 1960s and early 1970s, suddenly it was the conviction conservatives who baulked. Secretary of Education and former anti-drug czar William Bennett was one of the earlier defectors, but he led a steady stream of public – and private – expressions of dissatisfaction. Some conservatives became convinced that the nomination was not winnable. The 500 000-member Concerned Women of America wired the White House urging that Ginsberg's name be withdrawn to avoid another protracted confirmation hearing ending in defeat, and the Moral Majority began to prepare a statement withdrawing support. As the Republican Senator Charles Grassley put it: 'You like to think people who are appointed to the Supreme Court respect the law.'[22] Before Reagan could formally nominate him to the vacancy created by Powell's retirement, Ginsberg withdrew his name from contention.

Reagan now really only had one choice.[23] It was Anthony Kennedy. But there were plenty of other experienced and capable lawyers who might have been in that position. Kennedy's advantages over others of equal, or even superior, qualities were the normal ones of personal and political connections. The Justice Department is the major, often the sole, generator and selector of names for nomination to the judicial branch and a very large number of people is suggested. Within the Department, Kennedy had enjoyed the support of three of his former law clerks, Richard Willard (then heading the civil division), Alex Kozinski (who was appointed out of the Department to the Ninth Circuit Court of Appeals) and Carolyn Kuhl (then Deputy Solicitor-General). Politically he had good connections with the Reagan team in California when the President was Governor and the Attorney-General his Counsel. These networks ensured that his name was first suggested and then kept in the frame.

Kennedy had hardly returned to California from Samoa (which his Ninth Circuit covered) when he was summoned again to Washington. Everybody was suddenly more cautious. The White House arranged a thorough interrogation to ensure that no Ginsberg-like skeletons lay in Kennedy's cupboard; but his life appeared blameless. The conservative groups gathered at the White House to plan a strategy; the liberal groups gathered in the headquarters of one of the many public interest organizations concerned with judicial appointments. Neither was quite certain what the most appropriate tactics would be, for both sides had their problems. The conservatives were divided among themselves. Kennedy was probably a safe appointment but he lacked the passion and commitment of Bork, or even Ginsberg. In many minds was the example of Harry Blackmun, appointed by Richard Nixon also after two successive failures and chosen finally as a compromise candidate who would be nominated safely. And there was Senator Jesse Helms expressing his opposition. Yet, realistically, this was probably the last chance for Reagan to nominate anybody successfully. A Democrat-controlled Senate would surely postpone another nomination until after the November Presidential elections. Kennedy was the only candidate conservatives were being offered; however reluctantly, he had to be supported. Liberals, too, found it difficult to work out an agreed and coordinated position. While some individual groups had specific reasons for opposition, Kennedy's record was nothing like Bork's. Furthermore the interest groups of both sides were exhausted, psychologically and financially. There was not enough passion on either side to cause trouble and an impressive, if uninformative, performance during the hearings ensured that, at last, Lewis Powell's position on the Court was filled. This was Reagan's last opportunity to nominate to the Supreme Court. In November 1988, George Bush defeated Michael Dukakis, a success which had at one time seemed unlikely, and for the next four years had the responsibility, should any vacancies occur, to make nominations to the Supreme Court.

When William Brennan retired in the summer of 1990, after 34 years, the Court lost its most articulate liberal. Bush was therefore provided with the opportunity to shift the balance of the Court even more decisively than Reagan had been in 1987.[24] His choice was an almost unknown New Hampshire bachelor called David Souter. This decision can be explained once again by evaluating the two contexts in which such nominations are made: the uniquely Presidential one and the wider Washington one.

Bush, despite his many years of public service, did not have a long list of political contacts from whom he might make a personal selection. He turned to his advisers, most notably C. Boyden Gray, the White House Counsel, and John Sununu, his Chief of Staff. As is usual, his Attorney-General, Dick

Thornburgh, was also involved, but not to the same extent as the others. The Justice Department had considered several possibilities once the nomination of Robert Bork ran into serious trouble and these names provided the basic pool from which a nominee would be selected. The media speculated, but gave no attention to two names which had been reviewed favourably back in 1987: David Souter and Clarence Thomas.

One of the New Hampshire Senators in 1987 had been Warren Rudman and he carried important clout in Republican circles, especially among their more moderate members. Rudman had been the Attorney-General in New Hampshire who appointed Souter as his deputy and he had been his patron ever since then. Many names are put in the pool of possibilities; the successful ones need supporters within the small group which filters out the many to provide a very limited number of names from which the President can choose. At the heart of this process was Bush's Chief of Staff, John Sununu, who had been Governor of New Hampshire and had appointed Souter to its Supreme Court. He and Rudman had also been instrumental in getting a somewhat hesitant Souter successfully nominated earlier in 1990 to the Circuit Court of Appeals which sits in Boston.

The Presidential context is critical, but it is not determinative. The Washington context has also to be considered. Bush felt himself further constrained by his perception of the political context in which the nomination would be made. The fall-out from the Bork nomination had not gone away. The Democrats in the Senate, who would need to confirm any nominee, made it quite clear that they would look with great disfavour on anybody who was publicly and explicitly opposed to the major philosophical beliefs of the retired William Brennan. Even Bob Dole, the Republican minority leader, warned Bush that anybody who was publicly known as an opponent of abortion rights would have a very rough passage in an election year. The message was clear: seek out a nominee without a 'paper trail'.

At the same time, however, Bush was under pressure from the conservative wing of his party, especially since he had reneged on his 1988 election promise not to raise taxes. It wanted a truly conservative nominee. This requirement was difficult to reconcile with the lack of a 'paper trail', but Sununu's personal links with Souter helped him to convince Gray (who had met the nominee earlier in the year and been much impressed) and then Bush that Souter was a genuine conservative. Certainly his jurisprudential views appeared conservative, although they lacked any sense of zealotry. He was very much a lawyer's lawyer, cautious, pro-government, apparently little concerned with the human dimension of legal disputes on which he had to adjudicate. He had certainly had no qualms, in his professional capacity as state Attorney-General, in defending some of the indefensible policies of the Governor of the day, Meldrim Thomson.

Finally he had many of the experiential qualities the White House was seeking. He had distinguished himself at Harvard, both as undergraduate and graduate, and had been a Rhodes Scholar (yet without the athletic prowess associated with that distinction); he had also spent two years in private practice in New Hampshire's capital, Concord, before serving its administration in the Attorney-General's office. He had judicial experience as a member of New Hampshire's Supreme Court, where he was acknowledged to be its intellectual leader, and had just been promoted to a federal Circuit Court of Appeals judgeship. This background suggested someone who would not be an activist judge, would have sympathy for state governments and would fit intellectually into the mould of an Anthony Kennedy or Sandra Day O'Connor rather than the more proselytizing conservatism of William Rehnquist or Antonin Scalia. His confirmation hearings disclosed nothing additional and Souter fielded the questions with a cautious sincerity and shrewd refusal to commit himself in the sensitive areas on which he would soon have to cast votes. On 2 October 1990, the Senate voted 90–9 to confirm David Souter as the 105th Justice of the Supreme Court.

In the following year Thurgood Marshall retired. A legend in his lifetime, Marshall had made his name arguing cases for the National Association for the Advancement of Colored Peoples (NAACP) and had run its Legal Defence Fund. He had been successful in the revolutionary *Brown v. Board of Education* decisions in 1954 and 1955 and had masterminded the litigation strategy which gradually dismantled the legal edifices of racial segregation. Nominated to the Court by Lyndon Johnson in 1967, after experience both as a circuit court judge and Solicitor-General, Marshall had been an unwavering support for the underdogs, especially Afro-American underdogs, when their cases came before the Supreme Court. Implacably opposed to the death penalty and committed to affirmative action and strict procedural standards for law enforcement officers, he saw his role as a Justice as being to protect the individual, through the Bill of Rights, against governments and their agents. In short, he stood for just about everything which activists in the conservative movement disliked.

Marshall's unexpected announcement produced similar responses from both conservative and liberal quarters.[25] Boyden Gray, who was the most important of Bush's advisers, immediately touted the advantages of Clarence Thomas, an African–American who had been chairman of the Equal Employment Opportunities Commission before being nominated to the DC Circuit Court of Appeals. His name had been on earlier lists and Bush was already favourably disposed towards him, both for what he was (a man whose independent effort had raised him from humble beginnings to national prominence) and what he stood for (a fierce opposition to affirmative action remedies for discrimination). Although others, including a Hispanic, were considered, Thomas was quickly flown up to Bush's holiday home in Kennibunkport and the nomination made. The President and candidate who both preached individual merit and the inappropriateness of quotas stood side by side, ironically precisely because Clarence Thomas was a black man.[26]

On the liberal side, Nan Aron, who ran the Alliance for Justice (a public interest organization which researched into judicial appointments), had guessed that Thomas would be the nominee. There were few other black Republicans of any standing and his appointment, following his high-profile defence of administration ideology, to the DC Circuit Court of Appeals seemed a sure sign that a way was being prepared for further promotion. The Democrats in the Senate were unsure how to respond to what was a politically astute nomination. Despite his ideological position and, ultimately, the opposition of the NAACP and the Congressional Black Caucus, the opinion polls indicated that black voters generally favoured his appointment. The pivotal Southern Democrats, whose votes would be vital, were torn between an intellectual belief that Thomas was not well enough qualified (a view shared by some members of the American Bar Association's Committee on the Federal Judiciary) and a political calculation that black votes could not be forgone.

The Thomas hearings ultimately fell into two sessions. In the first, the nominee copied Souter's policy of non-committal responses, but it was less successful. Thomas had published and spoken publicly too much; he had a record. His responses were disingenuous at best, deceitful at worst. The Judiciary Committee split equally 7–7, but voted nevertheless to send his nomination to the full Senate. Before that happened, however, allegations of sexual harassment (which the Committee had ignored before) now entered the public domain and the American people were offered on their television screens an astonishing show in which a young female, black professor from Oklahoma, Anita Hill, charged Thomas with sexual harassment and the Republicans' nominee rejected the allegations with passion. This unseemly and unsavoury, but widely devoured, confrontation solved nothing. The public, black and white, believed Thomas more than Hill; a handful of Democrats decided not to support Thomas; the Republican Senators' commitment to demolishing Hill's testimony was stronger than the Democrats' concern to check Thomas's story. The vote was agonizingly close and Thomas took the place honoured by Thurgood Marshall, by 52 votes to 48.

The Thomas nomination again raised questions about the manner of the Senate's confirmation procedures and the values employed by Presidents in selecting Justices of the Supreme Court. The allegations against Thomas could not have helped ease his integration into the Court, nor did the somewhat unseemly haste in which he took the oath of office; Chief Justice

Rehnquist's wife had died after a painful illness just two days after the Senate vote, but the administration insisted on speed and would not wait a few days while the Chief Justice, and others on the Court, had their minds on sadder and more personal matters. The wider impact of the hearings is also only conjectural, but, for many articulate and educated women, the treatment of Anita Hill by an all-white, all-male Committee, manifestly out of sympathy with the reality of sexual harassment, galvanized them into action. The 1992 elections, both primary and national, brought more women to Washington as elected representatives than ever before. That was, surely, more than just a coincidence.[27]

The Consequences of Recent Nominations

Behind nearly every nomination to the Supreme Court lies a Presidential policy goal. For the most part such a goal will be closely related to specific decisions taken by the Court or to issues addressed by it and the nomination will be intended to advance that goal. In examining nominations, therefore, two distinct aspects need to be considered: first, the fit between a President's real goals and the person nominated to the Court needs to be studied; second, the degree to which the successful nominee then actually advances the President's goals can be estimated.

Ronald Reagan, well supported by those involved in the selection of judicial nominations, had a clear vision of his goals when selecting potential candidates. There were specific Supreme Court decisions with which he explicitly disagreed (*Schempp, Miranda, Bakke, Swann* and *Roe* are the most obvious) and he also shared the conservative view that the Court had been too keen to protect minorities and individuals against the laws and regulations passed by majoritarian institutions such as state governments. On the electoral stump in 1986, he made the point in almost every speech that his appointments to the federal courts were an essential part of his, and the Republican, agenda and that Rehnquist and Scalia had been two of his very best.[28] While George Bush was less explicit, he – and above all Boyden Gray, who advised him – was also committed to appointments according to the same principles as his predecessor. Judicial ideology was the starting-point, but other goals were also present on occasions. Thus representational symbolism affected the exact choice on some occasions (O'Connor, Scalia, Thomas) while confirmability was of importance on others (Kennedy, Souter).

The central truth about nominations is that Presidents prevail. And this was true of Reagan and Bush. Since Ginsberg was never actually nominated, the only failure was Robert Bork. His experience merely strengthens the general rules that apply, as they have always applied, to that single occasion in the American constitutional system when all three branches of government are momentarily linked. Presidents only face serious problems when they are perceived to be weak, when the opposition party (or contrary ideology) controls the Senate, and the candidate encapsulates and exaggerates the political differences of the day.[29] Reagan was entering his final year of office under the shadow of the Iran Contra controversy, a jubilant Democratic party had regained control of the Senate, and Bork himself epitomized what the most conservative politicians cherished and the most liberal politicians feared. The candidate himself was more significant than perhaps ever before because he activated the most widespread and passionate *popular* involvement in a nomination that the United States has ever experienced. In all the other cases, even those like Rehnquist's promotion and Thomas's nomination, not all the three critical factors were present. But, of course, one reason why they were not on other occasions follows from a conscious decision by the President to choose a confirmable candidate rather than somebody who reflected accurately his own judicial preferences. To some extent, therefore, political calculation weakened the fit between nominator and nominee.

Whether successful nominees will behave as their sponsors hope is another matter. Judging whether Reagan and Bush were able to 'pack the Court' with their nominees is difficult. In the first place, the criteria are unclear. At one end of the spectrum, it can be argued that Reagan's goal (and presumably Bush's as well), for instance, was simply to reverse *Schempp*, *Roe* and company. Reagan himself only changed three of the nine Justices (O'Connor for Stewart, Scalia for Burger, Kennedy for Powell) and it takes five Justices to form a majority. But Bush's additions (Souter for Brennan, Thomas for Marshall) not only made the number up to five, they also replaced the most liberal Justices, whereas Reagan had only been able to replace two moderate conservatives and one conservative. Using the overruling test, however, Reagan and Bush failed. Far from overruling the decisions they disliked, the Court in several cases went out of its way to reaffirm them.[30]

A weaker test would produce a different answer. This test looks at less high-profile cases (concerning access to the courts, anti-trust suits or prisoner complaints), at the real impact of what at first sight might appear disappointing judgements (*Casey* both reaffirmed *Roe* and upheld virtually all the Pennsylvania regulations) and at statutory construction (limiting affirmative action, cutting back on presumed civil rights). This perspective comes up with a very different picture. A close inspection of David Souter's votes during his first term, for example, reveals that, in twelve 5–4 decisions in which he formed part of the majority, he almost certainly voted in a way different from that expected of William Brennan, whom he replaced.[31]

The centre of a Court's gravity can often be discovered by seeing who dissents least and who dominates in the majority of 5–4 decisions. Table 5.1 provides some statistics to show how the jurisprudence of the Court is, by this test, dominated by the nominees of Reagan and Bush.

Table 5.1   5–4 votes, 1988 to 1992 terms

	1988	1989	1990	1991	1992
Rehnquist	27*	26*	15*	4	14*
White	27*	30*	9	8	10*
Blackmun	12	4	9	9*	7
Stevens	8	18	9	10*	7
O'Connor	25*	26*	15*	8*	8
Scalia	25*	24*	11*	5	14*
Kennedy	28*	25*	11*	9*	13*
Souter	—	—	14*	13*	4
Thomas	—	—	—	4	13*

Note: In each of these terms, one block of five voted together more than 50 per cent of the time in all 5–4 decisions. An asterisk represents membership of such a block. This table is compiled by the author from the annual statistics prepared for the first number of each volume of the *Harvard Law Review*.

What makes evaluating the fit between a nominator's hope and an appointee's performance difficult is that some Justices develop – that is, change – their judicial philosophy over the years.[32] Experience can be a great teacher, although this is by no means always the case. Some Justices have precommitted themselves, in the sense that their writings and speeches (and even their judgements) have solidified their views, from which a public repudiation would be almost unthinkable. In this category might be placed Rehnquist, Scalia and Thomas, all of whom had explicitly nailed their intellectual positions to a public mast. The others, however, came to the Court without fully developed, let alone publicly expressed, views on the great issues of the day. Nobody should imagine that O'Connor, Kennedy and Souter are developing into liberals of the Brennan, Marshall, even Blackmun mould, but their votes in the 1991 and 1992 terms seemed less conservative, less pro-government and anti-claimant, than expected.

It is possible, indeed, to make the counter-intuitive argument that the Court has become more liberal. Table 5.2 provides the statistics for such a position. There are several ways to read these figures. First, the brazen liberalism of Brennan and Marshall may have strengthened the unity of the conservatives. With their retirements and an equally brazen conservatism expressed by Scalia and Thomas, the moderate conservatives may have become more centrist. It is an open secret, for instance, that O'Connor was antagonized by the sharpness of Scalia's strictures on her abortion decisions. Second, the issues may themselves have changed. The gross number of civil liberties cases on the docket has fallen markedly and some of them required the reining in of over-enthusiastically conservative judges in the appeal courts. Third, some of the civil liberties cases were decided on grounds that were not civil libertarian; Rehnquist, for example, might defer to local politicians (one of his highly salient values) and so fortuitously support a liberal outcome. Finally, some Justices may actually have changed their view on the bench and there is some evidence that, at the margin, both Kennedy and Souter are now more likely to desert the true conservative block than they were in their first terms.

By the end of the 1992 term, the most important Justices were the trio of O'Connor, Kennedy and Souter, who provided, as Stewart and White had done in the early 1970s, the fulcrum round which different blocks rotated.[33]

Table 5.2   Decisions in civil liberties cases, 1980 to 1991 terms

Term	Direction of decision			
	Liberal		Conservative	
	%	no.	%	no.
1980	34.2	26	65.8	50
1981	41.8	38	58.2	53
1982	36.8	32	63.2	55
1983	33.7	35	66.3	69
1984	41.4	36	58.6	51
1985	37.6	38	62.4	63
1986	45.3	43	54.7	52
1987	48.0	36	52.0	39
1988	36.8	32	63.2	55
1989	36.6	26	63.4	45
1990	44.3	27	55.7	34
1991	46.2	31	53.7	36

Source: Christopher E. Smith and Thomas R. Hensley, 'Assessing the conservatism of the Rehnquist Court', *Judicature*, **77**, September–October 1993, p.85.

While the cautious conservatism shown by O'Connor (except in federalism cases) and Souter might have been anticipated from the facts surrounding their nominations, Kennedy's development has surprised some observers. His *Casey* opinion (and his new awareness of a place for the separation of church and state in *Lee* v. *Weisman*) is the most obvious instance. But, again, his background, which had not encouraged precommitment on the major issues facing the Court, allowed growth, a fear as to which those in the conservative movement in retrospect were correct to hold when they queried his nomination.

The focus on the Justices is natural, given the significance of the Supreme Court's judgement in some important areas of American life. But the political system is interactive and no single branch can be isolated from the others. Some of the judgements made by the Rehnquist Court, most obviously in the civil rights field in 1989, worried liberals and provided the basis for a widespread evaluation of the Court as, at long last, truly conservative; but it also disturbed the Democrat-controlled Congress, whose laws had been the subject of those conservative rulings. In 1991, despite George Bush's opposition, a major Civil Rights Act was passed which effectively overruled those decisions. It is also claimed that the spin-off from the hearings on Clarence Thomas's nomination galvanized many women not only to stand for public office but to vote for women, and so affected the results of the 1992 Congressional elections. That is difficult to show conclusively, but it is a reminder that the American political system is constantly responding to events and that the courts, dignified though they aim to be, are soon involved in the day-to-day business of politics.

Richard Nixon was right to remind Ronald Reagan that his judicial appointments would be a legacy which would be influential long after the end of his Presidency. He failed, however, to warn him about the possible consequences of an independent judiciary. Careful selection of candidates will undoubtedly enhance the likelihood of a President's goals being accurately reflected in later judicial decisions; but it cannot ensure an extended and close fit. William Rehnquist is intellectually sharper and personally more congenial than his predecessor, but he has not marshalled the Court.[34] The propensity to dissent or issue concurring opinions has not diminished. And the reason is simple: able men and women appointed to the Court will express their independence of thought because there are no sanctions – and no carrots – to persuade them otherwise. The final stocktaking of the Reagan–Bush legacy will not be made for many years yet, since we cannot know either what new issues will be faced by the Supreme Court at the century's end or how the Justices will continue to develop their jurisprudence. To complicate matters further, subsequent Presidents, like Bill Clinton, will dilute their appointments with appointments of their own.

Notes

1 Cited in William French Smith, *Law and Justice in the Reagan Administration: The memoirs of an Attorney General*, Hoover Institution Press, 1991, p.58.
2 Richard Hodder-Williams, *The Politics of the US Supreme Court*, Allen & Unwin, 1980, p.19.
3 See, generally, Louis Fisher, *Constitutional Dialogues: Interpretation as political process*, Princeton University Press, 1988.
4 *Brown* v. *Board of Education*, 347 US 484 (1954) outlawing segregated public schools; *Abington School District* v. *Schempp*, 374 US 203 (1963) outlawing prayers in public schools; *Miranda* v. *Arizona*, 384 US 436 (1966) detailing suspects' rights; *Reynolds* v. *Sims*, 377 US 533 (1964) requiring one man, one vote value; *Swann* v. *Charlotte-Mecklenburg School District*, 402 US 1 (1971) permitting busing as a means to desegregate; *Roe* v. *Wade*, 410 US 113 (1973) establishing a limited right to an abortion.
5 *Constitution*, Article III, Section 1.
6 See Henry Abraham, *Justices and Presidents: A political history of appointments to the Supreme Court*, Oxford University Press, 3rd edn, 1992, pp.5, 240–50.
7 See, generally, Abraham, *Justices and Presidents*; Jeffrey A. Segal and Harold J. Spaeth, *The Supreme Court and the Attitudinal Model*, Cambridge University Press, 1993, pp.125–64; Hodder-Williams, *Politics*, pp.19–33.
8 The account of the O'Connor nomination is drawn from Elder Witt, *A Different Justice: Reagan and the Supreme Court*, Congressional Quarterly Press, 1986, pp.29–43; Smith, *Law and Justice*, pp.62–9; David Savage, *Turning Right: The making of the Rehnquist Supreme Court*, Wiley, 1992, *passim*; Abraham, *Justices and Presidents*, pp.338–48; Susan Mann and Dan Fiduccia, 'Sandra Day O'Connor: The making of a precedent', *Stanford Lawyer*, **16**, Fall/Winter 1981, pp.5–8.
9 Cited in Witt, *A Different Justice*, p.33.
10 Beverley B. Cook, 'Women as Supreme Court candidates; From Florence Allen to Sandra O'Connor', *Judicature*, **65**, 1981–2, pp.314–26.
11 Mann and Fiduccia, 'O'Connor', p.5.
12 For the argument that Powell was, except for a few high-visibility cases, a firm member of a conservative block, see Janet L. Blasecki, 'Justice Lewis Powell: Swing voter or staunch conservative?', *Journal of Politics*, **52**, 1990, pp.530–47.
13 The quotations in this paragraph are taken from *Newsday*, 6 November 1987.
14 Donald Regan, *For the Record: From Wall Street to Washington*, Harcourt Brace Jovanovich, 1988, p.330.
15 The following account of the Rehnquist and Scalia nominations is taken from Savage, *Turning Right, passim*; Abraham, *Justices and Presidents*, pp.350–54.
16 Sandra Day O'Connor, 'A tribute to Justice Lewis F. Powell Jr.', *Harvard Law Review*, **101**, 1987–8, p.395.
17 This account of the Bork nomination is drawn from Richard Hodder-Williams, 'The strange story of Judge Robert Bork and a vacancy on the United States Supreme Court', *Political Studies*, **36**, 1988, pp.613–37; Ethan Bronner, *Battle for Justice: How the Bork nomination shook America*, Norton, 1989; Michael Pertschuk and Wendy Schaetzel, *The People Rising: The campaign against the Bork nomination*, Thunder's Mouth Press, 1989.
18 Cited in Segal and Spaeth, *The Supreme Court*, p.138.
19 Don Feder, 'Supreme Courts', Heritage Features Syndicate, 29 June 1987.
20 This account of the Ginsberg nomination is drawn from Herman Schwartz, *Packing*

the Courts; The conservative campaign to rewrite the Constitution, Scribner's, 1988, pp.144–8; Savage, *Turning Right*, pp.176–80; and the press files kindly lent to me by Patrick McGuigan.

21 Cited in *Washington Post*, 12 November 1987.

22 Savage, *Turning Right*, p.179.

23 This account of the Kennedy nomination is drawn from Savage, *Turning Right*, pp.174–82; Abraham, *Justices and Presidents*, pp.359–61.

24 This account of the Souter nomination is drawn from Robert McKeever, 'Courting the Congress: President Bush and the nomination of David H. Souter', *Politics*, **11**, 1991, pp.26–33; Savage, *Turning Right*, pp.350–58; Abraham, *Justices and Presidents*, pp.366–9; and two articles by Ruth Marcus and Joe Picharalli in *Washington Post*, 9 and 10 September, 1990.

25 The account of the Thomas nomination is drawn from Timothy Phelps and Helen Winternitz, *Capitol Games*, Hyperion, 1992; Savage, *Turning Right*, pp.423–58; Christopher E. Smith, *Critical Judicial Nominations and Political Change: The impact of Clarence Thomas*, Praeger, 1993, pp.45–122; *PS: Political Science and Politics*, **25**, 1992, pp.473–95.

26 Ironically Thomas had been admitted to Yale Law School on an affirmative action programme.

27 This is the central thesis of Smith, *Critical Judicial Nominations*.

28 See, for example, the series of speeches he gave in 1986 when campaigning on behalf of Republican candidates in *Public Papers of the Presidents: Ronald Reagan 1986* (Government Printing Office, 1988).

29 Segal and Spaeth, *The Supreme Court*, pp.125–64.

30 For example, *Morgan* v. *Illinois*, 112 S.Ct. 2222 (1992); *Planned Parenthood of Southern Pennsylvania* v. *Casey*, 112 S.Ct. 2791 (1992) (plurality); *Lee* v. *Weisman*, 112 S.Ct. 2649 (1992).

31 Christopher E. Smith and Scott P. Johnson, 'Newcomer on the High Court: Justice Souter and the Supreme Court's 1990 Term', *South Dakota Law Review*, **37**, 1992, pp.21–43.

32 William Mishler and Reginald S. Sheehan, 'The Supreme Court as a countermajoritarian institution? The impact of public opinion on Supreme Court decisions', *American Journal of Political Science*, **87**, 1993, pp.87–101.

33 See Christopher E. Smith and T.R. Hensley, 'Assessing the conservatism of the Rehnquist Court', *Judicature*, **77**, 1993–4, pp.83–9.

34 David W. Rohde and Harold J. Spaeth, 'Ideology, strategy and Supreme Court decisions: William Rehnquist as chief justice', *Judicature*, **72**, 1988–9, pp.247–50; Sue Davis, 'Power on the Court: Chief Justice Rehnquist's opinion assignments', *Judicature*, **74**, 1990–91, pp.66–72; Jeffrey A. Segal and Harold J. Spaeth, 'Rehnquist Court disposition of lower court decisions: Affirmation not reversal', *Judicature*, **74**, 1990–91, pp.84–8.

6 The Right After Reagan: Crack-Up or Comeback?

Nigel Ashford

In 1980, Ronald Reagan was elected as the most conservative President of the United States of the postwar period and many commentators believed that his Presidency would usher in a conservative era, ending the dominance of liberal New Deal ideas since 1932. However, since Reagan's period of office ended in 1989, there has been considerable talk of 'the conservative crack-up', to the effect that the conservative movement was falling apart. Conservative columnist R. Emmett Tyrrell Jr., in *The Conservative Crack-Up*, argued that the conservative movement had lost its sense of definition and purpose. Paul Gottfried in the 1993 edition of *The Conservative Movement* stated: 'The postwar conservative movement analyzed in the first [1988] edition had largely disappeared by 1990'. Liberal *New Republic* journalist John Judis claimed that 'the conservative movement that carried Reagan to victory barely exists any longer: it has dissipated into various cantankerous and confused factions; and the ideas associated with it have become obsolete, discredited, or heavily in dispute among themselves'. Edward Ashbee argued that the conservative coalition had splintered, while Alan Grant suggested that the Reagan coalition had fractured without the glue of anti-communism and prosperity to hold it together.[1]

The case for a conservative crack-up presented in this literature is, first, the crisis of the conservative issue agenda with the collapse of communism, an economic recession attributed by some to free market economics and the threat posed by unpopular social conservatism; second, the decline of many conservative organizations and the growing war between the remaining ones; third, the takeover of the Republican party by the Christian Right; fourth, a swing against conservatism by public opinion; and fifth, the lack of a clear leader.

After presenting the rise of conservatism, this chapter will critically examine the evidence for each of these claims and conclude that the conservative movement is more likely to make a comeback than to crack up and is in a strong position to capture political power in the rest of the 1990s and beyond.

The Rise of Conservatism

After the New Deal and the World War II, liberalism dominated American politics, with conservatism marginalized. Louis Hartz even argued that America was fundamentally liberal, and therefore conservatism was alien to the USA.[2] In the 1950s there was a revival of conservative ideas. In his excellent *The Conservative Intellectual Movement in America*, George Nash identified three streams of thought contributing to this revival: libertarianism, traditionalism and anti-communism.[3] Libertarians promoted a free market economy and criticized the growth of the role of government in economic and other aspects of life. The intellectual leaders were Milton Friedman, Friedrich Hayek and Ludwig von Mises. Traditionalists such as Russell Kirk and Peter Viereck lamented the demise of moral standards and the decline of virtue and its replacement by the satisfaction of wants and the pursuit of instant gratification. The third school were anti-communists, such as James Burnham and Whittaker Chambers, who viewed the defeat of communism as the central issue of their time, to which all other issues should be subordinated. Between these schools there were fundamental differences of principle and priorities.[4] Libertarians celebrated the freedom of the individual as the primary goal of politics and viewed government as the greatest threat to freedom, while traditionalists emphasized the pursuit of virtue as promoted through traditional institutions such as the family, church and voluntary associations, which were being undermined by the growing role of the state. However they were united against the threat of a centralizing, all-encompassing, bureaucratic and utopian state. Most accepted the idea of 'fusionism', that the protection of freedom was the political goal and the promotion of virtue was the goal of man as an individual in his or her private life, which enabled the three schools to largely agree on the appropriate policies of government. Frank Meyer and William F. Buckley Jr., in the magazine *National Review*, promoted this fusionist vision. In terms of policy, the three pillars of conservatism were an anti-communist foreign policy requiring a strong defence and a global presence, a free market economy and opposition to the power of the state undermining traditional values. In 1964, conservatism was widely viewed as having been rejected with the massive defeat of Barry Goldwater in the Presidential election, obtaining only 39 per cent of the vote. (Conservatives were later to note that it was only 4 per cent less than Clinton received in 1992.) However the campaign brought together a large number of activists into the conservative movement and helped turn the Republicans into a predominantly conservative party.

In the 1970s the movement was reinvigorated by the entry of three new groups: the neo-conservatives, the New Right and the Christian Right.[5] Neo-conservatives were former liberal Democrats who came to question many liberal policies in reaction to the New Left on campuses in the 1960s, the attack on US policy in Vietnam as morally corrupt rather than a tactical mistake, and the failure of many of the 'Great Society' government programmes introduced by President Lyndon Johnson in 1965–8.[6] Irving Kristol, known as the 'godfather' of neo-conservatism, described them as 'liberals mugged by reality'. They became increasingly sceptical about the capacity of government to solve social problems. They promoted an agenda of a consensus of political and moral values; a free market modified by basic welfare provision such as education; the revival of community structures; the restoration of a pluralist political system; and a strong defence and the vigorous promotion of American values in international affairs.

The second group was the New Right, which contributed a strongly populist tone to conservatism by appealing to working-class voters with social issues such as crime, abortion and the right to bear arms. The key figures were the direct-mail fund-raiser Richard Viguerie, Paul Weyrich of the Free Congress Foundation, Howard Phillips of the Conservative Caucus and Terry Dolan of the National Conservative Political Action Committee (NCPAC). Their strategy was to win elections by the use of direct-mail fund-raising, independent PACs, improved campaign organization, the use of single issues and the mobilization of fundamentalist Christian voters.

The last factor led to the creation of a third group, the Christian Right. Fundamentalist Christians are those who believe that the Bible is truth and inerrant, whilst evangelicals believe that they are 'born again' and have come into personal contact with God. They have normally been politically inactive, but a number of issues emerged in the 1970s which drew them into politics: abortion, the loss of tax exemption for religious schools, the Equal Rights Amendment, the promotion of homosexuality as an acceptable lifestyle, the ban on voluntary school prayer, feminism and pornography. The New Right strategists encouraged the creation of a number of organizations to appeal to these fundamentalists, such as the Moral Majority, headed by Jerry Falwell, Christian Voice, the National Christian Action Coalition and the Religious Roundtable. Many popular fundamentalist preachers on television and radio began to introduce political messages in between their religious ones. Conservative preachers included Falwell, with his 'Old Time Gospel Hour', Pat Robertson of the Christian Broadcasting Network, James Robison, and Jim and Tammy Bakker. They claimed to have registered millions of voters in 1980, brought many Christians into political activity for the first time and to have contributed to Reagan's decisive victory.

Reagan emerged as the candidate best able to unite this diverse coalition behind him in his 1980 election campaign around the themes of less government, strong defence and traditional values. His ten-point victory over incumbent President Carter was accompanied by Republican gains of 12 Senate seats, 33 House seats, four Governorships, 189 state legislative seats and five state legislative chambers. The greatest gains were among Democrat core voters, such as union families, manual workers, Southerners, Catholics, the old and the non-college-educated, who became known as Reagan Democrats. Some commentators believed that 1980 would usher in a conservative era to follow that of the New Deal as Reagan's victory reflected a shift to the right among both opinion leaders and the electorate.[7] It was this claim that the 'crack-up' literature in the early 1990s opposed.

Reagan himself pursued and articulated a clear conservative agenda in office: lower taxes, reducing the growth of federal government expenditure, deregulation and lower inflation in economic policy; in foreign policy, increased defence expenditure, and greater ideological and political competition with the Soviet Union in order to contribute to its demise and consign it to the waste-bin of history; and the restoration of faith in traditional values such as the family.[8] While his record in achieving these goals was mixed and frequently built on developments that preceded his period of office, nonetheless 'There can be described something called a Reagan Revolution: it constitutes a change in the political agenda and the options that may now be seriously considered by government.'[9] Mervin concluded that Reagan had been one of the most effective post-war Presidents in terms of achieving his key objectives.[10]

Reagan himself emerged from his period of office with widespread popularity among the American people. However the crack-up literature presents an image of conservative ideas and movement in a less healthy state than in 1980.

The Crisis of Ideas

Foreign Policy

Some observers have argued that the strongest uniting factor in the conservative movement was anti-communism, and that without that issue the coalition would collapse. Traditionalists viewed communism as a threat to Western civilization, libertarians opposed its demands for state control of the economy and society, anti-communists viewed the defeat of communism as the primary goal of the USA, neo-conservatives saw communism as the biggest obstacle to the spread of global democracy, the New Right viewed it as anti-American and the Christian Right saw it as atheistic and anti-Christian. All conservatives could agree on the necessity, and the priority, to combat communism as an ideology and the Soviet Union as the strongest military and political power behind it. Reagan substantially increased defence expenditure, from 5 per cent of GNP in 1980 to 6.4 per cent in 1988; launched the Strategic Defense Initiative ('Star Wars') of anti-nuclear weapons which culminated in the Intermediate Nuclear Forces (INF) treaty with the Soviet Union in 1987; and articulated the Reagan Doctrine of the promotion of the superiority of Western values over communism, backing for anti-communist guerrillas and support for the spread of democracy.[11] Conservatives believed that the collapse of communism in 1989 was a tribute to Reagan's policy of 'Peace through Strength'.

By the early 1990s, anti-communism had largely won, with the collapse of communism in eastern Europe and the crack-up of the Soviet Union. Communism remained in place in several countries, notably China, but it did not create a direct threat to the United States and communism had lost its appeal as an ideology. It was no longer a viable alternative to liberal democracy. Anti-communism was no longer suitable as the guiding principle of conservative foreign policy, and increased military capacity lost its appeal with the disappearance of the only other superpower. Three schools of thought emerged on what a post-Cold War conservative foreign policy should be in response to the collapse of communism.

The 'neo-isolationist', or 'new nationalist', school called for America First. This was a return to an earlier isolationist tradition of the Old Right in which America should avoid foreign entanglements. The Old Right had been opposed to US entry into World War II until the bombing of Pearl Harbor, and under Senator Robert Taft had initially opposed the Truman Doctrine of active anti-communist interventionism. Pat Buchanan, the television commentator and former Reagan Director of Communications, called for 'America First, Second and Third. When this Cold War is over, Americans should come home.'[12] The US involvement in the rest of the world had been a necessity arising from the unusual nature of the Soviet threat. With the decline of that threat, America should bring its troops home from Europe and Korea, and remove itself from its alliances. Most outbreaks of conflict in the world do not directly affect American national interests, according to Buchanan, and if they do America can act unilaterally. Buchanan had opposed the Gulf War until the US troops were in battle and he did not wish to undermine the war effort.

A second 'idealist', or 'democratic internationalist', school argued that the campaign against communism had not simply been a negative one against an alien power and ideology, but also a positive one for the promotion of universal values of democracy, free markets and human rights which were the fundamental principles of the United States.[13] It urged a strategy of the promotion of global democracy, which reflected the fundamental values of the USA (a prerequisite for popular support for interventionism), continued American leadership of the free world after the Cold War, and an enlightened understanding of the national interest. Compared to liberal internationalists, they are more sceptical about international institutions which may play a useful role but are no substitute for US leadership. Their argument is that democracies do not go to war with each other, so that a democratic world would be a peaceful one. The goal is universal dominance of Western ideals of liberal democracy, individual rights and market-oriented economies. This was the underlying theme of Francis Fukuyama's famous article, 'The End of History': that the future would lead to the universal acceptance of democratic capitalism.[14]

A third 'neo-realist' school articulated a foreign policy based on the promotion of the national interest but which would involve a much more extensive international role for the United States than the isolationists demanded.[15] It recognized the high degree of international interdependency of the USA and its extensive global interests, and rejected neo-isolationism. However it was critical of global democracy as a goal of US foreign policy because its advocates exaggerate the capacity of the United States to correct the moral imperfections of the rest of the world and the willingness of the American people to sacrifice men and money for such interventionism. The Heritage Foundation presented a detailed strategy on these lines, which stated that

> The United States should intervene around the globe only when vital national interests are at stake. To do more would violate our government's constitutional mandate: to protect and defend American lives, liberty and property. This does not mean however that the US should assume an isolationist stance.[16]

The neo-realist school is the one that best reflects the views of the majority of conservatives. It both expresses the belief that American values of liberal democracy, human rights and the free market economy are worthy ideals of universal value, which it is desirable for the United States to promote in its own national interest, and remains sceptical about the capacity of the United States to determine developments in other countries. Its views can be found expressed in the studies of the American Enterprise Institute and the Heritage Foundation and in the pages of *The National Interest*, in Bush's incoherent and inarticulate talk of a New World Order, and in conservative scepticism towards US action in Bosnia, Somalia and Haiti.

The Economy

Reagan summed up the conservative approach to the economy as 'Government is not the solution to our problems, it is the problem'.[17] Reagan pursued a policy of low taxes, a reduction in the growth of government expenditure, deregulation and the control of the money supply.[18] Most conservatives view the Reagan years as a great success story. Robert Bartley, editor of the *Wall Street Journal*, described them as *The Seven Fat Years*.[19] Between 1981 and 1989 there was a 31 per cent real growth in GNP, 18.4 million new civilian jobs, a 48 per cent increase in manufacturing output, a 10.6 per cent increase in productivity per hour of labour, a 32 per cent increase in gross private investment, a 5.1 per cent increase in charitable giving per annum, a 22.5 per cent increase in tax revenues, an 18 per cent increase in real disposable income per capita, an 11 per cent increase in median family income and the income of the poorest fifth rose by 5.6 per cent. Economic growth averaged 4.2 per cent from 1982 to 1988, the longest, strongest, non-inflationary economic expansion in world history. Inflation declined from 12.5 per cent in 1980 to 4.5 per cent in 1988, interest rates fell from 25.1 per cent to 10 per cent and unemployment declined from 7 per cent to 5.4 per cent despite the dramatic increase in 1981–2 to 10 per cent. However, whilst applauding the achievements of the Reagan years, conservatives were divided into three schools over the priorities for the future in economic policy.

A protectionist school felt that the gains had mainly been at the expense of ordinary workers in manufacturing industry, who suffered from unrestricted economic competition from low-waged workers abroad. They criticized the global free trade policies of both Republican and Democrat administrations, which they presented as a cosmopolitan and elitist Eastern Establishment under the influence of foreign lobbyists, especially from Japan, and remote from the interests of Middle Americans. Echoing back to an earlier tradition of the Grand Old Party (GOP) as the tariff party, they argued for a wall of tariffs, quotas and subsidies to keep out foreign goods, a Fortress America. Buchanan was the leading spokesman for protectionism on the right. Economic nationalists include the US Business and Industrial Council, the journal *Chronicles*, businessman Roger Milliken and some Senate and House Republicans. Former Republican strategist Kevin Phillips argued in his critique of Reaganism that economic nationalism rather than free trade was in the best interests of the average American and was the most successful electoral strategy for the Republican party.[20] They, together with Ross Perot, opposed the North American Free Trade Agreement (NAFTA) with Mexico and Canada. Most conservatives, in the think-tanks, magazines and among Congressional Republicans, however, remained free-traders and endorsed NAFTA. A few free-marketeers criticized NAFTA for being too interventionist with the creation of numerous bureaucratic committees on environmental and labour regulations, but they were a distinct minority. Conservatives remain overwhelmingly in favour of free trade.

The second group of critics were 'the deficit hawks' who were disturbed by the growth of the federal government deficit in the Reagan years, from $59.6 billion in 1980 to $155 billion in 1988, from 2.3 per cent of GNP to 5.1 per cent. They accepted the view that the tax reductions were a major contributory factor to the deficits and were willing to accept some tax increases to reduce the deficit. This contributed to the budget deal between President Bush and Congress in 1990 which increased taxes substantially, thereby breaking his 'Read my lips, no new taxes' pledge made during the 1988 campaign. Most conservatives reject this argument. They blame the deficit on the growth in expenditure. Tax revenues rose by $383 billion (22.5 per cent), defence expenditure by $149 billion (111 per cent) and domestic expenditure by $316 billion (70 per cent). They believe that it was the failure to control domestic expenditures that caused the deficit, that tax revenues grew sufficiently to pay for higher defence expenditure and still relieve some of the deficit if only domestic expenditure had been kept under control. They note that the 1990 budget deal led to much less revenue than predicted, a considerable increase in federal expenditure and a bigger budget deficit.

This leads to the third school of critics, 'the budget cutters', who claimed that the Reagan administration had been insufficiently vigorous in attacking expenditure. Indeed Reagan had declared in his first State of the Union address, 'It is important to note that we are only reducing the rate of increase in taxing and spending. We are not attempting to cut either spending or taxing to a level below that which we presently have'.[21] A variety of strategies were followed: the abolition or reduction of programmes, greater efficiency, returning responsibilities from federal to state and local governments, privatization and institutional reforms.[22] However the great increase in expenditure was in welfare entitlements, such as social security and health care, which were deemed 'uncontrollable expenditures'. The administration's failure to attack the welfare state was attributed by some conservatives to the malign influence of neo-conservatives, who criticize many failures of the system as it has developed but do not object to the welfare state in principle. Irving Kristol claimed that neo-conservatism

> feels no lingering hostility to the welfare state, nor does it accept it resignedly, as a necessary evil. Instead it seeks not to dismantle the welfare state in the name of free market economics but rather to shape it so as to attach to it the conservative dispositions of the people.[23]

One example of this was when Reagan's 1980 call for the abolition of the Department of Education on the grounds that education was a state responsibility was replaced by the department being used as a platform to promote conservative educational values by the neo-conservatives, such as his Education Secretary Bill Bennett.

Culture

Traditional values have been a constant theme of conservatives but, under fusionism, their attention was directed mainly at ways in which government had undermined such values. While some libertarians might defend a 'woman's right to choose' an abortion, they objected to the idea that taxpayers should pay for it, so they could support the Reagan administration's policies to prevent the use of public funds for abortion. There was also general agreement on the 'civic virtues' of hard work, self-discipline, a capacity for deferred gratification, the importance of the family, civic-mindedness and personal responsibility. Nearly all conservatives agreed that it was government actions of various sorts which had undermined these values. Furthermore social issues were a lower priority for the Reagan administration than lower taxes and a stronger defence, so libertarians unhappy with a stress on social conservatism did not feel threatened. The main actions of the administration were the appointment of conservative judges who opposed judicial activism, the promotion of educational reforms through public debate such as the report of the National Commission on Excellence in Education, and on abortion where federal funding both domestically and internationally was ended.[24] Social issues were viewed by most conservatives as primarily the responsibility of family, church and community, or if necessary state and local governments, so a limited federal agenda was accepted.

Crime has emerged as one of the major social issues of the 1990s. Conservatives attribute the increase in crime to the breakdown of traditional institutions such as the family and the pursuit of instant gratification. Liberalism has contributed to the devaluation of personal honesty by creating an entitlement culture, by excusing criminal behaviour as a result of difficult personal circumstances and by making changes in the law that restrict the capacity of law enforcement agencies to carry out their work. Conservatives call for the restoration of family values and personal responsibilities, clear condemnation of criminal behaviour and stricter penalties for criminals, such as mandatory penalties and capital punishment.

For many conservatives the 'culture wars' between traditional Western values and the accusation that those values are racist, sexist and oppressive, have emerged as the central issue of the 1990s.[25] Bill Bennett issued an Index of Leading Cultural Indicators, which sought to measure the 'the moral, social and behavioral condition of modern American society' with 19 social indicators.[26] He noted that, since 1960, 'there had been a 560 per cent increase in violent crime; more than a 40 per cent increase in illegitimate births; a quadrupling in divorce rates; a tripling of the percentage of children living in single-parent homes; more than a 200 per cent increase in the teenage suicide rate; and a drop of almost 80 points in the SAT scores' (high school results). Buchanan, in his convention speech, attacked the liberal social agenda and proclaimed:

> this election is about much more than who gets what. It is about who we are. It is about what we believe, it is about what we stand for as Americans. There is a religious war going on in our country for the soul of America. It is a culture war, as critical to the kind of nation that we will one day be as was the Civil War itself.[27]

He believed that liberals had started the culture war but conservatives have to recognize that it exists and to fight in it. Social conservatives believe that these are 'real' issues, as salient to people as the economy. Predictors of a conservative crack-up argue that an emphasis on social issues will split the coalition and alienate those primarily concerned with free markets and a strong defence.

Cultural issues are not as divisive as these predictions suggest. First, there is a consensus that government intervention, especially at federal level, has been the chief cause of social decline. Therefore the first principle, echoed by many conservatives, is 'Do No Harm'. Bennett notes that 'many of the most serious social and behavioral problems we now face … are remarkably resistant to government cures'. He quotes the British Tory Samuel Johnson: 'how small, of all the human hearts endure, that part which laws or kings can cause or cure'.[28] Conservatives are sceptical that social problems can be solved by throwing money at them. They therefore seek ways in which the role of government should be decreased to improve personal responsibility and reduce dependency, such as workfare, removing obstacles to adoption and enforcing fathers' responsibilities for their children.

Second, conservatives look to non-government institutions, such as the family, church, voluntary groups, businesses and neighbourhoods, called 'mediating structures', to challenge moral decline. The revival and strengthening of these institutions are seen as the most useful source of opposition to negative social trends, but this lies largely outside the ability of government to determine, except by getting out of their way. Those who can finish high school, avoid having a baby out of wedlock, hold down a job for one year and eventually marry do well on all the social indicators. The ability of government to affect these is strictly limited, according to conservatives.

Third, the culture wars are being fought primarily in television, films, plays, video games and books. Conservatives believe that there is a 'Kultursmog' in which the leading cultural institutions such as the major newspapers and magazines, television programmes and Hollywood films are dominated by liberal values and marginalize conservative ideas and values.[29] The government has, or should have, little to do in this realm. Withdrawal of support for the National Endowment for the Arts, with its grants for a crucifix in urine or pictures of a bullwhip up a man's anus, can be urged both by social conservatives who view it as obscene and libertarians who object to any government sponsorship of art. Tyrrell and others argue that conservatives need to concentrate on the culture rather than look to government to oppose these hostile values. Conservative magazines such as the *National Review* and *American Spectator* devote an increasing number of pages to cultural rather than directly political issues.

Fourth, there is a consensus on many of the specific policies in this area, if often for different reasons and with different long-term aims. There is unity on the need to strengthen the family. Economic issues are presented as pro-family, as in the American Family First Bill of 1993, an alternative budget plan which included $500-per-child tax credit for families with children. There is also a coalition behind school choice, which combines support for independent religious schools and the reduction of political control of education, and introduces an element of competition. Conservatives are also united against the phenomenon of political correctness, especially on university campuses, in which support for minorities is expressed in special financial, social and educational programmes and limitations on free speech.

The Conservative Movement

Some claim that the conservative movement has splintered. First, some organizations which were strong in the 1970s have disappeared or become weak. Second, some elements of the coalition have returned to the Democrats. Third, there is a bitter war for the heart and soul of the movement between neo-conservatives and the new paleo-alliance.

Decline of the Reaganite Right

Some of the organizations that were central to the Goldwater campaign in 1964 and were the focus of conservative activity in the 1970s, such as the Young Americans for Freedom, have disappeared or are enfeebled. Bush failed to pursue a conservative agenda, but it was difficult for conservatives to oppose a Republican administration. Of the foursome that were the chief architects of the New Right, only Paul Weyrich remains a major player. Dolan died of AIDS and his NCPAC has virtually disappeared. Viguerie went through a financial crisis as his fund-raising techniques were picked up by other conservative fund-raisers, many of whom he had trained, there was 'donor fatigue' as tried and tested methods began to be rejected by donors and he had an expensive, time-consuming and unsuccessful bid to win the nomination as Republican candidate for Lieutenant Governor of Virginia. He was forced to sell his equipment to, and rent back from, an organization owned by the religious cult leader Rev. Sun Myung Moon. Howard Phillips failed to develop the Conservative Caucus as an activist organization, and created the US Taxpayers Party in 1992. Only Weyrich and his organization, the Free Congress Foundation, remain a significant influence, as a media spokesman for conservative views and an organization of grassroots activism. Furthermore many of the Christian Right organizations created in the 1970s were wound up by the end of the 1980s, most notably Falwell's Moral Majority but also Christian Voice, National Christian Action Coalition and the Religious Roundtable. Even the US Chamber of Commerce, which had been a chief advocate of supply-side tax reductions, abandoned its strong anti-tax stance in 1993.

However some old organizations have become reinvigorated and many new organizations were created in the 1990s. The Intercollegiate Studies Institute and the Young America's Foundation, which both concentrated on students, became far more active and better funded. Conservative magazines such as *National Review, Reason* and *American Spectator* considerably increased their paid subscriptions. The *Spectator's* rose from 30 000 in 1992 to 200 000 at the end of 1993 before their exposé of Clinton's behaviour as Governor, and the *Review's* from 170 000 in 1992 to 240 000 by December 1993. New magazines, such as *The National Interest* and *Liberty*, were launched. Talk-show radio developed as a new medium for reaching and educating conservatives. One of the media success stories of the 1990s was the Rush Limbaugh Show, first on radio and then also on television, in which the populist presenter attracted up to 19 million listeners and his book, *The Way Things Ought to Be*, sold four and a half million copies in hardback.[30] National Empowerment Television was launched as a 24-hour conservative channel by Weyrich in 1993. Buchananites created the American Cause, Pat Robertson the Christian Coalition and neo-conservatives Empower America and the Project for the American Future. While the form of the movement had changed considerably, this was not a sign of weakness but of the natural developments with the movement.

Another major development was a renewed emphasis on activity in the states. This led to the formation of 30 state policy think-tanks in 26 states by 1992. They sought to apply the ideas of the established national think-tanks, such as Heritage and the American Enterprise Institute (AEI), to the particular circumstances of the different states. They were influential in the development of school choice and welfare reform in several states, such as Wisconsin. School choice became a major issue in a number of states, including California; the property rights movement emerged with 500 groups and over one million members to challenge the view that the environment was best protected by government regulations; and the term limits movement had a successful record in state referendums. A number of state-based Christian Right groups were organized, such as that behind the referendum against rights for homosexuals in Colorado.

A concentration on the conservative organizations of the 1970s and early 1980s gave a misleading impression of the state of the movement and ignored the multitude of developments that had occurred in the late 1980s and the 1990s.

Return to the Democrats

The second source of weakness in the movement was identified by some commentators as the return of many neo-conservatives and Reagan Democrats to their former party in the 1992 Presidential election, as well as some supporting Perot. Many neo-conservatives had been active in conservative Democrat organizations such as the Coalition for a Democratic Majority, which felt increasingly marginalized by a party that had moved decisively to the left since 1972. Some, such as Jeane J. Kirkpatrick, Reagan's UN Ambassador, joined the Republican Party, but others remained Democrats while supporting the Reagan administration on many issues, especially in foreign policy. There was a strong effort to move the Democrat party back to a more centrist position, led by the Democratic Leadership Council (DLC) and its associated think-tank, the Progressive Policy Institute (PPI). Clinton was chairman of the DLC and campaigned as a 'new kind of Democrat'. The DLC identified its principles as economic growth generated in the private sector instead of redistribution; individual rather than group rights; opposing minority quotas; the politics of responsibilities and duties instead of the politics of entitlements; global democracy and universal markets; and entrepreneurial rather than bureaucratic government, with more choice and responsiveness to consumers in the public sector, a development known as 'reinventing government'.

In a *New York Times* advertisement Clinton was publicly endorsed by a number of neo-conservatives, led by Richard Schifter, Assistant Secretary of State for Human Rights under Reagan, and including AEI fellow Josuah Muravchik, Penn Kemble, deputy director of the USIA, Carl Gershman, chairman of the National Endowment for Democracy, and political scientists Aaron Wildavsky and Samuel Huntington. Support for Clinton was based on three issues: commitment to a policy of promoting global democracy and human rights, most notably in the former Soviet Union, his strong support for Israel and his opposition to affirmative action.[31] They were also attracted to his positions on capital punishment, more police and welfare reform, all contributing to an impression that the Democratic party had moved to a more centrist position. Thus Clinton and the Democratic party seemed to have successfully won back some of those who contributed to the intellectual vitality and strength of the conservative movement.

However those neo-conservatives who endorsed Clinton quickly became disillusioned with his administration.[32] First, Clinton failed to appoint neo-conservatives or their allies in the DLC to significant positions within the administration; those who were appointed were in much lower positions than they expected. Second, neo-conservatives were disappointed with the quality and ideology of Clinton's appointments, in particular expressing dismay at the domination of the process by the 'EGG' principles, ethnicity, gender and geography, otherwise known as 'diversity'. Third, the administration failed to live up to the rhetoric of global democracy and human rights, notably over Bosnia. There is a strongly held feeling among many neo-conservatives and in the DLC that they were used to convey a centrist image for Clinton and the Democratic party, and then discarded after the election. This will make it more difficult for the Democrats to attract this group again.

The Paleo Challenge

The third evidence of weakness within the conservative movement was the bitter struggle between the neo- (or new) conservatives and the emerging paleo- (or old) alliance of a few traditionalists (known as paleo-cons) and libertarians (paleo-libertarians). The paleos blamed the perceived demise of conservatism on its takeover by the neo-conservatives. They accused neo-conservatives of wanting a 'welfare–warfare' state: a corrected capitalism ('democratic capitalism') which accepts the welfare state, an interventionist foreign policy based on spreading global democracy, a culture of liberal cosmopolitanism and internationalism which fails to respect local and national differences, and a belief in a strong federal government built around the President and managed by themselves. Gottfried attacked their 'globalist ideal of political and cultural homogeneity based on global equality'. He proclaimed the paleo principles as the national interest rather than internationalism, opposition to the welfare state, criticism of a 'civil rights' language that hides an egalitarian agenda, and the belief that self-governing societies must have cultural limits.[33] Paleos claimed that the movement had been hijacked by neo-conservatives using their financial control of the four main conservative foundations (Scaife, Olin, Smith Richardson and Bradley) and their access to the East coast media. Neo-conservatives were 'big government conservatives' who had given up the task of reducing the role of government and now simply sought to use its powers to promote their values. They were also attacked for manoeuvring to obtain appointments for their own people and for blocking their conservative critics. There was a particularly bitter battle over the appointment of the head of the National Endowment for the Humanities (NEH) in 1981 between traditionalist Professor Mel Bradford and the ultimately successful neo-conservative, Bill Bennett.

The paleo-con wing is based upon the Rockford Institute, its *Chronicles* magazine and editor Tom Fleming, journalists Samuel Francis and Joseph Sobran, Professor Paul Gottfried and the National Humanities Institute of Dr Claes Ryn. The paleo-libertarian wing is based upon the Ludwig von Mises Institute of economists of the 'Austrian' school, its director Llew Rockwell and Professor Murray Rothbard. Several organizations such as the Main Street Committee and the John Randolph Club, have been created to identify common causes and many were involved in Buchanan's campaign for the Presidency in 1992 and his group the American Cause.

Most conservatives, however, reject the paleo critique and welcome neo-conservatives into the movement, if not always agreeing with their policies. Most neo-conservatives have shed their initial reluctance to be defined or labelled as conservative or to be part of the conservative movement. They are no longer simply 'liberals mugged by reality'. They are strongly associated with supply-side tax cuts which remain at the top of the economic agenda of nearly every conservative. There has emerged a consensus around the empowerment theme which seeks to reform the welfare state by reducing its bureaucracy, reducing dependency and giving the recipients more responsibility for their lives. Many neo-conservatives believe that their conservative welfare state will remain a feature of US public policy, while many conservatives see it as only one stage in weaning Americans off dependence on the state.

The paleos have alienated most of their potential allies. Most libertarians are horrified at the paleo-libertarian attack on free trade developments such as NAFTA and on social freedoms such as the rights of gays to serve in the military, while many traditionalists see the paleo-cons as abandoning Reaganite principles on the free market. The paleos were accused of anti-semitism and racism, or at least of insensitivity, after the movement had worked hard to marginalize such elements in the past. *National Review* had defined conservatism as excluding anti-semitism and racism, as symbolized by the John Birch Society. Libertarian Ed Crane accused paleos of neo-fascism in the social arena, and neo-con Neuhaus alluded to their nativism and chauvinism. Bennett accused Buchanan of having 'flirted with fascism' and having 'practised political anti-semitism'. Before and during the 1992 election, Buchanan was accused of anti-semitism in the neo-con magazine, *Commentary*.[34] There was a bitter conflict between the paleo-conservative Rockford Institute and the director of its New York office, neo-conservative Richard Neuhaus, which ended in his removal. Furthermore the paleos' distrust of cultural pluralism has annoyed conservatives who are reaching out to groups in which the movement has been weak, such as blacks, Hispanics and Jews. This difference has become focused around the issue of immigration. The paleos are restrictionist, on the grounds that a multicultural society is unstable, lacking a common understanding of rules and behaviour. Other conservatives favour increased immigration as 'economic necessity and political morality', uniting neo-conservatives, traditionalist Catholics and libertarians. Ben Wattenberg declared the United States to be a successful melting-pot and a global microcosm. Fukuyama argued that recent immigrants supported and embodied family values and that those values were most threatened by native WASPS.[35] The paleos are a distinct minority within the conservative movement, as Gottfried acknowledges, although the explanations for that fact vary. They are unlikely to break the movement apart.

The conservative movement in the 1990s is certainly very different from that of the 1970s, with a high turnover of organizations, the potential attraction of a more centrist Democrat party for neo-cons and a bitter division over the proper direction for the future. However none of this is evidence of its demise, as many new organizations have arisen, the Democrats have failed to satisfy their conservative wing and the bulk of the conservative movement appears to have accepted a modified version of the neo-conservative vision.

The Christian Right

The Republican party is seen by some commentators as about to be torn apart by the growing role of the Christian Right and the fear by many Republicans that it will drive away many young and suburban voters, especially women. Religious conservatives are a significant force in a number of state parties, as in Texas and Minnesota, and played a major role in the nomination of Oliver North as the Republican candidate for the US Senate in 1994. The debate revolves around why the Republicans lost the Presidential election in 1992 with only 37.7 per cent voting for George Bush. Some Republicans placed the blame firmly on what they viewed as the intolerance displayed at the Republican convention in Houston, and the power of the Religious Right in the party. Others located the causes of defeat in the sluggish economy, a poor campaign that failed to mobilize their constituency and in Bush personally, particularly the breaking of his tax pledge.

Literature in the late 1980s had identified a decline of the Christian Right.[36] Steve Bruce, in *The Rise and Fall of the New Christian Right*, described it as having failed as the result of a small potential base, differences of theology, divisions on legislating righteousness, socioeconomic differences and the failure to control the issue agenda. Clyde Wilcox, in *God's Warriors*, claimed that the Religious Right was in decline because of divisions between fundamentalists, charismatics and conservative Catholics; the failure to mobilize its potential constituency because of its extremism; differences between different fundamentalist traditions; and their successful absorption into the Republican party. Financial and sexual scandals around preachers Jimmy Swaggart and Jim Bakker, the closure of several organizations, notably the Moral Majority, and the weak performance of Pat Robertson in the 1988 Republican primaries led most journalists and academics to write them off by the end of the 1980s.

However, to the surprise of many, the Christian Right played a major role in the 1992 campaign. The Christian Coalition, created in 1990 with Pat Robertson at its head, but largely run under the able young leadership of executive director Dr Ralph Reed, had, in 1992, 400 000 dues-paying members in 600 chapters, spending $13 million per annum. It was claimed that the Christian Coalition controlled 12 state Republican parties and was influential in many others. One-third of the national convention delegates had some form of association with Christian groups. A factor which led to underestimating their strength was a concentration on federal politics, when they had grown more influential at state and local level, sometimes without the support of strong national organizations. Focus on the Family, led by Dr Jim Dobson, had a small presence in Washington DC under former Reagan adviser Gary Bauer, but with two million members and activity in 18 states. Some groups, such as the American Family Association and the Traditional Values Coalition, are active in only a few states.

The accusation that the Christian Right was damaging to the Republican party came to be symbolized by the 1992 convention, which was portrayed in much of the media as captured by the fundamentalist right. Grant described it as 'a public relations disaster, giving the impression of a narrow and exclusive party that was not reaching out to a wider electorate'.[37] Buchanan appeared on television at prime time and announced that liberals had declared a Culture War against the American people. It was claimed that this close association with the Christian Right had alienated many voters. Rich Bond, Republican National Committee (RNC) Chairman during the 1992 campaign, complained that you cannot win elections by intolerance. This was illustrated by the debate on abortion. The Republican platform reaffirmed support for a constitutional ban on abortion. The attempt to soften this statement was decisively defeated on the platform committee by

84 votes to 16. Republicans for Choice were unable to speak from the platform and hostility was expressed towards pro-choice Governor of Massachusetts, William Weld.

The Republican Majority Coalition was created to wrest back control of the party from the fundamentalists. They accept the argument that the Christian Right drove away many potential voters, especially pro-choice middle-class women and some businessmen and women. Rudolph Guiliani, New York City Mayor, stated that 'abortion can't become a litmus test for the Republican party'. The leaders include Tom Campbell, defeated Senate candidate for California in 1992, Senator Nancy Landon Kassebaum, ex-Senator Warren Rudman and Senator John Chafee.

The case for the Christian Right is, first, that they are a loyal, core element of the Republican vote. Evangelicals consist of 25 per cent of the electorate, and 62 per cent voted for Bush; the fundamentalists are now a strong Republican voting bloc. Many evangelicals support the party primarily because of economic issues. They deny that they damaged Bush by noting that his support went from –24 points to –10 during the convention, and that the pro-life plank was the same as in 1984 and 1988.

Second, the key determinant of the 1992 election was the economy under Bush, not social issues. Most conservatives agreed with Clinton's campaign director James Carville, that 'It's the economy, stupid.' Some 12 per cent of voters in exit polls mentioned that abortion had affected their vote, but 56 per cent of them voted for Bush. Nearly all surveys of the 1992 election attribute the result to the economy. Pippa Norris concludes: 'The 1992 election can be seen to represent a referendum on the country's economic performance under the Bush administration.'[38]

Third, the Christian Right has become more professional. In the best recent book on them, Moen demonstrates that it has become both more sophisticated and more secular.[39] By sophistication, Moen means that they have learnt through experience how politics works and developed the structures and skills to be effective political operators, and by secular he means the ability to use a language of rights, choice and victimization that appeals to a wider audience in a pluralist society than biblical revelation.

Their strategists are aware of their weaknesses. The Christian Coalition's Ralph Reed explained the need for a broader agenda as 'Casting a Wider Net'.[40] He believed that 'the pro-family movement has limited its effectiveness in concentrating disproportionately on issues such as abortion and homosexuality' and should embrace an expanded agenda to include lower taxes on working families, crime, the failure of public education, deficit spending, health care, welfare reform and free trade. These issues not only enable coalition building with economic conservatives but also reflect the priorities of evangelicals and Catholics themselves: 'Their primary interest is not to legislate against the sins of others, but to protect the health, welfare and financial security of their own families.' Atwood contributed to this re-evaluation by identifying what he saw as the political sins of the Christian Right – the overestimation of strength, weak coalition building and cognitive immodesty – and by proposing a strategy to overcome them on similar lines to Reed's.[41]

Fourth, the Republicans have demonstrated that the mainstream party and the Christian Right can unite both in Congress and in elections. A solid Republican bloc voted against Clinton's budget plan and high party cohesion has developed. There were election victories in 1993, when Paul Coverdell was elected Senator in Georgia, and Kay Bailey Hutchison in Texas won a special election arising from the appointment of Lloyd Bentsen as Secretary of Treasury. Both Republicans were moderate pro-choice, but received the support of the Christian Coalition because of their opposition to taxpayer-funded abortions and to the Freedom of Choice Bill which would legislate *Roe* v. *Wade*. The ability to unite was demonstrated again in the election victories of 1993 in Los Angeles, New York City, Virginia and New Jersey.

Fifth, as discussed above, the greatest threat to Christian values is viewed to be government, so there is a consensus that the government should do less in these areas. For most fundamentalists, political activity is a defensive reaction against the infringement by government of their religious liberties. They believe that their children should be allowed to attend religious schools and avoid sex education and to pray in school, that they should not be forced to pay their taxes for blasphemous art or the conduct of abortions and that they should not be forced to employ homosexuals against their deeply-felt beliefs. Government is viewed by most of them as having become a force for the imposition of alien values, rather than as the means of achieving Heaven on Earth.

The Republican party can become a 'big tent' in which all are felt to be included. As Haley Barbour, RNC chairman, proclaimed, 'When I was elected chairman, I promised to focus on the issues that unite all of us. Taxes. The economy.' Any attempt to dilute the pro-life stance would probably alienate the Christian Right. However, as long as the Republicans are the more pro-life party and abortion does not become the central issue of an election campaign, the Republicans can unite around the economic issues.

Public Opinion

Some commentators state that the Republican position of social conservatism and economic laissez-faire fails to reflect public opinion, and that public opinion and the GOP are moving in the opposite direction.[42] Ashbee claimed that the 'package of social conservatism and 'hands-off' economics ran directly counter to the prevailing national mood in almost every respect ... Public opinion and the GOP were moving in opposite ideological directions.' Some political scientists argue that public opinion had moved to the left in the Reagan–Bush years. Howard Gold has suggested that, while the elite had moved to the right, public opinion had not. He attacked theories that attributed a shift in public opinion to a cultural backlash in the 1960s, institutional malaise in the 1970s and the sweeping mandate of the Reagan victories in the 1980s. He identified four dimensions of conservatism – the role of government, welfare, race and social issues – and presented poll evidence to support his claim. A similar argument, that the public mood has shifted towards liberalism since 1980, is made by Stimson.

However, there are serious problems with Gold's analysis. He ignored foreign and defence policy; failed to distinguish between support for civil rights and quotas; did not apply his argument to consistent time data; and ignored data which undermined his argument: for example, 70 per cent support for school prayer is used as evidence of weak conservatism!

Other polls, including the Voter Research and Surveys (VRS) exit poll taken on the 1992 election day, suggest a different story.[43] Some 55 per cent of voters said that they wanted fewer services and lower taxes, compared with 36 per cent who wanted more services and higher taxes, and the gap has grown in the late 1980s and the 1990s. A CBS/*New York Times* poll in January 1993 asked respondents whether they thought that, 'in general, the federal government creates more problems than it solves ... or solves more problems than it creates' and found 69 per cent favoured the former, while only 22 per cent supported the latter. The exit poll showed 75 per cent wanted government to encourage 'traditional family values', with only 25 per cent supporting 'tolerance of non-traditional families'. On abortion, according to a 1992 Wirthlin poll, 55 per cent favoured abortion either seldom (42 per cent) (only to save the life of the mother or after rape or incest) or never (13 per cent).

Americans are more likely to identify themselves as conservatives than liberals. In the exit poll the figure was 33 per cent conservative and only 18 per cent liberal, typical of the 1980s and 1990s. 'Conservative' does not necessarily mean voting Republican, as 35 per cent of such conservatives voted for either Clinton or Perot, whom they viewed as moderate or conservative. Clinton campaigned as a moderate candidate, echoing conservative themes on tax cuts for the middle class, law and order and welfare reform. As Kate O'Beirne, Heritage vice-president, said, 'What do you mean that conservative ideas didn't work in the 1992 election? They worked for Clinton.'

A key constituency for the future is the 19 per cent who voted for Perot in 1992, the 'Perotistas'. In terms of social status and political outlook, they tend to be Republican voters, although not identifiers; 56 per cent had voted for Bush in 1988, with only 17 per cent for Dukakis, while 27 per cent were new voters. Ladd notes that 'philosophically, the Perotistas resemble the Bushites, though with a more libertarian coloration'.[44] In the exit poll, they favoured smaller government by 66 per cent to 26 per cent; supported traditional values by 75 per cent; and only 14 per cent favoured expanding programmes: 'They just weren't much occupied by social issues, which left them more open to suasion on the economic dimension.' In a poll for the DLC, 44 per cent identified themselves as conservatives, 25 per cent liberals and 27 per cent moderates.[45] The Republican problem is how to win the Perotistas. Some Republicans try to establish an alliance with Perot by placing the reduction of the deficit as the main Republican plank and welcoming his supporters to Republican events. Others argue that Perot must be undermined and attacked as he is not a conservative. He attacked Reaganomics, is isolationist and protectionist, and favoured higher taxation. Bill Bennett and Fred Barnes have accused Republicans of 'Loving Perot Too Much'.[46] Perotistas need to be convinced that tax increases will fail to reduce the deficit. Conservatives point to the evidence from the 1990 Bush budget deal which increased taxation by $175 billion, the largest tax increase in American history, but was followed an increase in the deficit between 1990 and 1992, and argue that the Clinton budget will lead to the same.

Conservatives deny that the 1992 election demonstrated a repudiation of the Reagan–Bush years. They prefer to talk of the Bush–Clinton years. They point to the repudiation of Reaganomics under Bush with a considerable growth in regulations, including the Clean Air Act and the Americans for Disabilities Act; an 8 per cent growth in domestic expenditures, greater than under Carter; increased public expenditure as a percentage of GDP, from 12.2 per cent in 1988 to 14.9 per cent in 1992, higher than in 1980; and of course the abandonment of his anti-tax stance. Bush's approval rating dropped dramatically, from 75 per cent to 51 per cent, in the month after the budget deal.

Initiatives and referendums have been increasingly used by conservatives to promote their agenda and they claim that voters have usually endorsed their stance. In 1992, 11 out of 12 states voted down tax increases and seven out of eight voted for limitations on increased taxation and spending. Term limits were passed in 1992 in 14 states with an average of 66 per cent.

Leadership

The final argument for a conservative crack-up is the lack of leadership. No one dominates the conservative movement in the 1990s as Reagan did in the 1980s. Reagan held together a diverse coalition. Bush damaged conservatives by blurring the distinction between authentic conservatism and the policies of the Bush administration. Conservatives felt that Bush abandoned the Reagan economic agenda, increasing taxes and domestic expenditure, and creating 20 000 new regulatory officials. There is no obvious leader of the opposition. Leaders can be found in the Senate, the House, the National Committee, the states and among former administration officials. Some commentators believe that the party will tear itself apart, with so many claiming to be the true conservative leaders who will apply Reaganite views and rebuild the Reagan coalition in the 1990s. They belong roughly to three broad groups.

The Empowerment group includes Jack Kemp, former Secretary of Housing and Urban Development, Bill Bennett, former Secretary of Education, Newt Gingrich, leader of the House Republicans, former UN Ambassador Jeane Kirkpatrick, former Education Secretary Lamar Alexander and Governors Bill Weld of Massachusetts, John Engler of Michigan, Carroll Campbell of South Carolina and Tommy Thompson of Wisconsin. They are active in Empower America, created in 1993 under Vin Weber, which embodies an optimistic, 'can-do' style, and emphasizes their experience in office. Their primary policy focus is on economic growth with supply-side tax cuts at the forefront supported by deregulation and greater efficiency in government. They accept the need for a reformed welfare state, in health care, education and the relief of poverty, based on empowering the poor so they have more control over their lives, with, for example, tenant ownership or management and school choice, and by urging the responsibilities of recipients, as, for example, through workfare. They advocate new programmes that will be more decentralized and less bureaucratic than existing ones, rather than advocating that government should not be involved at all. They are pro-immigration, for free trade and believe in a conservative war against poverty. On social issues they tend to be conservative but give them a low priority, though Bennett has made cultural values one of his major themes, and Weld pursues a more libertarian stance on social issues, for example supporting choice on abortion and gay rights. On foreign policy they lean towards democratic internationalism, promoting global markets and democracy. They appeal to neo-conservative and 'progressive' conservatives, believe that they can appeal to Reagan Democrats, seek to be inclusive and a big tent, and support outreach to minorities. In 1993, they pointed to the 25 per cent black support for Christie Todd Whitman as Governor of New Jersey, 17 per cent for George Allen as Governor in

Virginia and to the 85 per cent Asian, 75 per cent Hispanic and 40 per cent black support for Bret Schundler as Mayor of Jersey City. Their conservative critics dismiss them as 'big government conservatives' who have given up the fight to reduce the size and role of government.

The second group is that of the deficit cutters, led by Senate Majority Leader, Bob Dole, ex-House Republican Leader Bob Michel, Senator Phil Gramm of Texas, Governor of California Pete Wilson, former Secretary of Defence Dick Cheney and former Chairman of the National Endowment for the Humanities, Lynne Cheney. Their main issue is reducing the deficit, preferably by cutting expenditure if possible but increasing taxes if necessary. Fiscal rectitude is the main stance. They note that a big majority of voters see reducing the deficit as more important than cutting taxes or introducing new programmes. They particularly note the 65 per cent support for this amongst Perot voters, and seek to woo Perot and his supporters. They view the 'empowerers' as offering easy options to cure economic problems. Phil Gramm and Dick Cheney are more optimistic about the possibility of reducing entitlements, the main item in the budget, while Dole considers this political suicide. This difference was reflected in the response to the Clinton health plan when some Republicans were prepared to accept a modified version of his plan whilst others opposed it and wanted to rely on greater competition. They all fear that social issues will damage the party and alienate voters. Supporters can be found in the Republican Majority Coalition. On foreign policy, they tend to be neo-realists and unenthusiastic about foreign adventures. This group believes that it represents both the mainstream of the party and the best chance of appealing to Perot voters. It represents the cautious and sceptical side of conservatism.

The third group is the Religious Right, centred around Pat Buchanan and Pat Robertson. The 'Culture Wars' are their top priority: pro-life, against gay rights, strong on crime, against pornography and anti-feminist. Protectionist in economic policy, they are willing to accept a more interventionist economic policy, for example federal aid to the unemployed. Isolationist in foreign policy, they are bitterly hostile to increasing the role of international institutions such as the UN. They argue that their politics will appeal to the populist and nationalist stance of voters, including the Perotistas. Buchanan could help to bring Catholics into the Christian Right. Some of the Christian Right, such as Ralph Reed, believe that the goal should not be to capture the Republican party but to ally themselves with candidates likely to be nominated and elected and to obtain concessions from them. Neither the Christian Coalition nor Jerry Falwell supported Buchanan in the 1992 primaries. Conservative critics claim that a programme of cultural war, protectionism, isolationism and nativism is not only an unelectable platform but a betrayal of the policies of Reagan – the politics of retreat.

There is the possibility that the factions could tear apart the party and the movement. However this ignores the differences that existed in the past. There has long been fierce debate between libertarians and traditionalists, and there has been a variety of candidates behind whom conservatives have rallied. They were divided between Eisenhower and Taft in 1952. In 1968, many did not support Reagan but Richard Nixon who, while not a conservative, was deemed the more electable. In 1972, Congressman John Ashbrook ran against Nixon in the primaries. In 1976, many conservatives were opposed to Reagan running against the unelected incumbent, President Ford. In 1980, there were several conservative candidates other than Reagan, with 11 other candidates, including the long-time conservative leader, Phil Crane. In 1988, the conservatives were divided amongst several candidates, including Kemp and Pete DuPont, and in 1992 most conservatives reluctantly supported Bush against his challenger, Buchanan. In other words, it has been the exception rather than the rule for the conservative movement to have a clearly recognized leader.

A multiplicity of leaders is beneficial because it widens the attractiveness of the party and increases the number of voters in the primaries, and they are more likely to become active and remain in the party. The danger arises if the party fails to obey Reagan's eleventh commandment: 'Thou shalt not speak ill of another Republican.'

Conservative Comeback

A comeback is a more likely proposition than the crack-up predicted by some liberals and conservatives. While conservatism has several major problems, as discussed above, they are not as serious or as potentially fatal as the crack-up literature implies. The conservative agenda can be reassembled with low taxation and less government as the priority, a cautious but nonetheless interventionist foreign policy and the removal of government obstacles to the promotion of traditional values, as through the reform of the welfare system to reduce dependency and the number of single-parent families. This could be 'the new fusionism'. The movement is reinvigorated by new and revived old organizations, magazines, ideas and personalities; neo-conservatives and Reagan Democrats are disillusioned by the Clinton Democratic party; and the aggressive challenge to mainstream conservatism from the paleos is limited to a few activists. The conservative movement has always had several strands but it demonstrated the capacity to unite in the 1970s. The Republican party can successfully integrate the Christian Right within its ranks, if the focus is on the negative impact of liberalism on the culture. The public, including the Perot voters, still expresses conservative values on most issues. There is a multiplicity of leaders to appeal to voters, which is an advantage provided the competition does not become too vicious. The case is supported by the evidence of the highly successful Republican campaign which led to gains at all levels in the 1994 elections. Of course, none of this guarantees that the Republicans will always win elections. There are so many factors that determine the outcome of an election, including many short-term factors and the qualities of the candidates. However the long-term trends continue to identify a strong conservative presence in US politics throughout the 1990s and into the twenty-first century.

Notes

1 R. Emmett Tyrrell Jr., *The Conservative Crack-Up*, Simon & Schuster, 1992; Paul Gottfried, *The Conservative Movement*, Twayne, 1993, 2nd edn, p.vii; John Judis, 'The Conservative Crack-Up', *The American Prospect*, (3), Fall 1990; John Judis, 'The End of Conservatism', *New Republic*, 1 August 1992, pp.28–31; Edward Ashbee, 'The Great Conservative Crack-Up', *Talking Politics*, 1993, pp.152–60; Alan Grant, 'The 1992 U.S. Presidential Election', *Parliamentary Affairs*, **46**, (2), April 1993, p.252.

2 Louis Hartz, *The Liberal Tradition in America*, Harcourt Brace Jovanovich, 1955.

3 George Nash, *The Conservative Intellectual Movement in America*, Basic Books, 1976.

4 Nigel Ashford and Stephen Davies (eds), *A Dictionary of Conservative and Libertarian Thought*, Routledge, 1991, pp.1–4.

5 Nigel Ashford, 'A new public philosophy', pp.7–20, and 'A new conservative majority?', pp.21–35, in Michael Turner and John D. Lees (eds), *Reagan's First Four Years*, Manchester University Press, 1988.

6 Nigel Ashford, 'The neoconservatives', *Government and Opposition*, Summer 1981, pp.353–69.

7 Ashford, 'A new conservative majority?', pp.31–4.

8 Nigel Ashford, 'The conservative agenda and the Reagan presidency', in Joseph Hogan (ed.), *The Reagan Years*, Manchester University Press, 1990, pp.189–213.

9 Ibid., p.212.

10 David Mervin, *Ronald Reagan and the American Presidency*, Longman, 1990.

11 Ashford, 'The conservative agenda', pp.200–208.

12 Patrick Buchanan, 'America First, and Second and Third', *National Interest*, **19**, Spring 1990.

13 Josuah Muravchik, *Exporting Democracy: Fulfilling America's Destiny*, American Enterprise Institute, 1991; Charles Krauthammer, *Cutting Edges: Making Sense of the 1980s*, Random House, 1985; Gregory Fossedal, *The Democratic Imperative: Exporting the American Revolution*, Basic Books, 1989.

14 Francis Fukuyama, 'The End of History', *National Interest*, Summer 1989.

15 Jeane J. Kirkpatrick, 'Beyond the Cold War', *Foreign Affairs*, **60**, 1990, pp.1–16; Robert Tucker and David Hendrickson, *The Imperial Temptation*, New York University Press, 1992; Owen Harries (ed.), *America's Purpose: New Visions of US Foreign Policy*, ICS Press, 1991; Max Singer and Aaron Wildavsky, *The Real World Order: Zones of Peace/Zones of Turmoil*, Chatham House, 1993.

16   Kim Holmes (ed.), *A Safe and Prosperous America*, Heritage Foundation, 1993, p.1.
17   Ashford, 'The conservative agenda', p.190.
18   Ibid., pp.190–200.
19   Robert Bartley, *The Seven Fat Years: And How to Have It Again*, Free Press, 1992. See also Lawrence Lindsey, *The Growth Experiment*, Basic Books, 1990.
20   Kevin Phillips, *The Politics of the Rich and Poor*, Random House, 1990.
21   Ronald Reagan, *A Time for Choosing: The Speeches of Ronald Reagan 1961–82*, Regnery Gateway, 1993, p.253.
22   Ashford, 'The conservative agenda', pp.194–6.
23   Irving Kristol, *Reflections of a neoconservative*, Basic Books, 1983, p.xii.
24   Ashford, 'The conservative agenda', pp.208–11.
25   James Davidson Hunter, *Culture Wars: The Struggle to Define America*, Basic Books, 1992.
26   William Bennett, *The Index of Leading Cultural Indicators*, Heritage Foundation, 1993, p.i.
27   Republican National Convention, Houston, July 1992.
28   Bennett, *Index*, pp.ii–iii.
29   Tyrrell, *The Conservative Crack-Up*; Michael Medved, *Hollywood versus America*, Pan, 1994.
30   Rush Limbaugh, *The Way Things Ought To Be*, Pocket Books, 1992.
31   Richard Schifter, 'Have the Democrats Changed? Yes', *Commentary*, **94**, (3), September 1992, pp.23–7; Josuah Muravchik, 'Why the Democrats Won', *Commentary*, **95**, (1), January 1993; *New Republic*, 3 August 1993.
32   Josuah Muravchik, 'Lament of a Clinton Supporter', *Commentary*, **96**, (2), August 1993, pp.15–22.
33   Gottfried, *The Conservative Movement*, p.159, 147.
34   Josuah Muravchik, 'Pat Buchanan and the Jews', *Commentary*, **91**, (1), January 1991; Norman Podhoretz, 'What is Anti-semitism?', *Commentary*, **93**, (2), February 1992; Norman Podhoretz, 'Buchanan and the Conservative Crack-Up', *Commentary*, **93**, (5), May 1992, pp.30–34.
35   For the debate on immigration, see *National Review*, 27 April 1992; *New Republic*, 13 September 1993; Ben Wattenberg, *The First Universal Nation*, Free Press, 1991; Michael Lind, 'Aliens Amongst Us', *New Republic*, 23 August 1993, p.22–3; Ben Wattenberg and Karl Zinsmeister, 'The Case for More Immigration', *Commentary*, **89**, (4), April 1990, pp.19–25; Francis Fukuyama, 'Immigration and Family Values', *Commentary*, **95**, (5), May 1993, pp.26–32; Julian Simon, *The Economic Consequences of Immigration*, Blackwell, 1990.
36   Steve Bruce, *The Rise and Fall of the New Christian Right*, Oxford University Press, 1988; Clyde Wilcox, *God's Warriors: The Christian Right in Twentieth Century America*, Johns Hopkins University Press, 1991.
37   Grant, 'The 1992 U.S. Presidential Election', p.245.
38   Pippa Norris, 'The 1992 American Elections', *Government and Opposition*, **28**, (1), Winter 1993, pp.51–68.
39   Michael Moen, *The Transformation of the Christian Right*, The University of Alabama Press, 1992.
40   Ralph Reed, 'Casting A Wider Net', *Policy Review*, (65), Summer 1993, p.31–5.
41   Thomas Atwood, 'The Political Sins of the Christian Right', *Policy Review*, (54), Fall 1990, pp.152–60.
42   Ashbee, 'The Great Conservative Crack-Up', p.160; Howard Gold, *Hollow Mandates:*

American Public Opinion and the Conservative Shift, Westview Press, 1992; James Stimson, *Public Opinion in America*, Westview Press, 1992.

43 Everett C. Ladd Jr., 'The 1992 Vote for President Clinton: Another Brittle Mandate?', *Political Science Quarterly*, **108**, (1), 1993, p.16; *American Enterprise*, January 1993, p.94; *American Spectator*, March 1993, p.41.
44 Ladd, 'The 1992 Vote', p.23, 24.
45 *New Republic*, 9 August 1993
46 Ibid.

7   Clinton and the Democratic Party: The 1992 Election and Beyond

Nicol C. Rae

The election of Bill Clinton as President in 1992 marked the culmination of a sustained effort by more centrist Democrats to gain control over the Presidential Democratic party. This chapter examines the nature of contemporary Democratic party factionalism, and explains how and why the moderates were able to prevail in 1992. The role of the Democratic Leadership Council (DLC) is also discussed, together with some reflections on the Clinton Presidency and the Democratic party at the end of Clinton's first period in office.

Factions in the Democratic Party

At least since the Civil War there has been a recurring pattern of intra-party cleavages within both the national Democratic and Republican parties. In Presidential nominating contests between the Civil War and the New Deal, both national parties, in Congress and at national party conventions, generally divided on a regional basis: Northeast/West/South in the case of the Democrats, and East/West in the case of the Republicans.[1] Analyses of Congressional voting over the same period by Sinclair and Bensel reveal a similar pattern.[2]

Since the 1930s, however, American party factionalism has been based more on ideological than on sectional divisions within the parties. The New Deal era (1932–68) temporarily replaced a party system based on regional/cultural divisions with a system based largely on socioeconomic class cleavages (outside the South). Yet, while the New Deal Democrats created a system of government intervention and welfare provision to benefit labour and the Northern working class, they left the Southern racial system untouched. Southerners in Congress reciprocated by allowing the passage of significant working class-oriented legislation which did not threaten their own electoral power base.[3] The evolution of the committee-seniority system within the Democrat-dominated Congresses also allowed the Southern Democrats – now a minority faction within the Congressional party – to achieve a dominant position within the Congress during the New Deal era.[4]

The Southerners were thus the major element in the 'conservative' faction within the Democratic party of this period. The party's New Dealers based in organized labour and the major state and local party organizations of the Northern states were generally regarded as the 'liberal' faction. However they still needed Southern Democratic support to win the Presidency and to pass their programmes in Congress. They thus acceded to the Southerners' domination of the Congress and their virtual veto on civil rights legislation.

As the New Deal party system evolved, the factional pattern began to change. The liberal Northern faction began to show signs of fragmentation as early as the late 1940s, when it became apparent that many of its adherents wanted to address the issue of civil rights for Southern blacks. The inclusion of a civil rights plank in the 1948 party platform precipitated the walkout by Strom Thurmond and the Dixiecrats from the Democratic party, though most of the South remained loyal to Harry Truman in November.

During the 1950s, younger active Democrats in the North and West became increasingly impatient with the cautious, pluralistic approach to politics of the New Deal liberals who dominated the party, and sought to emphasize a new politics of 'participation' and 'reform'. These were not blue-collar or 'ethnic' Democrats, but largely middle-class professionals employed in the talking, writing and thinking professions. Their focus was more on political style, single issues and ideology, than on the basic 'haves v. have-nots' politics of the New Deal and, by the early 1960s, they were already approaching an ascendant position within the Northern section of the party.[5] The New Deal era was thus a period of transition from a sectional pattern of Democratic party factionalism towards a more ideological type of conflict. Although a strong regional faction persisted in the South, among the Northern Democrats divisions between old New Dealers and reformers took on an increasingly ideological dimension.

The political upheaval engendered by Vietnam, the civil rights revolution and urban violence during the late 1960s, brought these divisions to the surface and divided the Democratic party into three distinct factions: the New Deal Regulars, the 'new politics' Liberals and the Southerners. The Liberal faction, which finally won the national Democratic party away from the traditional New Dealers and White Southerners in 1968–72, has since splintered into a New Left/Minorities faction and a Neo-liberal faction (see Table 7.1). The New Left/Minorities faction generally supports interven-

Table 7.1 Contemporary Democratic Party Factionalism

	New Left/ Minorities	Neo-liberals	Regulars	South
Economics	Populist	Cons.	Populist	Cons.
Foreign	Dove	Dove	Hawk	Hawk
Culture	Radical Mod.	Mod.	Trad.	Trad.
Leaders	McGovern Jackson Brown	Hart Tsongas Dukakis	Mondale Moynihan Rostenkowski	Nunn Gore Clinton
Constituency	N. blacks Latinos Feminists Gays	Professionals Suburbanites	Labour Catholics LSNW	LSSW SB
Strengths	Activists Caucuses Primaries Pres. Media	Activists Primaries Pres. Media	Congress States Local	Congress States Local
Weaknesses	Congress States	Congress	Primaries Pres. Media	Pres. Media

Notes
Cons. = Conservative
Mod.   = Modernist
Trad. = Traditionalist
LSNW = Lower status Northern whites
LSSW = Lower status Southern whites
SB   = Southern blacks
Pres. = Presidential politics

tionist government (particularly to promote the interests of 'disadvantaged groups' such as blacks, Latinos, gays and women), has an abiding distrust of American foreign and defence policy, and supports cultural modernism, being highly suspicious of all traditional cultures and values, and vehement in their defence of rights that they feel are threatened by traditional values. This faction of the party has its base among minority, feminist and gay activists on college campuses. Their most prominent national leader in recent years has been the Rev. Jesse Jackson.

The Neo-liberal faction also has its origins in the 1968–72 revolt against the Democratic regulars, but, unlike the New Left/Minorities segment of the party, the Neo-liberals have increasingly moved towards the centre of the political spectrum since 1972. Indeed many contemporary Neo-liberals have broken with traditional Democratic economic doctrine on social welfare, Keynesian economics and redistributive taxation, although they still believe that government has a critical role to play in promoting economic growth. Neo-liberals also tend to de-emphasize ideology and prefer to focus on a technocratic approach to government epitomized in 1988 Presidential candidate Michael Dukakis's phrase 'This election is not about ideology, it's about competence.' In contrast to the New Left and Regular factions, whose minority and working-class constituents have seen manufacturing jobs disappear as the result of Japanese and European competition, Neo-liberals remain ardent free traders. They also generally support New Left positions on civil liberties and the rights of women and minorities, although with much less stridency. Neo-liberals were dovish during the Cold War, but have since tended towards a more idealistic internationalism in foreign affairs. Their base of electoral support has lain within the educated, suburban, professional, middle class. Prominent Neo-liberals in recent years have included former Senators and Presidential candidates Gary Hart and Paul Tsongas, and 1988 Democratic nominee Michael Dukakis.

Regulars are those Democrats who still adhere to the fundamental premises of FDR's New Deal coalition emphasizing government intervention in economic and welfare issues to help the working class, a strong defence policy and respect for traditional values in culture. This faction has been greatly weakened at all levels of the party in recent decades because its electoral base – the unionized, white, working class outside the South – has been diminishing as a proportion of the electorate, and has also been wooed with some success by the Republicans in Presidential elections since 1968. While not being antagonistic towards civil rights for women and minorities, this section of the party does not share the New Left's fundamental ambivalence about the rectitude of American values and American patriotism. Recent leaders of the Regular faction within the Democratic party have been former Vice-President Walter Mondale, Senator Daniel Patrick

Moynihan, and House Ways and Means Chairman, Congressman Daniel Rostenkowski.[6]

The Southern faction is generally more conservative than other factions on all issues. Southern Democrats generally support free markets and free trade and oppose labour unions and government intervention in the economy except in areas important to the South, such as agriculture. This faction reflects the cultural conservatism of the Southern region, and Southerners are more likely than Democrats elsewhere to take the conservative position on issues of religion, civil liberties and personal morality. On foreign and defence policy, Southern Democrats also tend to adopt a conservative position, partly owing to the large number of military installations and defence industries in the South. On civil rights, as Democrats in the South have come to rely heavily on black voters, they have turned around 180 degrees to assume a very strong pro-civil rights position.[7] Thus on economic issues the Southern Democrats tend to be closer to the Neo-liberals, but on cultural and foreign policy matters they are generally to the right of the other Democratic factions. The electoral base of the Southern wing of the party lies among Southern white working-class and rural voters. Its most prominent leaders in recent years have been Senators Sam Nunn, Lloyd Bentsen and Charles Robb.

The factional balance varies at different levels of the party. In Presidential politics the Regular faction lost control to the New Left in 1972, but since then the latter have been unable to nominate another Presidential candidate. With the exception of the Regular Walter Mondale in 1984, Democratic Presidential candidates since 1972 – including the Southerner Jimmy Carter – have had a Neo-liberal cast of mind: more conservative than the Regulars on economics, liberal on social/cultural issues, generally dovish but internationalist on foreign policy.

The move towards a system of Presidential nominations through primary elections rather than in national conventions has enormously benefited the Neo-liberal and New Left factions, at the expense of the Southerners and the Regulars. In primary elections, which are determined by the ability of candidates to mobilize middle-class, single-issue and ideological activists, Neo-liberal and New Left candidates have inherent advantages. White-collar suburbanites, teachers and militant activists are much more likely to get involved in campaigns and show up at the polls, and in low-turnout primaries this advantage is decisive.[8] The crucial influence of the New Hampshire primary in the process particularly helps the Neo-liberals. Despite its conservative reputation, New Hampshire has consistently launched Neo-liberal Democratic Presidential candidacies which have converted New Hampshire momentum into eventual nomination (Carter, Dukakis, Clinton) or near-nomination (Hart). The urban, industrial states which constitute the geographic base of the New Left and Regulars, and the Southern states, have played a much-reduced role in the process.[9]

At the Congressional level, which is less focused on ideology and more on issues of constituency representation and service, the Regulars and the Southerners fare better, although the influence of both has eroded greatly since the mid-1960s, when the Southern Democrats controlled the Congress through the committee system and the seniority rule.[10] The Southern Democrats nevertheless remain a crucial voting bloc in Congress, despite their reduced numbers, and they have been consistently able to hold on to districts and states that have decisively repudiated Democratic Presidential candidates over the past quarter-century. In state and local politics, which is even less ideologically focused, we find a similar pattern: a growing Neo-liberal and New Left challenge to the Regular Democrats in most Northern industrial states and continuing conservative dominance in Southern state and local politics.

The Democratic party thus displays a complex but consistent factionalism in both geographic and class terms. However there are clear indications of a long-term erosion in the influence of the Regulars, and a much slower erosion of the position of the Southern Democrats. At all levels – but particularly in Presidential politics – the Neo-liberal faction is tending to dominate the Democratic party. The New Left faction, with its base among the militant issue activists, is an important presence in Presidential politics, but generally fails to win in the face of opposition from the other three factions. On Capitol Hill and in the states, by contrast, the New Left has little influence.

The Democrats' Presidential travails over the previous two decades did not inspire great confidence that they would finally be able to seize the White House in 1992. That they did so was due to an unprecedented mobilization of the national party elite behind the candidacy of the Southern moderate, Governor Bill Clinton of Arkansas, whose campaign strategy was brilliantly designed to take maximum advantage of the national anxieties of 1992. As we shall see, Clinton's success was also due to very weak opposition and a background that enabled him to appeal to the Neo-liberal and Southern conservative Democrats simultaneously.

The next section of this chapter will explain how the 1992 Clinton campaign originated in the formation of the Democratic Leadership Council (DLC) in the mid-1980s.

A Short History of the DLC

The DLC was founded by a group of largely Southern Democratic politicians in the wake of the landslide defeat of the Mondale–Ferraro Presidential ticket in the 1984 election, the prime movers being Virginia Governor Charles Robb, Congressman Richard Gephardt of Missouri, Governor Bruce Babbitt of Arizona, Senator Sam Nunn of Georgia and Florida Senator Lawton Chiles. Their attempt to organize and coordinate the more centrist forces within the Democratic coalition was prompted by the fear that similar defeats on this scale might eventually lead to a full-scale Republican re-alignment at the lower levels of electoral competition that would threaten their own electoral base. Yet the DLC from its inception was intended to be more than just a 'white boys' caucus' (as several of its detractors within Democratic ranks dubbed it) but instead to serve as a forum for debates on policy and new ideas to win back the middle-class voters who had been estranged from the party since the upheaval of the 1968–72 period. Insofar as they had a model, the DLC looked more to the conservative think-tanks such as the Heritage Foundation that had laid the intellectual basis for the 'Reagan Revolution' rather than pursuing a path of bland moderation.[11]

Despite initial hostility from the Democratic National Chairman, Paul Kirk, the DLC recruited an impressive roster of supporters from the upper echelons of the party's elected office-holders, including 36 per cent of the Democratic Governors, 28 per cent of the Democratic US Senators and 43 per cent of the Democratic House members by 1990.[12] It was also able to reach out beyond its Southern base to include several prominent minority politicians such as Congressmen William Gray and John Lewis, and Mayor Henry Cisneros of San Antonio. With funds raised partly from annual subscriptions but mostly from private businesses and lobbyists the DLC established a headquarters in Washington DC with a full-time staff of ten and a separate think-tank entitled the Progressive Policy Institute (PPI), and published a bi-monthly magazine entitled *The Mainstream Democrat* (later changed to *The New Democrat*).[13]

From the beginning the DLC's support from Democratic office-holders and its ideas-oriented approach gained the Council a high degree of attention – most of it favourable – from the national news media and Washington insiders in general. Yet strategic bungling and the absence of a clear national network of supporters led to the DLC's becoming almost peripheral to the 1988 Presidential campaign. The major problem was the reluctance of leading DLC figures such as Sam Nunn and Charles Robb to enter the campaign. Bruce Babbitt did run but was eliminated very early, and although Senator Albert Gore performed reasonably well in the Southern primaries he seemed inexperienced and got nowhere in the primaries outside the South. Richard Gephardt mounted a serious Presidential campaign but on vaguely protectionist themes that conflicted with the DLC's free trade orientation. Despite the consolidation of the Southern primaries on one date in early March, the failure of its paladins to get their act together ultimately confined the DLC to the margins in a nomination contest between the New Left/Minorities' candidate, Jesse Jackson, and the Neo-liberal, Michael Dukakis.

While many might have been ready to write off the DLC as a national political force after the 1988 débâcle, the Council was, in fact, re-energized by yet another Presidential election disaster for the party that seemed to confirm their oft-repeated warnings of the dangers of a naïve Democratic reliance on the tenets of what the DLC described as 'liberal fundamentalism'. Much of this revitalization was due to the impact of Arkansas Governor Bill Clinton as DLC chairman in 1990–91. A dynamic and ambitious politician with Southern roots and appeal to the Neo-liberal section of the party, Clinton saw the DLC chairmanship as a means to heighten his national Democratic profile while also gaining a base of organizational support for a national Democratic campaign. To this end Clinton encouraged the formation of DLC chapters at the state level, and by May 1991 over 20 states had followed his lead. DLC annual conventions in New Orleans in 1990 and in Cleveland in 1991 also attracted widespread and generally favourable media attention.[14]

The DLC's position on the Democratic Presidential spectrum as the 1992 election approached, however, remained somewhat ambiguous. Clearly the DLC was at odds with the traditional liberal nostrums of governmental interventionism and welfare programmes in economic and social policy, and represented a more robust stance on foreign policy than that represented by most recent Democratic Presidential candidates. On the other hand, the DLC was reluctant to be ghettoized as the section of the party reserved for Southerners and white males, and carefully avoided renunciation of the 1960s heritage of Democratic liberalism on cultural issues so as to avoid alienating minority and Neo-liberal Democrats. DLC policy proposals reflected this pattern. In its 1990 New Orleans Declaration the DLC endorsed free trade, workplace democracy, school choice, voluntary national service and a national system of youth apprenticeship. The overall theme of the document was the Democrats becoming the party of 'opportunity rather than government'.[15] Issues touching on the sensitive areas of race, religion and morality were studiously avoided, although at the Cleveland convention in 1991 the DLC denounced racial quotas while maintaining a commitment to civil rights and affirmative action.[16]

Emphasizing Neo-liberal economics while avoiding the cultural issues was further evidence of the DLC's moving away from its Southern roots. Moreover, when the DLC's magazine changed its title from *The Mainstream Democrat* to *The New Democrat*, an editorial explained, 'We're not trying to move the Democratic party to the centre, we want to move it forward.'[17] Of course this accorded perfectly with the purposes of Bill

Clinton, a young Southern Governor with Neo-liberal inclinations who had Presidential ambitions and could not afford to alienate the New Left and Neo-liberal sections of the party. In the summer of 1990, Alvin From, the DLC's Executive Director, was explicit as to the Council's outlook on 1992: 'In essence the strategy we're pursuing is to develop a message that a candidate can run on, and an infrastructure that a candidate can pick up.'[18] As 1991 proceeded and other contenders fell by the wayside, it appeared increasingly likely that Bill Clinton would be that candidate.

The 1992 Democratic Contenders

The Democratic field of candidates in 1992 was probably one of the weakest in recent years, as many of the Democratic party's most prominent national figures decided to bypass the 1992 race because of President George Bush's very high job-approval ratings after the 1991 Gulf War. Jesse Jackson's absence from the 1992 field (due to the apparent strength of Bush and a reluctance to appear as a three-time Presidential loser) critically weakened the New Left section of the party. The surrogates for Jackson were the populist Iowa Senator, Tom Harkin and the former California Governor, Jerry Brown, but neither had Jackson's appeal to black Democrats and Harkin was burdened by a lack of a national identity, the closeness of his ties to organized labour and his strongly protectionist positions on trade policy, while Jerry Brown's candidacy was not taken seriously by political insiders.

Among the Neo-liberals, Senator Bill Bradley of New Jersey had the highest national profile prior to the 1990 Congressional elections, but his surprisingly narrow re-election to the Senate, and Bush's triumph in the Gulf War (which Bradley had opposed) effectively ruled him out of contention. Senator John D. ('Jay') Rockefeller's campaign for health care reform drew the attention of the news media, but Rockefeller subsequently got cold feet and withdrew from the race in the summer of 1991. Senator Robert Kerrey of Nebraska appeared to be a potentially strong candidate. A Vietnam veteran who had later campaigned against the war, Kerrey seemed like the kind of charismatic 'outsider' who would appeal to the quirky New Hampshire Democratic primary electorate. Kerrey's lack of experience in national issues, several inconsistencies in his issue positions and doubts about his temperament with regard to the office of the Presidency were serious liabilities, however.

Former Massachusetts Senator, Paul Tsongas, had been one of the most prominent Neo-liberal Democrats in the early 1980s. After a remarkable recovery from the lymphatic cancer that forced his retirement from the Senate in 1984, Tsongas was the first Democrat to declare for the Presidency in 1991. Although he was rapidly dismissed by many political insiders as 'another liberal Greek from Massachusetts', it soon became clear that his campaign – built around the need for tough measures to deal with the budget deficit and strong liberal stands on social/cultural issues such as abortion and gay rights – possessed a particularly strong appeal to suburban, professional Democrats. Moreover the Presidential primary season would begin on his home turf of New England.

Perhaps the most prominent of all the Democrats on the liberal side of the party was New York Governor, Mario Cuomo. Cuomo kept the media and his fellow Democrats guessing about his intentions for 1992, and his hesitation probably served to keep some other Democrats such as Bradley and Rockefeller out of the race. The speculation was finally ended by Cuomo's announcement that he would not be a candidate on the very day of the filing deadline for the New Hampshire primary.

The absence of Cuomo, Bradley and Jackson left a field of largely unknown and untested candidates representing the Neo-liberal to New Left spectrum of the Democratic party. If the Southern Democrats and the DLC could rally their forces behind a single candidate, who could also appeal to the old-fashioned Regular Democrats (who had no obvious champion to support) and the more pragmatic Neo-liberals, they might be able to turn this situation to advantage. Yet, as in 1988, many of the South's 'top guns' failed to make the race. Despite his strength as the Vice-Presidential candidate in 1988, Texas Senator Lloyd Bentsen was considered too elderly at 71 and too linked to the corporate world to be a possible national nominee for the Democrats. Senator Sam Nunn had voted against the Gulf War – thus sacrificing some of his credibility to conservative voters – while still remaining too far from the Democratic mainstream on other issues to be a plausible Presidential candidate. Senator Charles Robb of Virginia had supported the Gulf War, but his political career had been set back by tawdry scandals. House Majority Leader, Richard Gephardt had also opposed the war and, given Bush's strong standing, was content to consolidate his position in Congress. Virginia Governor Douglas Wilder, the nation's first elected black state Governor and a fiscally conservative and socially moderate Democrat, was the most interesting Southern contender, but personal difficulties and disorganization led to his rapid withdrawal from the race before New Hampshire. Finally Senator Albert Gore of Tennessee, who had supported the Gulf War, was reluctant to risk another failed nomination campaign that might put paid to his Presidential prospects for good.

The one remaining plausible Southern moderate for conservative Democrats and the DLC to rally around was Governor Bill Clinton of Arkansas. Clinton's credentials as a Neo-liberal were stronger than his credentials as a Southern moderate, however. A Rhodes scholar educated at Georgetown and Yale, who had managed George McGovern's campaign in Texas in 1972, Clinton returned to Arkansas and won election as Governor of the state in 1978. After an unexpected defeat in 1980, Clinton came back and won re-election as Governor in 1982 and held on to the office for the next ten years. Clinton epitomized the 'New South' reformist generation in a state that had almost the worst record in terms of poverty and poor service provision in the nation. His 'pragmatic' approach to governing and his shedding of his cultural liberal associations after his 1980 defeat endeared Clinton to traditional white Southerners, as well as Neo-liberal reformers. With Jackson and Wilder out of the race, Clinton (like another white Southern Baptist, Jimmy Carter, in 1976) also had a potentially strong cultural appeal to black Democrats nationwide. So, despite Arkansas's remoteness from the national political scene, Clinton had already established a national political profile as an appealing and capable Southern, moderate, reformer.

Clinton had also done his cause considerable good through his service as chairman of the DLC in 1990–91, which gave him both a national platform and a national network of support for a Presidential campaign. However it should be re-emphasized that Clinton's political profile was also calculated to appeal to Neo-liberals and Regular Democrats. On civil rights and social issues like abortion, Clinton took clearly liberal positions, while simultaneously stressing an appeal to economically pressed 'middle-class families'. On foreign policy Clinton had not been forced to take positions as Arkansas Governor, while his opponents had all taken strong anti-interventionist positions on most foreign policy issues – particularly the Gulf War. No other contender was thus so uniquely placed as Clinton to appeal to all sections of the Democratic party.

In contrast to 1988, conservative/Southern/DLC forces had to rally behind Clinton because there was no alternative in the field. Thus, if Clinton could achieve a decent showing in the difficult terrain of New Hampshire, he might earn an enormous windfall of delegates in the Southern primaries that were largely concentrated in a two-week period in early March (after 10 March almost 40 per cent of the Democratic convention delegates would already have been selected).[19] The potential windfall became even greater with the absence of Jackson and Wilder, which released a large Southern black primary vote that Clinton (because of his good civil rights record and his strong social and cultural ties to Southern black political leaders) was poised to inherit. Clinton's problem as the Democratic frontrunner, however, was to survive the inevitable prolonged and detailed media scrutiny of his political career and private life. He would also have to survive the concentrated assaults of his fellow candidates and the perception that no Democrat could possibly defeat a Republican Presidential incumbent who had just won a foreign war.

The Primary Campaign

Paul Tsongas was Clinton's most serious challenger in the early primary season. Tsongas's combination of fiscal conservatism and social and foreign policy liberalism struck a chord with the Neo-liberal, professional, suburban Democratic constituency that had persistently responded to 'new politics' Democrats since 1968. As the primary campaign opened in New Hampshire, none of the other contenders had made much impression on the press or public. Harkin was too shrill, and too closely associated with old-time New Deal liberalism; Kerrey's campaign lacked a clear definition and theme; and Jerry Brown's low-budget effort was not taken seriously. The Democratic party establishment – leading office-holders and leaders of powerful interest groups – had already quietly coalesced around Clinton in the autumn of 1991, and Tsongas's economic conservatism, and ethnic and geographic associations with the disastrous Dukakis ticket in 1988, made him especially unattractive to Regulars, Southerners and New Leftists.

In the autumn of 1991, Clinton thus appeared to be comfortably placed. He rolled through a series of straw polls at state Democratic conventions, and opinion surveys in New Hampshire showed him ahead. The real test for the Clinton forces arrived when Gennifer Flowers (a former Arkansas state employee) alleged before the television cameras that Clinton had conducted a long-standing extra-marital affair with her. The Clinton campaign counter-attacked the news media for airing such a sordid and irrelevant story instead of focusing on the real issues facing the country, and Clinton and his wife Hillary also spoke frankly about their marriage on national television. No sooner had the Flowers story been surmounted, however, than the Clinton campaign had to endure a further barrage of bad publicity concerning his avoidance of the military draft at the tail-end of the Vietnam War.

While these stories dominated the headlines and the television news, Tsongas overtook Clinton in the New Hampshire opinion polls. What saved Clinton was the inability of any of the other contenders to capitalize fully on his weakened position and grab second place. The liabilities of Harkin, Kerrey and Brown remained so great that even a weakened Clinton was preferable to those sections of the party that could not abide Tsongas. The eventual result of the primary, with Clinton finishing only eight points behind Tsongas (33–25 per cent), was cleverly converted by the Clinton campaign into an unexpected triumph for a candidate who had appeared doomed only two weeks earlier. The media perception of Clinton as New Hampshire's 'Comeback Kid' gave him the momentum he needed for the critical primary tests in his home region.

As Kerrey and Harkin had been essentially eliminated by poor showings in New Hampshire, the race was apparently reduced to a two-man contest between Clinton and Tsongas (Jerry Brown's candidacy was still generally regarded as little more than an irritation): both essentially Neo-liberals but with contrasting regional bases. However the dynamics of the campaign had altered Clinton's strategic position. When Clinton originally entered the Presidential race, the strategy had been to campaign as a Southern 'New Democratic' alternative to a Northeastern 'liberal fundamentalist' like Mario Cuomo. With Cuomo's non-appearance and the emergence of Tsongas as the favourite of Clinton's original target constituency of suburban, professional, Neo-liberal Democrats, Clinton was compelled to change course and run as a Regular, with support from Southerners (for cultural reasons) and New Leftists (for ideological reasons).

Despite the approach of the Southern primaries, Tsongas also had several advantages in the primary calendar. Prior to 'Super Tuesday' (10 March) there were primaries and caucuses in several Northern and Western states where Tsongas expected to do well – Maine, Maryland, Colorado, Washington state, Massachusetts and Rhode Island. The 1988 race had also demonstrated that the batch of Super Tuesday primaries in the South would not necessarily deliver the desired 'bloc' vote to the regional favourite. There were several areas in the South where Dukakis had run strongly in 1988 – suburban and migrant-dominated Florida, high-tech North Carolina, the Atlanta suburbs and the college towns – where Tsongas also had the potential to do well. Clinton thus had to work hard to deliver his home region, but he still had several advantages denied to Gore and Gephardt in 1988. For a start, the absence of Jesse Jackson who had cornered most of the Southern black vote in 1988, was a major plus. Although the black turnout might be reduced, those blacks who did vote would vote overwhelmingly for Clinton, who had strong regional/cultural ties to Southern black voters. Moreover Tsongas's campaign, with its strong emphasis on fiscal rectitude and economic retrenchment, had little appeal to minority voters, many of whom were heavily dependent economically on federal social programmes. For similar reasons the elderly Jewish Democratic primary voters in Southern Florida were concerned that Paul Tsongas's harsh economic medicine might include reductions in their social security benefits, an anxiety that was fully exploited by the Clinton campaign in this crucial state. Finally the moving of the Georgia and South Carolina primaries to the week preceding Super Tuesday enabled Clinton to translate his comfortable victories in both states into a major degree of momentum for the Super Tuesday contests.

Clinton was also fortunate that Tsongas could not exploit his regional/ cultural base as effectively as he might have done, owing to the surprising resilience of the Jerry Brown campaign. In states such as Maine and Colorado, Brown's shoestring 'anti-establishment' campaign had a strong appeal to counter-cultural/New Leftist voters who formed a significant portion of the active Democrats in such states. In a desperate scramble for votes across a vast expanse of territory, Clinton's formidable campaign infrastructure was also a major asset. The Clinton campaign had the money, the television advertising, and the state and local office-holders, already in place in the Southern states before the New Hampshire primary. Tsongas, who had concentrated all of his resources in New Hampshire, had nothing comparable to Clinton's resources for Super Tuesday.

In what transpired to be an uneven contest, Clinton swept the board on Super Tuesday, winning eight of the ten primaries, 54 per cent of the total primary vote (to 28 per cent for Tsongas) and 432 (62 per cent) of the 700 delegates at stake.[20] This propelled him into a formidable lead in the delegate count over Tsongas and Brown. If Clinton could demonstrate strength outside his home region by winning the two major Midwestern industrial states of Illinois and Michigan, his path to the nomination looked secure. This Midwestern 'rustbelt' territory contained many unionized Democrats in traditional manufacturing industries (particularly motor cars) who feared job losses as the result of competition from foreign imports, and were thus not at all receptive to Paul Tsongas's austere, militantly pro-free trade economics. While Jerry Brown secured significant local union support by eagerly coming down on the side of more managed trade and a rejection of the North American Free Trade Agreement (NAFTA), Clinton, not wishing to alienate Tsongas's pro-free trade, suburban Neo-liberal constituency, adhered to a more ambivalent position. Electorally this proved to be the wisest course, as he easily defeated Tsongas in Illinois and Brown in Michigan. Tsongas reacted by announcing his withdrawal from the race, thus effectively guaranteeing Clinton's nomination.

However there were still several obstacles for the Clinton campaign to surmount before the nomination was finally assured. The Flowers and draft allegations still had a negative effect on Clinton's national ratings with Republican and Independent voters, and fears of further revelations and Republican propaganda led many senior Democrats to doubt whether Clinton, despite rave notices from political insiders as the most formidable Democratic campaigner since John F. Kennedy, could run a serious race against George Bush in the autumn. Rumours continued to circulate in the press about the possible late entry into the race of a senior national Democrat such as Texas Senator and 1988 Vice-Presidential nominee Lloyd Bentsen, Congressman Richard Gephardt or even (yet again) Mario Cuomo, if the Clinton candidacy should suddenly disintegrate.

The unlikely vehicle on which such speculations rested was the ever-enigmatic and surprisingly resilient Governor Jerry Brown, the former Neo-liberal hero of the 1970s, now running for President on an unabashedly New Left platform. If Clinton were to lose a major-state primary to a candidate with as many liabilities as Brown, then his viability against Bush in November would be put into question. Anxiety in the Clinton camp was enhanced when Brown secured a surprise victory in the Connecticut primary, the dress rehearsal for New York. In the dynamics of the 1992 campaign New York looked like possibly fertile territory for Brown. He had a potential base of support among New Left Democrats, union leaders and minority activists, and had the additional advantage that white, Southern Baptists like Clinton had not traditionally found favour with New York's cosmopolitan and polyglot electorate (Carter lost the New York primary in both 1976 and 1980).

Once again, however, the Clinton campaign showed itself to be at its most formidable under pressure. Clinton went on the offensive against Brown in televised debates for raising the issue of Hillary Clinton's business associations in Arkansas and asserted that Brown's 'flat-tax' proposal would increase, not reduce, the fiscal burden on middle- and working-class voters. Brown's courting of the black vote by offering the Rev. Jesse Jackson the Vice-Presidential nomination gained him little encouragement from Jackson, but guaranteed a high level of hostility from the large Jewish primary electorate in New York City. Finally Brown's chances of defeating Clinton in New York were probably fatally damaged by a flurry of speculation that Paul Tsongas (whose name was still on the New York ballot) would re-enter the race in the event of a Clinton defeat.

Clinton's convincing victory in the Empire state (with non-candidate Tsongas edging Brown into third place) more or less concluded the Democratic primary campaign. By demonstrating strength in big states outside his Southern base, Clinton snuffed out potential trouble from more established Democrats. Brown stayed in the race and continued to harry Clinton through the rest of the primaries, but, with no serious prospect remaining of impeding his progress towards the nomination, the Californian was little more than a nuisance candidate.

Why Clinton Won

The success of the centrist Bill Clinton in winning the 1992 Democratic nomination reversed the trend of recent Presidential nominating politics. Does this indicate a fundamental change in the structure or environment of Presidential nominations that will favour centrist candidates during the 1990s?

From the evidence of the 1992 campaign, the answer appears to be negative. Clinton won in 1992 for reasons that were specific to the circumstances of that campaign and his own candidacy. The most obvious reason for his success was the weakness of the Democratic field. Prominent New

Left or Neo-liberal candidates such as Jesse Jackson, Mario Cuomo, George Mitchell, Patricia Schroder or Bill Bradley were non-runners. The New Left was barely represented in the race, as the Harkin candidacy, with its associations with organized labour and protectionism, had limited appeal to the minority, feminist and gay activists that constituted the core of the New Left constituency. Leadership of the New Left forces fell by default upon Jerry Brown, but, given his past record, it was impossible for him to arouse the fervour of the activists as McGovern or Jesse Jackson had done.

Jackson's absence did Clinton a further favour by releasing the large black Democratic primary vote. This was an enormous advantage for Clinton who, given his Southern background, had by far the most experience in courting black voters of any candidate in the field. By adding a large black vote to the white Southern conservative Democratic base, Clinton was able to capitalize on Super Tuesday to an extent that had been impossible for Gore in 1988, and amass a formidable lead in delegates.

When the competition moved to the decisive battlegrounds of Illinois, Michigan and New York, Clinton was fortunate that his remaining opponents were Paul Tsongas and Jerry Brown. Tsongas had associated himself so strongly with fiscal conservatism and free trade that he alienated the large labour and black voting blocs in each state, and Brown's counter-cultural associations mitigated the effects of his latter-day conversion to protectionism and the cause of organized labour. After his decisive victories in these three Northern states, Clinton was unstoppable barring a catastrophe.

Clinton's success was due to contingent factors: the leadership vacuum on the New Left, the absence of a strong black candidate, the fact that he had the centre-right field of the party all to himself, and the fact that in terms of fundamental ability and electoral appeal he stood head and shoulders above an extraordinarily weak field of opponents. Clinton's unique political background – the Southern moderate who had opposed Vietnam, worked for McGovern and had an exemplary record on civil rights – also meant that, unlike his major opponents, he was acceptable to all factions of the party. He had the benefit of being everybody's second choice: Neo-liberals preferred him to Brown if they could not have Tsongas; New Left-ists preferred Clinton's populist rhetoric to Tsongas's fiscal stringency and associations with big business; and Clinton was much closer rhetorically and culturally to the Regular wing of the party than the other two alternatives.

Despite Clinton's success, the Democratic nominating process still has an inherent structural bias against centrist candidates. The activist base of the party, the powerful interest groups that participate in Presidential nominating campaigns, and the basic Democratic Presidential primary electorate are still to the left of centre. Other things being equal, that situation still favours the more liberal candidate over the moderate. But other things were not equal in 1992: as we have seen, the New Left and Neo-liberal alternatives to Clinton were weak and the absence of a serious black contender delivered the black vote to the Arkansas Governor, who had more cultural affinity with black voters in his home region despite his more 'conservative' position on the ideological scale.

One final factor that also made an impact in 1992 was the end of the Cold War, which mitigated the divisions within the Democratic party on national security that had formed the main basis for intra-party conflict since Vietnam and the 1968 election. With those divisions being far less relevant, it was easier for the other Democratic factions to accept a Southern moderate. The fact that, as a small-state Governor, Clinton had not been compelled to take strong stances on foreign and defence policy issues during the 1980s also worked to his advantage, whereas a Southerner with a higher foreign policy profile, such as Sam Nunn, would never have been accepted by the other sections of the party.

None of the longer-term factors that have worked against Southern Democrats in Democratic Presidential politics since 1968 disappeared with Clinton's victory in 1992. Clinton is also more liberal than the average Southern Democrat, and he could not have been nominated without establishing close ties to Neo-liberal Democrats and Regulars outside his home region. Looking to Clinton to overhaul the Democratic party organizationally and redirect it organizationally also seems to be misguided. American political parties are not rigidly hierarchical organizations, but elusive and amorphous entities, incapable of being 'turned around' even by a powerful incumbent President, and it is unlikely that Clinton as party leader would be very interested in making fundamental changes to a nominating process that worked so well for him in 1992.

Postscript: The General Election and the New Administration

As the nomination was settled relatively early, candidate Clinton had sufficient time to rally the Democratic party behind him, and to write a vague party platform that alienated the smallest number of November voters. The selection of another youthful white, Southern, male, DLC-oriented Democrat – Tennessee Senator Albert Gore – as the Vice-Presidential nominee strengthened the ticket even further among the key voting blocs that had been drifting away from the Democrats since 1968 – white Southerners, white males and white Northern middle-class voters. It also placed the Republicans on the electoral defensive in the South, the base of their Electoral College strength in recent Presidential elections.

After an autumn campaign that brilliantly exploited the widespread public concern over the economy, declining living standards, competitiveness
and the lack of vision of the Bush administration, and with more than a little
help from Independent candidate H. Ross Perot, Clinton was elected with
370 electoral votes to 168 for Bush, and with 43 per cent of the national
popular vote to Bush's 38 per cent. In the South, Clinton carried Arkansas,
Tennessee, Louisiana and Georgia, and came very close in Florida and
North Carolina, raising the Democratic Presidential vote in every Southern
state except Texas. Clinton also scored a little better than 1988 candidate
Michael Dukakis among white Southerners, although his national popular
tally was three points lower in a three-way race.[21]

In the 1996 Presidential election, Clinton needs to win over the lion's
share of the 1992 Perot voters (19 per cent of the electorate). He thus has the
delicate task of trying to balance the interests of the discontented white,
suburban, middle-class voters with those of the 'minorities' – blacks, Latinos,
feminists, gays – that constitute the base of the Democratic coalition. Clinton's
Cabinet choices reflected this dilemma. Most of the key positions – State,
Defense, Treasury – were filled by white male Democrats of a generally
moderate-to-conservative stamp. The other senior position – Attorney-General – was filled by a woman, while blacks gained four Cabinet posts,
Latinos two and women six. The selection process did not run entirely
smoothly. Women's groups protested that Clinton was not appointing enough
women during the process, and Clinton apparently changed his nominee for
Secretary of Energy in response to this pressure, although he made a calculated outburst against the notion of Cabinet 'quotas' at a news conference.
In the foreign policy area, neo-conservative Democrats who had deserted
the party because of its 'dovishness' during the 1970s and 1980s, but who
had been wooed back with some success by Clinton following the end of the
Cold War, were upset that three of the four major foreign policy positions
were filled by veterans of the Carter administration with dovish reputations
– Warren Christopher (Secretary of State), Anthony Lake (National Security
Advisor) and Madeleine Albright (UN Ambassador).

During Clinton's first year in office the tensions between the Democratic
factions were reflected on a variety of issues, with the White House generally adopting a Neo-liberal position and finding different factional allies on
an issue-by-issue basis. The first week of his Presidency was dominated by
a fracas over Clinton's pledge to end the policy of indiscriminately dis-
charging homosexual personnel from the armed forces. Southern conservative Democrats, led by the powerful Senate Armed Forces Committee Chairman, Sam Nunn of Georgia, made it clear that they could not support ending
the ban and, fearful of alienating culturally conservative, middle-class
voters, the White House settled for a compromise position that differed only

marginally (gays would not be discharged unless they were sexually active) from the status quo and which, in turn, infuriated gay rights activists who had been loyal and enthusiastic supporters of Clinton during the 1992 campaign.

Tensions also arose over Clinton's 1994 budget, which did not go far enough in reducing spending to satisfy some of the more conservative Democrats in Congress, although the President was able to call upon a sufficient degree of party loyalty to ensure passage of the measure by the narrowest possible margin in both House and Senate. On the North American Free Trade Agreement, many on the party's New Left, the labour unions and many of their allies among the Regulars in the party deserted Clinton, as a majority of Democrats in each chamber voted against the President's position. Southerners and Neo-liberals generally stood by the White House, however, and with more than a little help from the GOP Clinton was able to prevail.

But if the DLC, the Southerners and the Neo-liberals had stood together with Clinton on the budget and NAFTA, as 1994 approached major differences emerged on Clinton's proposal to reform the health care system – the centrepiece of his domestic legislative programme. The White House proposal guaranteeing universal medical coverage for all Americans, through reliance on employer mandates and large regional 'health alliances' for the purpose of negotiating insurance rates, found little favour with the DLC and its chairman, Congressman Dave McCurdy of Oklahoma, to whom the Clinton package seemed overly bureaucratic and imitative of past Democratic 'big government' programmes. Their preferred approach was closer to the alternative plan proposed by Congressman Jim Cooper of Tennessee, that relied more on market incentives rather than government mandates. This was essentially a strategic disagreement. The White House was betting that middle-class voters would respond to the establishment of a universal programme similar to Social Security and Medicare, from which they would gain as well as the indigent. McCurdy and Al From, on the other hand, were wary of creating a massive new entitlement programme that seemed to contradict the whole tone of DLC policy and rhetoric.

Democratic factionalism thus did not vanish with the election of Clinton to the Presidency, although there was evidence of increasing fluidity among the factions, with different alliances being formed on different issues – New Left, Neo-liberals and Regulars for the Clinton budget, Southerners opposed; New Left and Regulars opposed to free trade, Neo-liberals and Southerners more enthusiastic. On health care the party divided three ways, with the New Left and Regulars supporting a Canadian-style 'single-payer' system, Southerners supporting the more modest market-oriented Cooper plan and Neo-liberals standing by Clinton's compromise 'managed compe-

tition' scheme. Clinton's lack of identification with any one faction ultimately turned out to be an asset in government, as it had been in seeking the
nomination, enabling him to form different alliances of Democrats on an
issue-by-issue basis. He was also assisted, of course, by the comfortable
Democratic majorities in Congress, which gave him some room to spare.

Notes

1 For reasons of clarity and consistency I have chosen to refer to American intra-party
   groups as 'factions', although in American history they have rarely possessed the
   degree of organization that the term would imply in a European context. On American
   party factionalism, see Nicol C. Rae, *The Decline and Fall of the Liberal Republicans:
   From 1952 to the Present*, Oxford University Press, 1989, pp.10–45; Earl Black and
   Merle Black, *The Vital South: How Presidents Are Elected*, Harvard University Press,
   1992, pp.79–115.
2 Barbara Sinclair, *Congressional Realignment: 1925–1978*, University of Texas, 1982,
   pp.18–50; Richard Franklin Bensel, *Sectionalism and American Political Development: 1880–1980*, University of Wisconsin Press, 1984, pp.60–174.
3 On party factions in the New Deal Era, see Bensel, *Sectionalism*, pp.104–74; James T.
   Patterson, *Congressional Conservatism and the New Deal: the Growth of the Conservative Coalition in Congress*, University of Kentucky Press, 1967, pp.32–76; Frank
   Munger and James Blackhurst, 'Factionalism in the National Conventions, 1940–
   1964: An Analysis of Ideological Consistency in State Delegation Voting', *Journal of
   Politics*, **27**, 1965, pp.375–94.
4 See V.O. Key, Jr., *Southern Politics in State and Nation*, Knopf, 1950, pp.345–82;
   Donald R. Matthews, *US Senators and Their World*, Vintage, 1960, pp.92–117, 162–6;
   William S. White, *Citadel: the Story of the US Senate*, Harper & Brothers, 1956,
   pp.67–79, 179–97, 199–211.
5 James Q. Wilson described the conflict between the reformers and the old New
   Dealers as one between two distinct types of party activists: 'amateurs' and 'profes-
   sionals'. See James Q. Wilson, *The Amateur Democrat: Club Politics in Three Cities*,
   University of Chicago Press, 1962, pp.1–31. On the Republicans, see Aaron Wildavsky,
   The Revolt Against the Masses: And Other Essays on Politics and Public Policy, Basic
   Books, 1971, pp.246–69.
6 The tension between the Regulars, the New Left and the Neo-liberals within the
   Democratic party also reflects a broader tension between modernizing and traditional
   cultures in American society, which was anticipated by James Q. Wilson in the early
   1960s. See Wilson, *The Amateur Democrat*, pp.258–370. See also James Davison
   Hunter, *Culture Wars: the Struggle to Define America*, Basic Books, 1991, pp.1–51;
   Everett Carl Ladd, Jr., with Charles D. Hadley, *Transformations of the American Party
   System*, 2nd edn, Norton, 1978; Jonathan Rieder, *Canarsie: the Jews and Italians of
   Brooklyn Against Liberalism*, Harvard University Press, 1985, pp.1–9, 233–63;
   Christopher Lasch, *The True and Only Heaven: Progress and Its Critics*, Norton,
   1991, pp.476–532.
7 On the Southern volte-face on civil rights within Congress, see Charles S. Bullock, III,
   'The South in Congress: Power and Policy', in James F. Lea (ed.), *Contemporary
   Southern Politics*, Louisiana State University Press, 1988, pp.177–93.

8 On the upper-middle class, white-collar bias of Democratic primary electorates, see Nelson W. Polsby, *Consequences of Party Reform*, Oxford University Press, 1983, pp.157–67.

9 On the 'momentum effect' of the New Hampshire primary, see William G. Mayer, 'The New Hampshire Primary: A Historical Overview', in Gary R. Orren and Nelson W. Polsby (eds), *Media and Momentum: the New Hampshire Primary and Nomination Politics*, Chatham House, 1987, pp.9–37.

10 Bullock, in Lea (ed.), *Contemporary Southern Politics*, pp.177–93.

11 Material from interviews with Senator Robb (28 June 1990) and the DLC's Executive Director since its inception, Alvin From (18 July 1990).

12 DLC membership list.

13 Information from interview with DLC Policy Director, Bruce Reed, 2 July 1991.

14 *The Economist*, 11 May 1991, pp.21–2.

15 See *The New Orleans Declaration: A Democratic Agenda for the 1990s*, Democratic Leadership Council, 1990.

16 See *The Economist*, 11 May 1991, pp.21–2.

17 *The New Democrat*, May 1991.

18 From interview, 18 July 1990.

19 The 'Southern primary' in 1992 was staggered, with Georgia voting on 3 March, South Carolina on 7 March and Florida, Louisiana, Mississippi, Tennessee and Texas on 10 March; the remaining Southern states were voting later in the season. This arrangement diluted the influence of New Hampshire and enhanced that of Georgia, thus assisting the prospects of any Southern regional contender.

20 *Congressional Quarterly Weekly Report*, 14 March 1992, p.632.

21 See Voter Research and Surveys (VRS) poll in 'Portrait of the Electorate', *New York Times*, 5 November 1992, p.B9.

8　Political Action Committees in American Politics

Alan Grant

Throughout American history there has been concern about the influence of big money on elections and the democratic process. In the 1980s, as the cost of running for Congress spiralled, demands for reform of the campaign finance system grew to include not only public interest groups such as Common Cause but also the parties in Congress and even the President himself. The focus of much of the criticism as well as the proposals for reform were political action committees (PACs), organizations that have been set up with the specific role of channelling funds from pressure groups to candidates for public office. This chapter seeks to explain how and why PACs developed, the strategies they adopt in making financial contributions and their role in relation to the overall funding of elections, and examines the debate about their influence on the legislative process and the political system. Finally recent legislative proposals to reform election campaign finance are analysed, with particular reference to the working of PACs.

The PAC Explosion

Political action committees were born in the 1940s out of what at the time was perceived to be political necessity. Trade unions were prohibited from spending money from their regular funds to support candidates for office and so they invented the idea of pooling donations from their members and presenting that money to candidates instead. Business organizations followed suit with the establishment of BI-PAC (Business–Industry PAC) in 1963, but it was not until the period after the passage of the 1974 amendments to the Federal Election Campaign Act, which officially sanctioned the idea of political action committees, that the huge expansion of PACs took place. The reforms of the 1970s were introduced in the aftermath of the Watergate scandal, when it was revealed that large amounts of money had been donated to the Nixon campaign in return for past or expected future favours. Legislation tightened up the rules for disclosure of campaign receipts and the administration of elections, while seeking to restrict the influence of wealthy 'fat cats' by placing limits on contributions. Individuals could give up to $1000 to a particular campaign (with primary and general elections counting as separate campaigns) and a total of $25 000 to all campaigns in a single year. PACs were restricted to donating $5000 to any individual campaign, but no limit was placed on the overall amount they could contribute. By favouring PACs giving in this way, as compared with individual donations, the law effectively increased candidates' reliance on them.

Any remaining doubts about the legitimacy of corporate PACs were dispelled when the newly-created Federal Election Commission determined in 1975 that the Sun Oil Company could form a PAC and that a sponsoring group such as a business corporation could pay the PAC's administrative and overhead expenses as long as its direct political activities were supported by a separate fund. A year later the US Supreme Court's ruling in *Buckley* v. *Valeo* upheld parts of the 1974 law but overturned others. Most significantly the Court found that mandatory limits on the amounts candidates could spend on their campaigns were an unconstitutional restriction of free speech under the First Amendment. In addition, a provision of the Act that had placed limits on 'independent expenditures' made on behalf of a candidate without his or her cooperation was also struck down, thus opening the door to another method of PAC funding.

In 1975, there were 608 PACs in existence, but after the Sun Oil case the number of business PACs soared, from 89 to 1600 in the next decade. By 1980, 2551 PACs had been established, with the numbers reaching a peak in 1988, when 4268 were registered with the Federal Election Commission. Since the late 1980s, the number of PACs has remained fairly stable after the vast expansion of the previous decade. In 1991, 4094 PACs were registered, of which 1738 were set up by business corporations, 338 by trade unions, 742 by trade and professional associations or similar membership bodies and 1083 were non-connected.[1] Corporate, labour and trade/professional association PACs are all connected to their parent body, which remains in charge, whether through a chief executive or a committee or board reflecting the membership of the organization. These organizations can raise money from their employees, shareholders or members, which they do principally through payroll deductions, direct mail appeals or face-to-face solicitation for donations. They sometimes try to motivate involvement in election campaigns by persuading people to work voluntarily for candidates, and may also make 'in kind' donations such as lending staff or office equipment for a campaign. Some of the overhead costs of the PAC may be absorbed either within the lobbying budget of the pressure group or through the organization's general treasury and by sharing buildings, staffing or equipment. Non-connected PACs, on the other hand, are different in that they have no parent body. They are often ideological, with a clear political philosophy, or have been formed to campaign on a single issue. Unlike other PACs, they can appeal directly to the public at large for funds and do so through extensive direct mail operations. Being unconstrained by a parent body, decisions may be made by a small group or even an individual. Some of these groups also establish non-profit educational or research foundations, which leads to tax advantages as well as the sharing of costs in running the PAC.

Politicians may also set up their own organizations, known as leadership PACs. This may be done to prepare for a Presidential election campaign and to avoid legally limited expenditure before the formal announcement of a candidacy. It may be established by a Congressman to contribute to other politicians' campaigns in order to secure their gratitude and support later in furthering their own legislative or leadership ambitions. Ronald Reagan created the first Presidential PAC in 1977 to prepare the groundwork for his successful 1980 campaign. In the next year, Citizens for the Republic PAC spent over $4·5 million, with contributions to 400 conservative candidates while financing Reagan's own speaking tours and publicity. Senator Jesse Helms's Congressional Club PAC has supported not only his own highly expensive Senate campaigns but those of other right-wing candidates. Congressional leaders are expected to show they are effective fund-raisers as well as legislative strategists and their PACs have helped them secure colleagues' backing in leadership elections. For example, Democratic House Whip, Tony Coelho, gave over $500 000 to candidates for the House in 1987–8. Ross K. Baker argues that, although there are relatively few leadership PACs, they do have a significant influence, dispersing $3·5 million in 1986, an average of $70 000 for each recipient. This in turn may have been decisive in the leadership elections for positions such as House Majority Whip and Chairman of the House Democratic Caucus which are chosen by the Democratic members of the House of Representatives.[2] As the number of PACs increased rapidly after the 1974 Act so did their spending on campaigns. In 1972, they gave $19·1 million to Congressional candidates; in 1986, the figure was $139 million; and by 1992 the total of PAC contributions had risen to $188 million. At the same time the percentage of campaign funding coming from PACs compared with other sources has steadily increased, particularly for House members. In 1976, winning candidates in House elections received an average of 26 per cent of their total funding from PACs; by 1990 this had risen to 46 per cent.[3] Concern has therefore been expressed, not only about the rise in numbers and spending overall by PACs, but also the growing dependence by legislators on PAC funding compared with individual contributions and support from political parties, and the potential influence of special interests on both elections and the legislative process.

PAC money has the great advantage for candidates that it is relatively easy to collect compared with soliciting donations from a large number of individuals. In effect PACs do the collecting from individuals – members, employees, supporters – and bear the administrative cost of doing so. They then distribute the money to those candidates they feel are most likely to support the collective interests of the group in Congress. Baker believes that PACs are best understood as a political mutual fund:

> As the investor relies on a mutual fund manager to invest his or her money in a variety of companies the political contributor can give money to a PAC and have the PAC director donate the funds to a variety of candidates. Because many donors have neither the time nor the knowledge to evaluate the records of more than a few candidates, it is efficient to use the PAC as an intermediary.[4]

Contributing to Candidates

PACs may follow one of three broad strategies when making decisions as to which candidates to support financially, or combine these approaches in such a way that they maintain credibility with their donors as well as having an impact on policy making.[5]

1 *Partisan/ideological*: the PAC may support candidates of a sympathetic party or those who have demonstrated their backing for the group's view on a particular issue or a broad ideological approach that the organization favours.
2 *Access/legislative*: the PAC supports candidates on a pragmatic basis that the individuals have or are likely to have influence in the policy-making process in areas of interest to the organization and it wishes to retain or gain access to these legislators.
3 *Organizational/local*: the PAC backs candidates who are favoured by donors or contributes to local members of Congress where the group has a base or supporters living within their constituencies.

The access/legislative strategy is mostly aimed at simply maintaining or continuing relationships with those members to whom the group already has access, although it may also be designed to expand the number of members with whom the organization has ready contact.[6]

Most PACs have tended to concentrate on a pragmatic approach aimed at ensuring that they have access to the people who will be in a position to affect the groups' interests. This has inevitably led to a concentration of PAC contributions going to incumbent members of Congress and only a small percentage of their money going to challengers in elections. In 1978, 57 per cent of PAC contributions went to incumbents; this had risen to 70 per cent by 1988 and approximately 80 per cent in 1990. Senate incumbents raised $33 million from PACs in 1990, while House members received $88 million and their challengers only $8 million.[7] This huge financial advantage helped contribute to the 95 per cent success rate of House members in securing re-election in that year. House members receive on average almost half their total campaign funding from PACs, while Senators, with their larger, more diverse constituencies and greater number of potential donors, obtain just under a quarter of their finances by this route. Figure 8.1 demonstrates the pattern of PAC contributions to Congressional members in 1991–2.

In 1990, only 14 House members and four Senators refused to accept any money from PACs. They were able to argue that they were free from the influence of any sectional interest and were totally dedicated to serving their constituents, although it is worth noting that some members in this position do receive many large individual donations from the executives and employees of corporations based in their constituencies, but, because they are not channelled through a PAC, they are less readily traceable.

Influenced by the group's lobbyists in Washington, supporting friendly incumbents is often a PAC's top priority, followed by contributing in open races where no incumbent is running. Those following a pragmatic approach usually only give to the opponent of an unfriendly incumbent if he is already believed to be in electoral trouble. PACs will give most heavily to those members who are on committees relevant to their interests and the chairmen of committees and sub-committees will attract the largest donations. Party leaders who have influence across the range of policy areas usually attract the largest overall sums from PACs. Incumbents often built up a formidable war chest of campaign funds well before the next election, which may well deter serious challengers in the party primary or even the general election. While there is pressure on PACs to donate early in the election cycle, they may also make contributions to legislators after the election, even in some cases where they had backed an opponent in the run-up to the election. This will help the candidate pay off campaign debts and is particularly welcomed by those successful challengers who spent heavily to secure their victories, but it is a practice that is much criticized because it appears to be a clear attempt at influence-peddling.

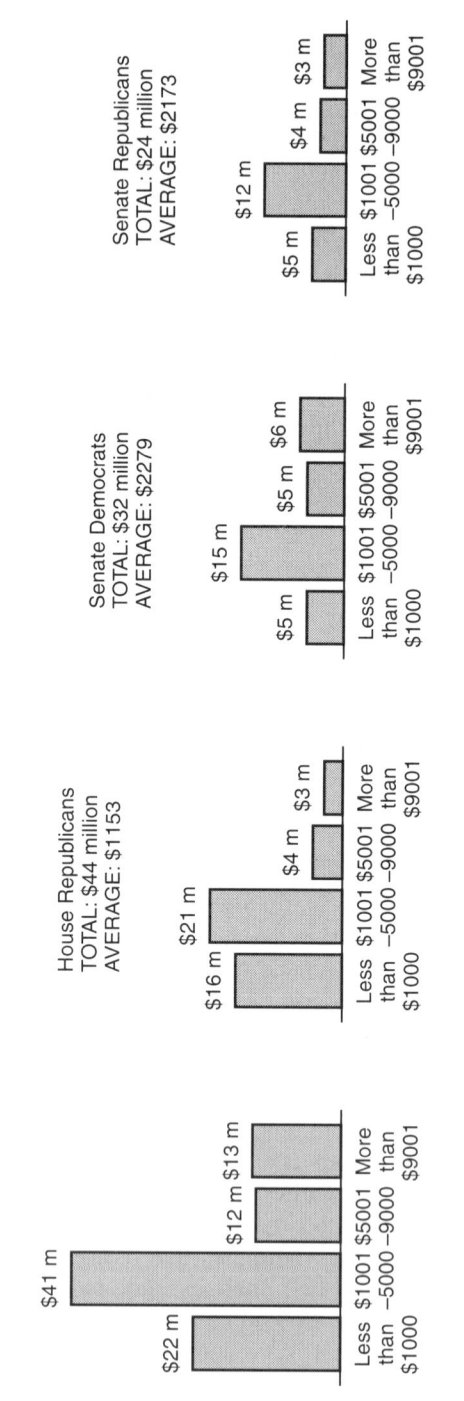

House Democrats
TOTAL: $88 million
AVERAGE: $1602

$41 m

$22 m

$12 m $13 m

Less $1001 $5001 More
than   –5000 –9000 than
$1000 $9001

House Republicans
TOTAL: $44 million
AVERAGE: $1153

$21 m

$16 m

$4 m $3 m

Less $1001 $5001 More
than   –5000 –9000 than
$1000 $9001

Senate Democrats
TOTAL: $32 million
AVERAGE: $2279

$15 m

$5 m $5 m $6 m

Less $1001 $5001 More
than   –5000 –9000 than
$1000 $9001

Senate Republicans
TOTAL: $24 million
AVERAGE: $2173

$12 m

$5 m $4 m $3 m

Less $1001 $5001 More
than   –5000 –9000 than
$1000 $9001

Source: Federal Election Commission, reported in *Washington Post*, 13 June 1994, p.A17.

Figure 8.1   PAC contributions to Congressional Members, 1991–2

Although $5000 has remained the upper limit for PAC contributions or $10 000 for the primary and general election campaigns (and with the effect of inflation it is worth considerably less in real terms than when it was set in the mid-1970s) only labour PACs regularly give the maximum amounts. The average PAC donation to a candidate in the 1992 elections was $1600 and the most common contribution was $500. Just over 3000 of those PACs registered in 1990 actually contributed to Congressional campaigns and of these many are small-scale operations sponsored by political clubs, small businesses and local branches of trade unions or only give to candidates in their own state or region. Only one PAC in four gave $20 000 or more to federal candidates in 1990, but those that did accounted for over 93 per cent of all PAC donations.[8] Table 8.1 shows the largest PAC contributions in 1993–4. Candidates seek out contributions from a range of different groups in order to raise enough money to fight a serious campaign and they have to do so on a regular basis, particularly in the House with its two-yearly election cycle. A form of reverse lobbying takes place, with legislators and their staffs trying to persuade PAC managers to support their campaign

Table 8.1   Biggest-spending political action committees Jan. 1, 1993–March 31, 1994

PAC	Disbursements
EMILYS's List	$4,863,424
DRIVE (Intl. Brotherhood of Teamsters)	4,174,355
American Federation of State County & Municipal Employees	2,971,152
Campaign America (leadership PAC of Sen. Robert Dole. R-Kan.)	2,475,247
National Rifle Association Political Victory Fund	2,073,175
Association of Trial Lawyers of America	2,050,398
Machinists' Non-Partisan Political League	1,964,957
District No. 1-PCD MEBA (Marine Engineers Beneficial Association)	1,706,891
National Education Association	1,704,345
National Conservative Club (formerly the National Congressional Club)	1,648,834

Source: Federal Election Commission, reported in *National Journal*, 2 July 1994, p. 1580.

fund. For incumbents, Washington fund-raising events, where tickets for a dinner or reception sell for $500 to $1 000 or more, are a common method of PAC funding. PACs rarely donate to a campaign except in response to a request and are often inundated with invitations to do so. PACs often feel under an obligation to support an incumbent Congressman, particularly if he holds a powerful position in the legislature, because they fear he or his staff will otherwise be offended and refuse future access.

Those groups for whom the ideological 'purity' of the candidate is the most important factor are more likely to take risks and support challengers. They will also examine the voting records of incumbents – either on the key issue they are concerned with or their overall political stance – and look at the ratings given by groups such as Americans for Constitutional Action (a conservative pressure group), Americans for Democratic Action (a liberal group), the AFL-CIO or BI-PAC as indicators of members' ideologies. In 1990, ideological PACs gave 68.2 per cent of their donations to Democratic candidates and 31.7 per cent to Republicans, while trade union PACs, long-time supporters of the Democratic party, favoured its candidates with 92 per cent of their contributions. With the Democrats controlling both houses of Congress, labour PACs have not faced a conflict when deciding on strategy for giving; both an access/legislative approach and an ideological approach lead them to support Democrats. Business, on the other hand, has not had this happy congruence and in recent times the majority of corporate PACs have taken a pragmatic approach, with their contributions going to the parties' candidates almost equally. For example, in 1990, business PACs donated $54·7 million to Democrats and $53·4 million to Republicans.[9] Corporate PACs gave nearly twice as much as labour and ideological PACs combined but, because their contributions were split evenly, Democratic candidates received 61.7 per cent of total PAC funding in 1990, compared with the Republicans, who were given 38.2 per cent. Not only has Democratic control of the legislature meant that access to their members has been more advantageous but their majority status also, of course, has meant the Democrats have had larger numbers of candidates for re-election.

The growth in the number of corporate PACs and increased political activism by business in the 1970s resulted from what executives saw as a threat to their interests from a liberal Democratic Congress, increased government regulation and the rise of public interest groups. Dan Clawson, Alan Neustadtl and Denise Scott have carried out detailed research on business PACs, concentrating on 309 of the largest corporations.[10] They point out that well known giants such as IBM and Procter and Gamble have not felt it necessary to establish their own PACs. They also argue that those corporate PACs following an ideological strategy, which is aimed at influencing the political composition of Congress, have two key criteria when determining to which campaigns they should contribute. They will direct their resources to 'pro-free enterprise' candidates (in practice always conservatives) who face opponents who are perceived to be unsympathetic to business and they will concentrate on competitive elections where the money has the potential to influence the result. They will often give to challengers or candidates for open seats where no incumbent is running. Some corporate PACs, such as Cooper Industries PAC (CIPAC) and Political Action Coors Employees (PACE), are known for their commitment to give only to conservative candidates. An ideological strategy means that supporting free enterprise as a philosophy takes priority over the immediate corporate interest and is not related to the company's lobbying activities.

In practice most business PACs have followed an ideological strategy only in the run-up to the 1980 elections when Ronald Reagan won the Presidency, the Republicans took control of the Senate and made important gains in the House of Representatives and when their support was a significant factor in the party's success. In subsequent election years most corporate PACs reverted to a pragmatic access strategy which has led to the pattern of donations where the parties benefit equally. Clawson, Neustadtl and Scott argue that a number of factors explain this dramatic change of approach in corporate giving after 1980. Following the enactment of much of the Reagan agenda in the early 1980s, with its emphasis on deregulation and pro-business policies, corporate PACs felt that their most pressing concerns had been addressed, while the Democrats in Congress moved to more moderate positions that accommodated business interests. Democratic leaders, and particularly Tony Coelho the Majority House Whip, persuaded the PACs that, not only did the Democrats deserve support, but it was not sensible for business to ignore the reality of Democratic control of the House and the likelihood that this would continue. Consequently business leaders felt that the most hostile Democrats had either been defeated or had been marginalized and that the political situation meant that they had more to lose than they were likely to gain by aggressively seeking to defeat Democrats across the board. Brooks Jackson described the approach of corporate PACs: 'As a group they remained far more interested in currying favour with the ruling faction than in promoting the free market ideology the Republicans championed.'[11] Republican leaders and the more ideological business PACs attacked the timidity of such an approach, which they saw as appeasement. The frustration felt by House Republicans was voiced by Rep. Guy Vander Jagt, Chairman of the Republican Congressional Campaign Committee, when during the 1986 elections he declared, 'The PACs are whores!'[12] Business PACs have not given to Democratic incumbents because they wanted them to win but because they thought they would win. When it comes to open races their preference for Republicans is clear, with approximately three times as much money going to the party's candidates than to Democrats.

The most controversial form of PAC funding has been that known as 'independent expenditures': if spending is truly independent and is 'without consultation with, or the cooperation of, any candidate or campaign' then there are no limits to the amount that can be spent in either promoting or seeking to defeat a candidate. While comprising only a very small part of total PAC funding, it has been significant not only in Congressional races but also in Presidential elections. Generally PAC money has concentrated on Congressional elections because of the availability of public funding for Presidential contests. Ronald Reagan particularly benefited from independent expenditure on his behalf by the National Conservative Political Action Committee (NCPAC). The notorious Willie Horton advertising campaign during the 1988 Presidential election, in which the Democratic candidate, Michael Dukakis, was depicted as being 'soft on crime', cost $8·5 million and was paid for by the National Security PAC, a conservative group which was technically independent of the Bush campaign. In Presidential primaries, where the candidate has reached or almost reached the official spending limit allowed, such funding can be influential. However the main criticism has been that much of the expenditure has been used, as in the Willie Horton case, for negative advertising aimed solely at defeating individuals who have alienated a PAC and, it is claimed, often distorting their voting records or positions on the issues in the process. In 1980, NCPAC spent over a million dollars on a campaign to oust six liberal Senators. Four of them (Bayh, McGovern, Church and Culver) lost their seats, but it is difficult to say how far NCPAC contributed to these results, given the Reagan landslide in that year. Former Senator Lloyd Bentson has argued that: 'These so-called independent groups ... reap the advantage of lies and distortions and then force the candidate to spend funds to set the record straight.'[13]

In 1990, 110 PACs spent $5·1 million on independent expenditures during the Congressional elections, with only 11 running campaigns that exceeded $100 000, and most were small and localized.

The Debate About PACs

As Larry Sabato has pointed out, PACs have superseded the 'fat cats' of old as the public focus and symbol of the role of money in politics and have inherited the suspicion that goes with that territory.[14] In fact many of the criticisms levelled at PACs are actually better directed at the campaign finance system as a whole, in which PACs play an important but not dominant role. Until recently PACs did not actively lobby on the issue of campaign finance reform but, during the early 1990s, they began to put forward their own case and submit their own proposals for changing the system.

The activities of PACs are criticized on a number of different levels. We shall examine their role in relation to the political parties and the legislative process in greater detail later in this chapter, because in many respects these aspects are central to understanding the impact of PACs on democratic government. Opponents of PACs have argued that their gifts come with strings attached and that Congressmen's votes are effectively being bought to secure the passage of favoured pieces of legislation (or possibly, just as importantly, the defeat of unwelcome bills). They believe that when PACs say that they seek access they really mean that they are expecting influence over the legislative process; they put Congressmen under a sense of obligation in return for past or future donations so that, when a bill comes before their committee or the full chamber, they have to think how their vote will effect their fund-raising rather than whether it is in the national interest or even in the interests of their constituents. PACs may themselves feel trapped by the system, but fear of losing out compels them to continue. In research carried out among PAC directors by the Center for Responsive Politics, one lobbyist interviewed quoted an unnamed Senator as saying, with the deepest cynicism, 'I've had people who contribute to my campaign and they get access; the others get good government.'[15] According to Philip Stern, in his book entitled *Still the Best Congress Money Can Buy*, the capacity to aggregate donations is the crucial new element PACs have introduced and it endows interest groups with two new and important powers. First, it enables them to magnify their groups' political influence without relationship to the number of members or the merits of their arguments and, second, it allows the groups to impose huge costs on the rest of the public, for example by successfully lobbying for subsidies paid for by the taxpayers to particular industries or sectional interests.[16] This latter argument is also emphasized by C.W. Griffin, who comments:

> Collectively the PACs constitute a huge coalition of special interest groups dedicated to perverting the political process for private gain. They provide the political mechanism through which special interest groups exploit society at large, the means by which small, well-organised minorities assert their economic tyranny over the disorganised, apathetic majority.[17]

Legislators may also be deflected from their proper representational and legislative work because of the need to spend so much time and effort in raising campaign money, a demeaning chore that has contributed to the

recent growing disillusionment among Congressmen with Washington politics. It is also suggested that PAC money can undermine the relationship
between law-makers and their constituents. When so much of their funding
comes from national PACs rather than from people in their own districts or
states, they are more likely to be attuned to PAC interests and less sensitive
to shifts in home town sentiment. Philip Stern argues that the money-built
connection between interest groups and legislative committees has altered
the meaning of the term 'constituency'. Members of Congress now represent not only a geographical constituency made up of the voters who elected
them to office but legislative or economic constituencies as well. For example, the members of the Armed Services Committees in Congress have the
defence contractors as their natural economic 'constituents', which Stern
describes as 'an ugly, undemocratic new concept'.[18]

As we have seen, PAC money goes predominantly to incumbents, as the
majority of PACs follow an access or legislative contribution strategy. This,
it is argued, undermines the democratic process by reducing the competitiveness of elections, deterring challengers or making the odds against them
so great that voters are denied a proper choice. What is more, some PACs
are so unprincipled that they have even been known to hedge their bets by
supporting both major party candidates in the same race and, in other cases,
helping to pay off a candidate's campaign debts after the election if they
backed the wrong horse beforehand.

Sara Fritz and Dwight Morris argue that the easy availability of PAC
money has been a major factor in the spiralling of expenditure on Congressional elections. Their research indicates that it is not, as widely believed,
that the real costs of campaigning on such items as television advertising
have rocketed, but that legislators have used the money available to build
themselves political empires with staffing and offices which consolidate
their positions in their constituencies and make them almost impervious to
electoral challenges. They point out that more than half the money spent in
the 1990 Congressional elections went on purchases that were virtually
unrelated to contacting voters and, of all the money spent by House incumbents, 55 per cent was invested by those with little or no opposition. House
members seeking re-election spent on average $390 000 and incumbent
Senators $4 million in 1990. Rep. Martin Frost (D – Texas) spent almost
$600 000, even though he had no major party opponent, while Rep. Joseph
Kennedy II (D – Massachusetts) used $826 000 in his efforts to defeat a
Republican challenger with less than $5000 in his campaign coffers. Fritz
and Morris argue: 'Money from special interests has enabled most incumbent members to create their own state of the art permanent political
machine'.[19]

PACs have also been criticized for being internally undemocratic and unaccountable to their own donors for their decisions and activities. Some employees, such as corporate executives, may feel under pressure to contribute to the PAC whether they want to or not, because it is expected of them. Only a minority of PACs allow donors to earmark their contributions for candidates of their choice and even then they do not usually publicize this facility. Decisions about which candidates to support are made by a small group of leaders, or even by individuals. In 1984 the AFL-CIO decided to back Walter Mondale in the Democratic party Presidential nomination contest, while less than a quarter of trade union members were asked their preference.[20]

Some PACs have actively sought to bypass the $5000 limit by indulging in the practice known as 'bundling'. This involves the PAC collecting a large number of individual donations, some of which will be up to the $1000 limit, each cheque being made out to the candidate's campaign fund, and sending them together to the candidate so that he and his staff are aware that the PAC should have the credit for the gifts. This practice can lead to very large collective contributions and resulted in, for example, a PAC known as EMILY's List (EMILY being an acronym for 'Early Money Is Like Yeast') raising substantial sums for female candidates in Congressional elections. Finally PACs have been accused of undermining the role of political parties, which many see as vital elements of democratic government. By providing so much funding for election campaigns PACs have increased candidates' dependence on them while at the same time making politicians more independent of parties. This in turn, it is argued, reduces the parties' influence over campaigns and weakens cohesion in the legislature, strengthening the trend to law-makers becoming more like independent political entrepreneurs, rather than members of a united and responsible party of government or opposition.

Supporters of PACs argue that they are simply the modern method of channelling money into expensive election campaigns and that the limits on contributions and regulations, including public disclosure of their gifts, prevent the type of corruption that may have existed in the past, when undisclosed and untraceable donations were the norm. The very fact that the media, the public and watchdog groups can find out which groups have given to whom has meant that PACs have taken almost all the blame for the ills of the campaign finance system, whereas the re-emergence of 'fat cat' contributors who donate to party funds (often known as 'soft money') and the practice of corporate executives (and their spouses) giving large personal donations up to the $1000 limit for individuals, which are more difficult to trace, have been largely ignored. Larry Sabato also stresses the need to see PAC funding in the context of the overall spectrum of campaign finance: individual donations and parties provide around three-fifths of the money for House candidates and three-quarters of that given to Senate campaigns, and PACs appear less awesome when looked at from this perspective.[21]

As the $5000 limit in PAC contributions has not been increased, the costs of campaigning have risen considerably since the mid-1970s and relatively few PACs give the maximum amount allowed, politicians have to seek out donations from a diversity of different groups. It can be argued that this prevents them from becoming dependent on any particular sources and weakens the influence of any PAC on an individual legislator. Given the amounts spent in total on campaigns, PAC supporters suggest that it is hardly credible that a Congressman's vote could be bought for a campaign contribution of a few hundred or even a few thousand dollars. PAC proponents also believe that they reflect the vast range of different interests within the United States and that they have legitimacy as part of the pluralistic political system. Competition between them and the vigilance of a free media prevent the dominance of any particular group and abuse of their positions. Herbert E. Alexander says that, while PACs are a relatively new phenomenon, they fit naturally into the larger stream of the nation's political life which, ever since De Toqueville noted Americans' propensity to form groups dedicated to furthering their interests, has often witnessed the creation of new forms of association.[22]

PACs also claim to have increased political participation and awareness and to have helped millions of Americans to exercise their constitutional rights of free expression and association. The vast majority of PACs communicate with their members and supporters about issues and candidates, thus providing a valuable method of political education and involvement at a time when there has been increasing concern expressed about low turnouts and voter apathy. In a recent advertising campaign, the Ad Hoc PAC Coalition (AHPAC) and the National Association of Business Political Action Committees (NABPAC) argued that it was not unusual for 60 per cent of PAC donors to be newcomers to the political arena, and reminded legislators that most PAC members are also active voters as well.[23] At the same time, PACs argue that proposals for reform which seek to ban or restrict their activities would make communicating with voters more difficult, while replacing their funding would be more expensive and time-consuming for legislators and their staffs.

In response to the argument that PACs concentrate their resources on incumbents, supporters point out that the same bias exists among individual contributors, whether large or small, and yet critics usually ignore this when proposing regulation of PAC funding. Moreover there are many different factors which explain the high re-election rates among Congressmen. The advantages of incumbency translate into an expectation of re-election and, as a result, a further advantage of being more readily able to raise funds. Larry Sabato argues that limiting PAC donations further would actually handicap challengers in competitive races who need to spend more to become known against an incumbent whose name is familiar to the public, while also favouring wealthy opponents who can spend their own money without limitation under Supreme Court rulings.[24] It has also been pointed out that members from poorer areas of the country and those with urban constituencies where individual political contributions are scarce benefit particularly from PAC funding to run viable campaigns.[25] In 1992, black candidates raised 52 per cent and Hispanics 40 per cent of their funds from PAC donations.

Therefore PAC funding should be seen in context. Some observers believe that PACs have been unfairly singled out for criticism and that proposals for reform have often not been fully thought through as to their possible consequences. After all, the current system came in the wake of the last period of reforming zeal in the post-Watergate era. PAC supporters point out that there is a danger that changes may lead to less accountable and open ways of financing elections, while allowing powerful interest groups to find new methods of channelling money to candidates.

PACs and Political Parties

The growing role of PACs in the financing of campaigns has raised issues about the relationship between organized interests and American political parties. Some observers have seen the explosion of PAC numbers and expenditure as an important factor in the decline of parties, a trend that political scientists have noted and monitored over recent decades. The relationship between the two forms of political organization is a complex one: part competitive, part cooperative and part accommodating.

Frank J. Sorauf has pointed out that during the twentieth century political parties and interest groups struck an historic bargain. The parties dominated the politics of the electoral process, choosing candidates and organizing campaigns, while interest groups concentrated on the politics of policy making by making representations and lobbying officials in power. While there was never a complete division (for example, parties had a role in proposing policies and some interest groups, particularly labour, did recruit candidates and help directly in campaigns), Sorauf notes that the rise of PACs did see the first major challenge to this division of effort. Political parties had already begun to lose their effectiveness by the mid-1970s, when PACs really started to make an impact on the political scene. Party organization had declined, voter loyalty, as reflected in the increase in split-ticket voting, had weakened and parties had much less control over the selection of candidates and the running of their campaigns. The rise of candidate-centred organizations meant that many of the tasks that had previously been performed by party volunteers had now to be paid for, with the resulting increase in costs. With greater emphasis on media advertising as well, candidates looked to PACs as a source of finance to help them meet the bills of their new organizations. Sorauf concludes:

> In no sense then did the rise of PACs contribute to the decline of political parties. ... The fortunes of PACs and political parties intersected in the 1970s both because of the decline of the parties and because of the transformation of American campaigning.[26]

Parties adapted to the new situation by providing services to candidates on a quasi-commercial basis, raising money through direct mail solicitations to supporters and developing the new skills of media-based campaigning. The Republicans led the way under the leadership of William Brock, who was Chairman of the Republican National Committee in the late 1970s, but by the mid-1980s both major parties had effectively developed a new relationship with their candidates. Parties also acted as intermediaries between PACs and the candidates, by organizing events which brought together potential donors and beneficiaries and, using their wider political intelligence as to the most likely winners, by giving cues to PACs in order to try and direct their contributions to their worthiest and most deserving candidates. Party organizations tend to concentrate their own funding on challengers and candidates in open seats, in the belief that most incumbents can find sufficient funds for their own campaigns and because they are seeking to maximize the number of legislative seats the party holds, rather than simply aiming at the re-election of incumbents. At the same time they promote their best hopes among these candidates to the PACs, particularly in what are likely to be close races.

Sorauf points out that, although PACs have on occasions raised more than twice as much as both the national parties combined (for example, in 1987–8 $384·5 million, compared with $182·2 million), parties can mobilize Americans for a much broader range of activities in addition to contributing funds to campaigns. With the exception of labour PACs which have traditionally helped candidates, nearly always Democrats, with volunteer efforts, most PACs have in practice remained fairly simple organizations based on the raising and distribution of money. In addition Sorauf notes that parties attract more involved and committed individuals, while PACs are supported by people who, although they are better informed and more aware than the population generally, have lower levels of interest in and commitment to politics.[27]

Because PACs have generally followed a play-safe strategy of giving to incumbents and likely winners, they have not developed into the type of electoral organizations political parties are. This would involve more risk taking, only giving to candidates with similar views and concentrating resources on races where the result was likely to be close and the additional money might make a difference. As we have seen, ideological PACs, labour PACs and a minority of corporate PACs can be said to follow this approach to some extent, but the majority, encouraged by the ever more aggressive fund-raising of incumbents and their ease of re-election, have found it worthwhile to abandon electoral goals and concentrate on legislative access. It appears that, although political parties and PACs have in some respects been in competition in the electoral arena, the two types of political organization generally still have distinctive objectives and differing approaches to achieving their goals.

PACs and the Legislative Process

Industrialist Justin Dart once observed that talking to politicians 'is a fine thing but with a little money they hear you better'.[28] Supporters of PACs admit that there is a link between their contributions and their activities in seeking to influence Congressional policy making, but maintain that the main advantage they secure is access to legislators and their staffs and the chance to put their case in person on an issue. Congressmen's appointment diaries are always under considerable pressure, with a plethora of meetings, invitations to attend events and media interviews, as well as rounds of committee and sub-committee meetings, party caucuses and votes in the chamber to attend. Staff inevitably have to ration both time and access to the member but a legislator is most likely to be willing to see contributors to his campaign, especially if he feels comfortable politically with the cause the PAC supports. However it is also true that, for important organizations, contributions are not necessary for such access if a member's district or state interests, his issue concerns or other reasons make it advantageous for them to meet.

As we have seen, critics of PACs believe that an unhealthy relationship exists between legislators and contributors which affects the legislative process in a direct way. Public interest groups such as Common Cause have pointed to what they see as a clear correlation between PAC donations and the way legislators vote on bills of direct interest to their contributors. C.W. Griffin argues that these correlations, when correctly analysed, point to causation and evidence of PACs effectively buying votes. He emphasizes that, with many close votes in Congress on controversial issues, even one or two votes, particularly in the Senate, can make all the difference.[29] Philip Stern questions the extent to which members of committees, who are so crucial in the legislative process, can take a balanced and even-handed approach on the issues when their 'economic constituents' have supported them financially in the past and may be expected to do so in the future.[30] Candidates seeking campaign contributions are often required to indicate how they would vote on particular bills, sometimes in written question-naires, and then as members they feel beholden to the groups who helped them get elected, particularly if they are freshmen or legislators without much seniority.[31] The public at large also seems convinced that pressure group money has a major impact on the legislature. A CBS/*New York Times* poll in October 1990 found that 71 per cent of those surveyed agreed that 'most members of Congress are more interested in serving special interest groups than the people they represent'.[32]

This popular perception that PACs can buy votes in Congress is signifi-cant, but research studies carried out in this area offer relatively little sup-port for this view. Political scientists have been able to analyse the inde-pendent effects of PAC contributions on Congressional voting, while con-trolling variables such as party, ideology, constituency interest and past voting record, which are recognized as playing a role in legislators' decis-ions. The evidence accumulated from these studies on whether contribu-tions generally influence legislative outcomes is conflicting and the issues raised are complex. M. Margaret Conway points out that insufficient re-search exists to permit a definitive answer to the question. Some studies have concluded that PAC money did affect recipients' support on roll call votes on issues such as minimum wage legislation, the B1 bomber, trucking deregulation and bills of interest to doctors and car-dealers. Other studies, however, on questions such as the Chrysler Corporation's loan guarantee, the windfall profits tax and dairy price supports, found that contributions were not a significant factor in voting behaviour.[33]

Janet M. Grenzke argues that, because so much of the research on PAC contributions consists of case studies, it is difficult to establish whether specific examples of PAC influence are indicative of a general pattern on much of the legislative agenda or whether these cases are exceptions to the norm.[34] Her own research study, conducted across a range of issues and over an eight-year period, concluded that there was little evidence that contributions affected the voting patterns of members of the House who served continuously from 1975 to 1982. She found that during the 1982 election cycle the average member received donations from 138 PACs, as well as many individuals. There was no statistical evidence to suggest that large contributions systematically caused members to consider the donors' arguments more carefully and positively. She concluded that, in the few cases in which a clear relationship between contributions and a member's vote was established, the analysis indicated that contributions were a surrogate measure of a more important and larger package of support for the member from the interest group concerned. The organizations involved had widespread support in members' districts and consequently had a variety of resources available:

> All of the PAC officials agreed that, in order to turn access into influence, the PAC must convince the House members that a particular position will improve their election prospects. Members' electoral prospects are improved by issue positions that generate support from district elites and voters, by contracts that provide jobs, and by a home style that matches the district. A particular PAC's contribution is not critical because a sizeable warchest and votes are forthcoming if there is general support in the district for the candidate.[35]

Larry Sabato also believes that, while 'PAC-bashing is undeniably a popular campaign sport', it has distracted attention from other more fundamental campaign finance issues. He concludes that the vote buying allegation is not supported by a careful examination of the facts. Whereas PAC contributions can make a difference in access and influence, such an effect is not as frequent or as widespread as is often suggested. PACs affect legislative proceedings to a decisive degree only when certain conditions prevail. PAC influence appears to be greatest when the issue is not a highly visible or controversial one, when the public and the media are not so interested or attentive, when technical or specialist matters are involved and when a large number of PACs are allied in pushing a cause. PAC money may also have more effect in the early stages of the legislative process, such as agenda setting and sub-committee meetings, than in the later floor deliberations and roll call votes in which there is more public interest. Sabato concludes:

> It is worth stressing that most Congressmen are *not* unduly influenced by PAC money on most votes. The special conditions simply do not apply to most legislative issues and the overriding factors in determining a legislator's vote include party affiliation, ideology and constituents' needs and desires.[36]

Sabato emphasizes the fact that PAC contributions are a means to an end for the legislator: re-election. If the PAC has a number of members or supporters living in the constituency or a stake in the area, the member is likely to be voting the PAC's way principally because it constitutes an important part of his electorate rather than because he received a donation from it.

Much of the research has concentrated on the roll call votes of the full House or Senate. While research on PACs and committees is now beginning to emerge, John R. Wright's study of the House Ways and Means and

Agriculture Committees found little evidence of a direct link between money and voting, but that campaign contributions influenced voting decisions indirectly through lobbying. Groups often structure their lobbying activities around prior contributions and these gifts, once in place, may facilitate access and amplify lobbying messages. Therefore the political and technical information representatives receive from groups' lobbying efforts is shaped to some extent by campaign money.[37] Analysis of the working of three House committees by Richard L. Hall and Frank W. Wayman indicated that money did have an important effect at committee level. They contend that the objective of PAC strategy is not simply the direction of a legislator's vote but the vigour with which this preference is promoted in the legislative process. What PACs want (and often get) is the Congressman's time, commitment and staff resources so that he may act as an agent or mobilizer of support in the committee. He may sponsor a bill, submit amendments or try to build a coalition of support among colleagues. Hall and Wayman argue that this explains, not only why PACs give to those who are almost certain to win anyway, but also why their contribution strategy sometimes extends to a group's known opponents: 'the intent of the money is not persuasion but demobilization: "We know you can't support us, but please don't actively oppose us."'[38]

The influence of PAC money may therefore not be so direct as to be actually buying law-makers' votes. There are more subtle ways in which it can influence the legislative process. Ellen S. Miller, the director of the Center for Responsive Politics, argues, 'It buys silence, hearings not held or amendments not introduced.'[39] This view is supported by former Senator William Proxmire, who claims:

> It [the influence of a campaign contribution] may not come in a vote. It may come in a speech not delivered. The PAC pay-off may come in a colleague not influenced. It may come in the calling off of a meeting that otherwise would result in advancing legislation. It may come in a minor change in one paragraph of a 240-page bill. It may come in a witness not invited to testify before a committee. It may come in hiring a key staffer for a committee who is sympathetic to the PAC. Or it may come in laying off or transferring a staff member who is unsympathetic to a PAC.[40]

PACs and Campaign Finance Reform

Every year since 1987, Congress has examined the issue of election campaign finance reform as public and media criticism of the spiralling costs of the current system have increased. However finding agreement within the Democratic party that has controlled both houses of Congress and between the parties has proved to be extremely difficult. Although almost all of the ideas considered would reduce the contributions allowed to be made by PACs or even seek to ban such funding altogether, the differences of interest among legislators have complicated the task. As we have seen, House Democrats have generally been more dependent on PAC money than their Senate counterparts and have been far less willing to give up this source of funding, while Republicans have wanted to ban or severely restrict PAC money which they believe has helped to keep the Democrats in power in Congress. Democrats have seen the ever-increasing costs of campaigns as the most significant problem under the current system and have therefore backed proposals to restrict spending on individual campaigns. The 1976 Supreme Court ruling against mandatory limits makes it impossible to construct a bill that limits spending without inducements to candidates to comply, and the introduction of public financing of Congressional campaigns has been the incentive proposed. Republicans have criticized spending limits on campaigns because they argue that it unfairly disadvantages challengers who lack the benefits of incumbency such as high name recognition, while opposing public funding on the basis that taxpayers should not have to foot the bill for politicians' election expenses.

In June 1989, President Bush announced a plan that he claimed would free the electoral system from the grip of special interests. He proposed the elimination of contributions from corporate, labour, trade and professional association PACs that provided almost 30 per cent of the money raised by Congressional candidates in 1988. His plan would have retained the right of ideological and single-issue PACs to contribute, but would have reduced the maximum donation to $2500. It would also have doubled the amounts parties could spend on behalf of a candidate, added disclaimers paid for by independent expenditures, restricted the practice of 'bundling' and required candidates to empty their campaign treasuries at the end of each election cycle so that incumbents would not start off a new campaign with a large financial advantage. Because the Bush plan did not include overall spending limits on campaigns or public funding, the Democrats in Congress not surprisingly failed to act on the proposals.

In 1990, both houses did pass measures, but they differed markedly on several important principles and they died in conference committee. The Keating Five scandal, in which Charles Keating, the powerful boss of a savings and loan empire, used his fund-raising skills to exert influence over five US Senators, focused attention on the issue and the 102nd Congress was under considerable pressure to pass a reform package, particularly after further scandals involving the House bank and post office came to light and public esteem of Congress sank to new lows. The House and Senate initially passed bills which both included sweeping changes designed to limit campaign spending but which again differed substantially on the details of how this was to be achieved. The Senate version of the bill, passed in May 1991, banned PACs from spending money to influence any federal election by direct contributions to campaigns, although they could continue to give to political parties. Because of the concern that such a ban might be ruled unconstitutional by the Supreme Court, the bill included contingency provisions that would reduce the maximum PAC contribution to $1000 per election and set an aggregate limit on the total of PAC gifts a candidate could accept. The final version of the Campaign Finance Bill of 1992, passed by both houses, contained separate regulations for House and Senate campaigns in recognition of the differences in the way such elections had been financed. In Senate campaigns candidates could accept no more than an aggregate of 20 per cent of the general election limit set for each state from PACs, with no more than $2500 from any one PAC. In House races candidates could accept no more than $200 000 overall from PACs, an amount equal to one-third of the spending limit of $600 000, and the maximum amount from any one PAC was to remain at $5000. President Bush had stated his objections to a bill based on spending limits on campaigns, public funding and separate rules for House and Senate elections. The proposed legislation contained all three of these elements, although it was silent on how public funding would be financed, and as expected he vetoed the bill on 9 May 1992. In doing so he contrasted its provisions with those in his own proposals and particularly criticized the bill for its failure to eliminate special interest PAC contributions. Democrats in Congress finally reached a compromise because they wanted to demonstrate to voters that they could pass a reform package before the 1992 elections, while knowing that its chances of becoming law were virtually nil. Some Democratic members undoubtedly voted for the measure, despite their own misgivings, because they knew Bush would veto it.

Bill Clinton said during the 1992 Presidential campaign that he would have signed the bill into law if he had been in the White House and he made election reform an issue in his contest with George Bush. His campaign document, 'Putting People First', differed in detail from the 1992 bill and he suggested reducing the maximum PAC contribution to $1000, the same as for individuals. After the elections, with federal deficit reduction and proposals to increase taxes at the centre of political debate, it was clear that many Democrats, particularly conservatives and moderates in both houses, were becoming increasingly nervous about asking the taxpayers to pay for public funding of elections, a scheme the Republicans were characterizing as 'food-stamps for politicians', and yet this had been a central plank of the 1992 reform bill. After months of discussions between the White House and Democratic Congressional leaders, the new President announced his own proposals for change on 7 May 1993. The main principles were in line with those of the 1992 bill. There were to be spending limits of $600 000 for House elections and between $1·2 million and $5·5 million for Senate races, depending on the size of the state; candidates who complied with the limits would receive federal communications vouchers to help pay for media advertising, printing costs and postage; Senate candidates would be given vouchers for up to 25 per cent of the spending cap and House candidates up to 33 per cent of the limit; to receive public funding a candidate would have to raise a significant proportion of his funding from small donations of less than $250. The proposals also included provisions to prevent the flow of unregulated 'soft money' to political parties, even though the Democrats had raised $30 million in this way to help Clinton win the Presidency. The main provisions with regard to PACs were identical to those in the 1992 bill, with the House Democratic leadership persuading the President to retain the $5000 maximum contribution to their campaigns. A new proposal was included in the package which would limit PAC donations to Presidential campaigns to $1000 and there was to be a ban on bundling by PACs and lobbyists. Clinton also wished to prevent anyone who had lobbied a legislator or his staff within the last year from donating to a campaign. He proposed to resource the public funding element of the plan, estimated to cost between $150 and $200 million in an election cycle, in two ways: by increasing the taxpayer check-off fund which finances Presidential elections from one to five dollars per individual, and by ending the tax exemption for lobbying expenses which pressure groups enjoy.[41] However revenues from a new tax on lobbying expenses were pre-empted in the deficit reduction package passed by Congress in August 1993.

The Senate considered the plan in June 1993 and, in order to face up to the political realities in their chamber, where Republican opponents had promised to filibuster and block the bill, Democratic leaders were forced to make concessions in a bid to win over sufficient Republican moderates to pass a cloture motion with the necessary 60 votes. The bill was eventually passed 60–38, with seven Republicans supporting the amended version. The cost of their backing was the stripping of almost all the public financing provisions, so that such funding would only be available to those candidates who complied with the spending limits but whose opponents exceeded them. In practice it was argued that the limits had been set sufficiently high for public finance to be rarely necessary. In addition the Senate introduced a new 35 per cent tax on all receipts of campaigns that reject spending limits, a provision that critics argued was unconstitutional. The other major change in the Senate bill was the imposition of a total ban on PAC contributions in all federal elections, with provisions similar to those of the 1992 bill if such a restriction was found to be unconstitutional.

After considerable delay, during which the House task-force on campaign finance and Democratic leaders in that chamber worked hard to write a bill that could win majority support in a floor vote, the House of Representatives passed its version of the legislation 255–175 on 22 November 1993. Despite the months of bargaining, the House bill was very similar to the 1992 legislation and, without the controversial new Senate tax provision, contained no proposals on ways to finance the public funding elements without which any reform could not be implemented. The House insisted that the current $5000 PAC contribution limit should remain, along with the one-third aggregate cap. The House bill did not include a ban on leadership PACs contained in the Senate version, and it would allow an exemption that permitted 'bundling' by EMILY's List, whereas the Senate had banned the practice completely.[42]

Because of disagreement between the two houses and the pressure of other legislation, particularly on health care reform and crime, no further action was taken on campaign finance for almost a year. When the Democratic leadership eventually agreed a compromise in September 1994, including a $6000 limit on PAC donations in an election cycle, it came too late and exposed the bill to the highly charged end-of-session political pressures. The Republicans in both houses had decided upon a strategy of obstructing legislation for which the Democrats might claim credit in the November elections. They also argued that the bill was partisan, pro-incumbent and unconstitutional. An attempt to break a Republican-led filibuster in the Senate against sending the measure to a conference committee to formally iron out differences in the bill failed by 52 to 46, eight votes short of the 60 necessary. Six Democrats joined the Republicans because of their objections to the public-funding provisions of the bill, while some moderate Republicans who had previously backed the Senate version defected because of what they saw as insufficient curbs on PAC funding.[43]

The failure of campaign finance reform in the 103rd Congress was a major defeat for both President Clinton and Congressional Democrats. Although the party inevitably sought to blame Republican obstructionism the major factors were the failure of the President to publicly lobby for his proposals and the inability of the Congressional leadership to reach a compromise, particularly over the limits of PAC funding, until too late in the session. With the Republicans gaining control of both houses in the 104th Congress, Democratic House members in particular may well regret that they missed the opportunity to create a fairer system for non-incumbents. It remains to be seen whether Republican hostility to PAC funding in Congressional elections survives their newly acquired majority status in the legislature.

Notes

1   Figures from the Federal Election Commission; Statistical Abstract of the United States 1992, p.274.
2   Ross K. Baker, *The New Fat Cats; Members of Congress as Political Benefactors*, Priority Press, 1989, p.1.
3   Larry Makinson, *Open Secrets: The Encyclopedia of Congressional Money and Politics*, Center for Responsive Politics/Congressional Quarterly Inc, 1992, p.6.
4   Baker, *The New Fat Cats*, p.9.
5   Frank J. Sorauf, 'PACs and Parties in American Politics', in Allan J. Cigler and Burdett A. Loomis (eds), *Interest Group Politics*, Congressional Quarterly Press, 1991, p.221.
6   M. Margaret Conway, 'PACs in the Political Process', in Cigler and Loomis (eds), *Interest Group Politics*, p.204.
7   Makinson, *Open Secrets*, p.3.
8   Ibid., p.18.
9   Ibid., p.20.
10 Dan Clawson, Alan Nuestadtl and Denise Scott, *Money Talks: Corporate PACs and Political Influence*, Basic Books, 1992.
11 Brooks Jackson, *Honest Graft: Big Money and the American Political Process*, Farragut, 1990, p.77.
12 Ibid., p.82.
13 Larry Sabato, *PAC Power: Inside the World of Political Action Committees*, Norton, 1984, p.101.
14 Ibid., p.186.
15 Jackson, *Honest Graft*, p.89.
16 Philip M. Stern, *Still the Best Congress Money Can Buy*, Regnery Gateway, 1992, p.8.
17 C.W. Griffin, *Cleaning Out Congress: The Case For Term Limits*, Griffin Associates, 1992, p.61.
18 Stern, *Still the Best*, pp.44–5.
19 Sara Fritz and Dwight Morris, *Gold Plated Politics; Running for Congress in the 1990s*, Congressional Quarterly Books, 1992, p.3.
20 Sabato, *PAC Power*, p.168.
21 Larry Sabato, *Paying for Elections: The Campaign Finance Thicket*, Priority Press, 1989, p.10.
22 Herbert E. Alexander, 'The PAC Phenomenon', in Edward Zuckerman (ed.), *The Almanac of Federal PACs*, Onwards Publications, 1992, p.ix.
23 *Congressional Quarterly Weekly Report*, 5 June 1993, p.1416.
24 Sabato, *Paying for Elections*, p.19.
25 Sara Fritz and Dwight Morris, *Campaign Spending: Money in the 1990 Congressional Races*, Congressional Quarterly Books, 1992, p.74.
26 Sorauf, 'PACs and Parties' p.219.
27 Ibid., p.220.
28 Sabato, *PAC Power*, p.122.
29 Griffin, *Cleaning Out*, chap. 6.
30 Stern, *Still the Best*, p.64.
31 Fritz and Morris, *Campaign Spending*, p.73.
32 *Congressional Quarterly Weekly Report*, 2 February 1991, p.277.
33 Conway, 'PACs in the Political Process', p.211.

34   Janet M. Grenzke, 'PACs and the Congressional Supermarket: the Currency is Complex', *American Journal of Political Science, 33,* February 1989, p.3.
35   Ibid., p.20.
36   Sabato, *Paying for Elections*, p.13.
37   John R. Wright, 'Contributions, Lobbying, and Committee Voting in the U.S. House of Representatives', *American Political Science Review*, **84**, June 1990, p.434.
38   Richard L. Hall and Frank W. Wayman, 'Buying Time: Moneyed Interests and the Mobilization of Bias in Congressional Committees', *American Political Science Review*, **84**, September 1990, p.803.
39   *National Journal*, 16 June 1990, p.1479.
40   Stern, *Still the Best*, p.49.
41   *Congressional Quarterly Weekly Report*, 8 May 1993, p.1121.
42   *Congressional Quarterly Weekly Report*, 5 February 1994, p.217.
43   *Washington Post*, 1 October 1994, pp.A1, A4.

9   Parties and Presidential Nominations

Dean McSweeney

Mass participation has been a feature of the selection of Presidential nominees for most of the twentieth century, but from 1972 onwards the influence of voters over the nominating process rose sharply. The result was a transformation in both the process and the products of the Presidential nominating system. The process used prior to 1972 is described at the beginning of the chapter. Next the forces propelling a reform of that system are documented. Then the features of the new nominating process are specified, along with the objections to it raised by numerous critics. The chapter ends with an evaluation of the reformed process. It is argued here that there have been two phases to the brief history of the nominating process from 1972. Many of the criticisms are more persuasive for the earlier phase (1972–80) than for the later contests (1984–92). Such discontinuity within the reformed process indicates the impact of historical contingencies as well as rules in shaping the way the nominating system operates.

A Party-dominated Process

In most democracies party leaders are selected by small numbers. For example, John Major was chosen as leader of the British Conservatives in 1990 by the party's 312 members of parliament. The United States is exceptional in the mass participation in the selection of party leaders, the parties' Presidential nominees. There were over 12 million participants in the process which gave George Bush the Republican Presidential nomination in 1992. Over 20 million people were involved in the Democrats' nomination of Bill Clinton the same year.

Mass participation has been a feature of the US Presidential nomination process since the inception of Presidential primaries in 1912. In that year twelve states used primaries generating a total turnout in Republican contests of over two million voters. But for 60 years Presidential primaries did not decide Presidential nominations. For most offices the primary replaced the party convention as the method by which candidates were selected. The Presidency remained an exception, for at this level primaries were grafted on to national conventions. Few convention delegates were chosen by primaries, for usually only a minority of states held them, the majority continuing to be selected by processes controlled by party organizations. Within these intra-party processes the parties' officials and public office-holders were the dominant influences, advantaging the candidates who were popular with them. Candidates whose support was largely external to the party organizations were unable to convert public popularity into the nomination, as exemplified by Theodore Roosevelt in 1912 and Estes Kefauver in 1952. But support within the party could immunize favoured candidates whose public popularity was unproven or demonstrably absent, as with Hubert Humphrey in 1968 and Barry Goldwater in 1964, respectively.

By the 1960s many delegates came to conventions with informal commitments to support a particular candidate for the nomination. Commitments emerged out of the bargaining between candidates and either delegates or the party elites who controlled blocs of delegates in some states. Few commitments were the product of the binding results of primaries. Nor were the commitments sufficiently secure or numerous to remove uncertainty about the outcome before the national convention met.[1] One indication of this uncertainty was the continuation into the 1960s of strategies designed by candidates and delegates for more than one ballot (an absolute majority of the delegate vote is required for nomination), suggesting that the protagonists did not see the result as a formality.[2]

The Conventional Wisdom and the Wisdom of the Convention

The mixed system of a minority of primaries, a majority of party-controlled processes and a decision by the national convention had gained widespread acceptance shortly after its inception. Neither party sought to overhaul their Presidential nominating processes. Particular states adopted or relinquished primaries, but after the 1920s there was no consistent trend in their favour. Congress intermittently considered but consistently rejected a national Presidential primary. The political science profession was almost uniformly supportive of the mixed system.[3] Praise centred on the dominance and judiciousness of parties and party leaders, and the benign effects of their controlling influence. Bargaining for support and flexibility in the exercise of choice, both seen as virtues, were facilitated by the paucity of binding primary results. Free to negotiate, leaders could resolve their differences, unifying the party in preparation for the election. By accommodating and reconciling diverse interests the nominating process was able to incorporate the heterogeneity of the United States within a two-party system. Preserving their duopoly, the two parties, of necessity of the catch-all type, fostered social consensus. Two such parties lubricated an institutionally fragmented constitutional system which would have been immobilized by a multi- or polarized party system.

When parties controlled the nomination process the choice of nominee was designed to promote their long-term interests. Survival required long-term electoral success. Irresponsible, temporarily electorally rewarding behaviour was deterred by party leaders' concern to retain public confidence into the future. Personalist politics and demagoguery, potentially productive for individual candidates, was subdued by the farther horizons of those within the party organizations. Whilst individual Presidents might escape retribution for their excesses, the party was less likely to escape eventual punishment. Statesmanship, moderation and constrained ambition followed from a process structured around parties. Electoral concerns also ensured the selection of appealing candidates. Even though direct popular influence within the process was modest, sensitivity to public opinion was required to nominate candidates who could win the election. Here the interests of party elites and the public converged.

The mixed nominating system ended when a near consensus in its favour existed amongst political scientists. In 1968, the Democratic nominating process was subject to such stresses that some reform was inevitable to prevent a repetition. But the magnitude of reform, bloated by some of the unanticipated reactions to it, inaugurated a qualitatively different nominating process from 1972 onwards. A plebiscitary, or voter-dominated, process emerged to replace the mixed system.

Reform

Under the mixed system voter participation had been constrained by the paucity of primaries, their neglect by some candidates and concentration upon a handful of the primary states by others, and the impermeability of or low public interest in the processes controlled by party organizations. Even where voter participation occurred it rarely resulted in national convention delegates mandated to support a particular candidate.

For over half a century the absence of direct voter influence over a nominating process dominated by elites was uncontroversial. But in 1968 the legitimacy of the process was widely questioned. For the first time since the inception of the mixed system an insurgent movement made an attempt in every state to select delegates backing their preferred candidates. Formerly, insurgent efforts had concentrated on the primaries, demonstrating popularity to make converts among election-conscious officials in the non-primary states. In 1968, the campaign of Senator Eugene McCarthy represented a cause: opposition to the war in Vietnam. The cause preceded the candidacy and McCarthy was the first willing, rather than first choice, candidate of those who sought to use the nominating process to advance their aim.[4] That cause possessed a nationwide constituency. The object of the McCarthy campaign was to mobilize that constituency into the delegate selection process to prevent, first, the renomination of President Johnson (who did withdraw in early 1968) and, subsequently, the nomination of his faithful Vice-President, Hubert Humphrey. But translating the anti-war constituency into delegates encountered numerous procedural impediments. In some states participation was confined to party officials. In others, broader participation was permitted, if not encouraged, but party officials controlled the proceedings. In 20 states rules of procedure were non-existent, meagre or unobtainable in written form, affording discretion to officials in conducting delegate selection meetings, disadvantaging the inexperienced McCarthy supporters. The candidate preferences of the delegates were often unpublicized at the time of selection. Where preferences were apparent at selection meetings, delegates were not allocated proportionately, resulting in McCarthy's under-representation or exclusion. Past service to the party was often a condition of selection as a delegate, excluding the McCarthy insurgents.

The alignment of party insiders with Humphrey, insurgents with McCarthy, produced two simultaneous, largely reinforcing conflicts. There was a conflict over the nomination between the supporters of the rival candidates which became overlain by a conflict about control of local and state party organizations. The party organization controlled delegate selection, therefore the party organizations had to be controlled to win a majority of delegates. Power within the party was at stake. The advantage of control over procedure exerted by Humphrey supporters fostered a sense of injustice in the McCarthy campaign. The sparseness of their share of delegates was attributed to the procedural advantage of the Humphrey forces rather than the merits of their candidate or the numbers they mobilized to attend meetings. Formerly arcane delegate selection procedures became controversial. Calls for procedural reform were carried to the national convention, which approved some remedies (abolishing the unit rule used in some states to bind the minority to vote for the candidate favoured by the majority) and authorized a committee to review delegate selection procedures.

The creation of a committee is often a way of deferring the resolution of a controversy and committees are rarely associated with radical innovation.

But the committee authorized by the 1968 convention proceeded to carry through what one author has termed a 'quiet revolution'.[5] Known after its successive chairmen as the McGovern–Fraser (officially the Commission on Delegate Selection and Party Structure), it so overhauled procedures that the mixed system came to an abrupt end. Defeat in the Presidential election, Humphrey winning 12 million votes less than Johnson in 1964, added to the pressure for change. The existing system appeared flawed on grounds of both procedures and results. Within the Commission the impetus for reform was strengthened by a membership selected with a bias towards innovation, augmented by an active and influential staff committed to transforming the process.[6]

Entitled *Mandate for Reform*, the Commission report sought to avoid a repetition of the controversies over delegate selection in 1968. Reforms aimed to ensure access to delegate selection meetings and the accurate translation of participants' preferences into the allocation of delegates. Specific reforms included the abolition of ex-officio delegates; requirements that selection meetings should receive advance publicity and be conducted according to written rules; fair representation of minority preferences was required; the selection of delegates before the beginning of the election year was prohibited; only 10 per cent of a state's delegates could be selected by a party committee; and representation amongst delegates of women, young people and minorities in numbers comparable to their presence in state populations was mandatory.[7]

The Commission focus was to reform the caucus process. Few of the reforms pertained to primaries, nor did the Commission advocate the adoption of primaries. A national Presidential primary was explicitly repudiated. The type of insurgent excluded or discounted in 1968 was singled out for inclusion and fair representation for the future. But an unintended consequence of the reforms was the spread of primaries, prompted by rules which either outlawed previous selection methods (party committees) or required complicated new procedures which primaries largely circumvented whilst fulfilling their aim of increasing access. By switching from a caucus or committee to a primary, states extended participation beyond the insurgent activist to any voter willing to go to the polls. The spread of primaries, though motivated by *Democratic* rules, permeated the Republican party. Required by law, a primary applied to both parties, intensifying the reformation of Republican as well as Democratic procedures. In 1972, two-thirds of Democratic and more than half of Republican delegates were selected in or bound by primaries.

McGovern–Fraser inaugurated a dynasty of Democratic rules commissions. The Mikulski, Winograd, Hunt and Fairness (the latter from its title) commissions followed in the line of succession. Several subsequent reforms were consistent with the aims of the original reform. For example, Democratic winner-take-all primaries were prohibited after 1972, allowing for the representation of minority preferences. Some reforms made a partial retreat from the McGovern–Fraser innovations. Affirmative action plans replaced what had been, in practice, quotas to encourage the representation of minorities and young people. Other reforms reversed McGovern–Fraser. From 1976, ex-officio delegates were restored, though they were required to vote in the same proportions for candidates as the elected delegates from their states. From 1984, unmandated ex-officio delegates returned in the form of superdelegates – Governors, Senators, Representatives, state party chairs and members of the party's governing national committee.

None of the successor commissions evinced an enthusiasm for primaries, yet states continued to adopt them. In 1980, 35 states held Democratic Presidential primaries which chose or mandated over 70 per cent of the delegates to that year's national convention. In 1992, two-thirds of the states held primaries, providing substantial majorities of the delegates to both parties' national conventions.

Restructuring of delegate selection during the 1970s coincided with the reform of the funding of elections. The 1971 Federal Election Campaign Act (FECA) required that campaigns disclose the source of every contribution over $100, and limits were placed on expenditure on media advertising in each state. Amendments to FECA in 1974 provided for the partial public funding of campaigns for the Presidential nominations. On raising $5000 in 20 states from individual donations of under $250 a campaign was entitled to matching funds from the federal government. Every subsequent individual contribution under $250 was matched by an equal amount of government funding. In campaigns for the nomination, as in all federal elections, donations from private sources were limited to $1000 from individuals and $5000 from groups (political action committees). Reforms of delegate selection and campaign finance inaugurated a shift from elite to mass politics. Prior to reform small numbers of wealthy individuals funded most campaigns and party elites decided nominations. Post-reform campaigns were funded by thousands of modest-size donations (and the federal government) and millions of voters decided the nominee.

Changes in rules propelled changes in candidates' strategies. Pre-reform campaigns were directed at party leaders. Many candidates shunned primaries. Other candidates entered a few primaries to prove their electability to the watching party leaders. Money-raising efforts relied on wealthy donors. After reform candidates entered many primaries because large numbers of delegates were mandated by their results. Money raising became a prolonged effort at tapping thousands of supporters for donations. Features of pre-reform campaigns, such as seeking support for the second ballot in case the first failed to produce an absolute majority, became anachronisms. Table 9.1 summarizes the principal differences between pre- and post-reform campaigns.

Table 9.1   Major changes in rules effected by reform

Pre-reform	*Post-reform*
Majority of delegates selected through non-primary process.	Majority of delegates selected in or bound by primaries.
In some states non-primary process confined to party officials.	Non-primary process open to voters.
Delegate selection process spread over several years.	Delegate selection process confined to the election year.[1]
Racial discrimination in selection; under-representation of women and the young.	Positive discrimination/affirmative action programmes to increase participation of racial minorities, women, the young etc.
Participants unable to express candidate preferences in many states.	Participants able to express candidate preferences.[1]
Winner-take-all primaries; unit rule in Democratic party.	Proportional representation in distribution of delegates.[2]
Rules often absent; party officials exercise discretion.	Rules provided.[1]
Campaigns financed from private sources.	Federal matching funds available.
No limits on size of donations.	Limits on size of donations.
No federal limits on expenditures.	Federal limits on expenditure for candidates accepting matching funds.

Notes

1   Not required by Republican party rules but generally accurate as a description of its selection process in practice.

2   Not required by Republican party rules and not observed in practice in many states.

Reformed or Deformed?

Political scientists, journalists and political elites have delivered overwhelmingly negative judgements on the post-reform nominating process. They have identified effects damaging to parties, party competition and the quality of government emanating from the selection system. Ambition and stamina, it is argued, have become prerequisites for the nomination, rather than Presidential calibre. Disproportionate influence is said to be exerted by the small states which start the sequence of delegate selection, by unrepresentative minorities among voters and by the mass media. Critics maintain that divisions within the parties are widened by the new process, undermining the preparations for the general election. The process is said to require political skills and supportive coalitions to win the nomination which are unrelated to those necessary for governing. An informed choice, it is suggested, cannot be made under the conditions of the contemporary nominating process.[8] We look at each of these arguments in greater detail below.

According to critics, reform removed the moderating effects of party upon those seeking the nomination.[9] Under the mixed system, party leaders, sensitive to their party's long-term interests, deterred demagoguery by candidates. Leaders bargained with candidates for support, enabling the former to impose conditions and require responsible behaviour. In the reformed process there are fewer constraints on candidate behaviour. Extremism and implausible promises may win votes, and voters cannot bargain with candidates to extract compromises from them. Nor are voters concerned for the reputation of the party in the future. They may be attracted by irresponsible appeals which, in the longer term, will undermine respect for the party when their damaging effects are revealed.

Post-reform campaigns require years of preparation to raise funds, build a nationwide organization and cultivate a mass constituency. Candidates have to mount unrelenting campaigns to win the nomination. Some have been deterred by the demands of competing for the Presidency rather than the demands of the office. Senator Walter Mondale ended his campaign for the nomination, saying he 'did not have the overwhelming desire to be President which is essential for the kind of campaign that is required'.[10] Mondale's announcement of withdrawal from the 1976 nominating contest was made in *November 1974*. (Ten years later, he had developed the 'overwhelming desire to be President', winning the Democratic nomination in 1984.)

For incumbent office-holders campaigns demand a prolonged neglect of official duties. Candidates travel the country, which means frequent absences from Washington or their state capitals. In contrast, candidates who have left office lack the competing demands on their time, allowing them to campaign full-time. Republican Senate Leader Howard Baker complained that only the politically unemployed had the time to be serious candidates for the Presidency.[11] Conscientious incumbents either forgo candidacy or run campaigns at a disadvantage. Neither is conducive to ensuring the election of the most able President from the talent available.

Opening the nominating process to wider participation had the paradoxical effect of decreasing its representativeness of the party rank-and-file.[12] Party leaders were not a demographic microcosm of the party's voters but their goal of winning elections compelled sensitivity to popular preferences. After reform the greater scope for participation in the nominating process was utilized unevenly across the electorate. Voters higher in the social structure participated at higher rates than those less advantaged on measures of income, education and occupational status. 'New class' white-collar professionals participated in high numbers. Within the Democratic party this shift in participation had political consequences, for the 'new class' professionals are more liberal than those lower in the class structure, heightening the possibility for the party to select a nominee unacceptable to many of its general election followers. McGovern's nomination followed by landslide election defeat in 1972 turned this possibility into reality.

'New class' activists also tend towards a distinctive political style. They exhibit a purism characterized by an uncompromising commitment to principle. Bargaining, compromising to increase support and shaping appeals to maximize votes are seen as disreputable. Committed to their own conceptions of political virtue, purists refuse to adjust their own preferences to increase the chances of winning elections. Purism compounds the impact of ideological unrepresentativeness to yield unelectable nominees.

Internal party divisions grew after reform.[13] Primaries multiplied, increasing the number of divisive contests. In candidate-centred campaigns intense loyalties develop, hindering the task of reconciling supporters of losing candidates to the nominee. Purism also intensifies conflicts, with preferences on candidates and issues being invested with righteousness. Opponents are viewed as immoral, unsupportable if they win. Particularly in multi-candidate contests there are incentives to seek the nomination by carving niches amongst the voters to construct an electoral base. Such strategies fragment the party into factions defined along lines of candidate preference, ideology and demographic constituencies. The coalitions necessary to win elections are destroyed by strategies which segment the party, impairing their performance in the general election.

Long though the nominating process is, outcomes are heavily influenced by the earliest stages of the delegate selection timetable. Caucuses in Iowa and the primary in New Hampshire inaugurate delegate selection each year and begin the winnowing which eventuates in a clear winner of the nomination in advance of the convention.[14] New Hampshire, in particular, has acquired a formative influence over the nomination. Between 1976 and 1988, the winner of the eight New Hampshire Presidential primaries (four per party) went on to win the nomination on seven occasions. Yet this formative influence over nominations coincides with an irrelevance in Presidential elections. Like other small states, New Hampshire is neglected in the election, where candidates concentrate on the large states with the most weight in the Electoral College. Nor is the state a microcosm of the United States. Compared to the nation as a whole, its population is disproportionately white, its taxes are untypically low and it is one of the few states where registered Republican voters outnumber Democrats.

New Hampshire derives its prominence from the devotion of candidates and the mass media. Most candidates compete in the state. Relative to the number of delegates at stake, they spend lavish amounts of time and money there. The small electorate enables candidates to meet large numbers of voters through personal campaigning. Traditional, inexpensive campaign techniques such as canvassing remain effective means for reaching voters. These characteristics facilitate successes in the primary of candidates unknown to a national audience, lacking the finances of rivals who are recognized across the country. Candidates such as Jimmy Carter and Gary Hart, the former unknown to much of the Washington political elite, rose from obscurity to become contenders for the nomination aided by victory in New Hampshire.

Media coverage exaggerates the impact of the New Hampshire primary. In 1984, the state in which 0.4 per cent of the US population live attracted 19.2 per cent of all the network television news stories devoted to the nominating contests.[15] Candidates deemed by the press to have performed successfully receive extensive and favourable coverage, projecting them to a national audience which lacks knowledge of many of the competitors on which to base a choice when the sequence of primaries and caucuses reaches their state. Favourable publicity begins to generate larger voter appeal, financial support, campaign personnel and the aura of a potential nominee—assets collectively referred to as 'momentum'.[16] Candidates deemed to be unsuccessful withdraw or are neglected by the media, deprived of the currency of momentum that can be converted into further success in later contests. Thus voters in later states have a shrunken range of alternatives to choose from, and their remaining choices compete in a handicap race where the first primary stacked the odds in favour of some candidates.

Media coverage has also been faulted for its interpretation of results and inattention to the candidates' records and programmes.[17] On occasions the media has designated a front runner for the nomination who competes not only against the other candidates but also against the expectations of the press. A front runner who comes first in a primary or caucus may be judged to have failed if their share of the vote is lower than the press anticipated. When front runner Muskie won the 1972 New Hampshire Democratic primary by an 11 per cent margin, but with under half the vote, the media interpreted his performance as a setback.[18] Voters' learning about candidates was thus framed by press judgements of strength and weakness rather than objective standards of defeat or victory.

'Horserace'-style journalism predominates in press coverage. News stories are preoccupied with the candidates' prospects of winning the race for the nomination. Indicators of strength such as opinion polls, funds raised, efficiency of the campaign organization and primary and caucus results feature in the reporting of the contest, and candidates' prospects for nomination are regularly redefined in the light of new evidence. 'Horserace' journalism overwhelms attention to substance. Voters learn more about how candidates are doing than what they stand for, which deprives them of the information with which to test their suitability for the Presidency. Such a style of reporting increases voter susceptibility to the effects of momentum. Voters learn disproportionately about candidates deemed successful in previous contests and what they learn is disproportionately favourable because successful candidates receive positive treatment. Paucity of information about policy stances or candidates' records propels voters into a reliance on 'horserace' indicators of the contestants' virtues.[19]

Whilst press influence in evaluating candidates rose after reform, that of party elites fell. Neither the process of delegate selection nor voter judgements about candidates were shaped by party elites. The consequence was removal of influence over the nomination of those with first-hand knowledge of candidates, familiar with their skills and knowledge of government. Dealing with elites is an indispensable part of the Presidency but they ceased to have an impact in deciding who the President would be. Their removal from influence also depleted the value attached to winning the election when choosing a nominee. Elites want election success for the entire party ticket, which can be assisted by the coat-tail effects of a popular Presidential candidate. In post-reform nominations the participants are not sensitive to the party's election prospects. Voters support the candidate who most appeals to their preferences, a choice heavily conditioned by the 'horserace' presentation of the race by the press. The purists who populate conventions support candidates out of principle. In neither case are choices mediated by electoral considerations, which can result in the nomination of a candidate such as McGovern, unacceptable to many of his party's voters in the general election.[20]

Reform disjoined the requirement of governing from that of winning the nomination. To win pre-reform nominations, candidates had to construct a coalition of party elites, bargaining with Governors, members of Congress and party officials. At the convention concessions were made to losing contestants to unify the party for the election. A new President entered office supported by party elites who proceeded to constitute a governing coalition, staffing the executive branch and providing support in Congress. To win post-reform nominations, candidates had to mobilize factions of voters. Forging a governing coalition became a separate task. The governing coalition no longer accompanies the President into office. It has to be created after the new President takes over. Moreover the greater likelihood of the nomination being won by an outsider increases the prospects for the Presidency to be won by a novice unaware of the need for or ill-equipped to create the elite coalition necessary for governing. Carter exemplified the naïve belief that only support amongst the people was necessary to convert promises into policy.[21]

Reform After Twenty Years

Much of the highly critical conventional wisdom about the impact of reform was informed by the evidence from the early post-reform nominations. These contests provided plentiful evidence of the deficiencies of the new process. McGovern alienated many of his own party's supporters. Carter was propelled from obscurity to the Presidency despite his naïvety about the way the office worked. Presidents Ford and Carter engaged in prolonged struggles to retain the Presidency against challenges from within their own parties. Falls in election turnout and party identification, increases in split-ticket voting and the desertions by party identifiers from their own party's ticket – dealignment – registered the detachment of voters from the new participatory parties.[22]

Yet by the 1990s the conventional wisdom looked considerably less wise if no less conventional. Its validity was undermined, modestly, by some new research findings and, more substantially, by the evidence supplied by later contests for the nomination. The new research suggests that some of the shortcomings identified in the new process were either erroneous or exaggerated. More recent contests suggest that the process can work in a variety of ways. The new structures are not so powerful as to determine a single campaign dynamic or outcome. These later contests indicate that the earliest nominations did not exhaust the possibilities under the reformed rules. Whilst deficiencies were exposed as possible by the earliest contests, subsequent experience suggests they were not inevitable. The variations in the operation of the reformed process, evident after six post-reform nominations for each party, suggest that the rules interact with particular historical circumstances. When circumstances alter, the rules can yield different dynamics and outcomes.

New research refuted or qualified claims of the unrepresentativeness of primary voters, the divisiveness of contests and the insensitivity of participants to electoral considerations. Primary electorates have been shown to resemble the voters who support the respective parties in Presidential elections. Earlier studies compared primary voters with primary non-voters, party identifiers or all general election voters irrespective of the party they supported.[23] These studies neglected the potential general election constituency to which nominees have to appeal to win the election. Rather these early studies compared primary voters with those who do not even vote, vote for the other party or who identify with the party (missing those independents who vote for the party without identifying with it). Later studies sought more accurate measures of each party's general election constituency – the voters who have to be mobilized if the election is to be won. By this standard the party's constituency consists of both its identifiers and voters who support the party but do not identify with it. Compared with the general election constituency, primary voters, contrary to the conclusions of previous studies, are politically more moderate.[24] Where primary electorates are compared with that section of the party's general election constituency which does not vote in Presidential primaries, no issue or ideological differences distinguish the two groups.[25]

New research showed that contests were less divisive for the parties than originally argued because most supporters of losing candidates retained their party loyalty in the general election. In shifting from the choice of which candidate should represent the party to which party should control the Presidency, party loyalty usually prevails. During the election campaign supporters of losing candidates develop a more positive view of their party's nominee. Where a more positive view of the nominee failed to develop, as amongst Kennedy supporters' evaluations of Carter, the deficiencies of the President rather than antagonisms generated by the nominating contest appear to explain their inertia. A negative view of the Carter Presidency was the origin of Kennedy's campaign for the nomination, not its consequence.[26]

Despite the failure of their preferred candidate to become the nominee, campaign activists remain active in the general election. Having been mobilized into campaign activity by the nominating contest, they switch their activism to the nominee for the Presidential campaign. Losing the nomination does have an effect. Supporters of losing candidates are less active in the Presidential campaign than the nominee's original supporters but they do not lapse into inertia. This evidence suggests that allegiance to the party outweighs loyalty to a particular candidate.[27]

Electability has been found to weigh heavily in determining preferences amongst post-reform convention delegates. The widespread incidence of purist attitudes discovered by earlier researchers led to the conclusion that the pre-reform preoccupation of finding an election winner had been relegated in importance. Such conclusions were extracted from responses to abstract questions about the relative importance of various criteria in choosing a Presidential candidate. But when later researchers probed for candidate choices in practice, rather than selection criteria in the abstract, they found that electability outweighed ideology. Many delegates closer to Kennedy on issues in 1980 supported Carter, whom they thought more likely to win. Similarly many Republican delegates opted for Reagan, whom they thought more likely to win, than for Bush, to whom they were closer on issues. Re-examination of the 1972 Democratic national convention, a peak in purist attitudes, found a similar electoral pragmatism at work. Delegates who considered a candidate more electable than the one to whom they were closest ideologically usually resolved the conflict in favour of the former.[28]

The evidence provided by the later nominating contests, particularly beginning in 1984, demonstrated that the features of earlier years were not inevitable. The mixed system had exhibited diversity too. It had produced an outstanding President in Franklin Roosevelt as well as the inadequate Warren Harding. It had yielded united parties on occasions and divided parties on others. Rules induce tendencies rather than determine a particular type of campaign or outcome. Organization, strategy, preferences and political moods operate within and upon rules to produce decisions.

The first two post-reform nominations, on which so many of the conclusions about the effects of the new rules were based, were shaped by the formative influences of the Vietnam War and Watergate. These historical contingencies interacted with the reformed procedures to produce nominating contests and outcomes distinctively different from not only the pre-reform era but also the later post-reform nominations. Opposition to continued involvement in Vietnam enabled McGovern to capture the allegiance of the anti-war movement which provided the candidate with both a constituency and nationwide organization. McCarthy's campaign in 1968 had demonstrated the emotional intensity and activism that anti-war opinion generated. Having harnessed that devotion, McGovern showed that the reformed process was sufficiently permeable for an organization outside the party structure to capture the nomination. But the conditions that facilitated his nomination have not recurred. No subsequent issue has energized and unified liberal activists on the scale that the war did. No liberal candidate has reproduced McGovern's success in injecting an existing issue constituency into active support for a candidate for the Presidency. The inimitability of McGovern's success indicates that the reformed procedures were a necessary but not sufficient condition of his victory.

McGovern's campaign also benefited from a more acute understanding of the implications of the new rules than his competitors. Several members of the campaign had served as staff of the reform commission which McGovern chaired. The appreciation of the need for grassroots support compared favourably with the campaign of the front runner Muskie which engaged in the anachronistic pursuit of endorsements from the party elites. Campaigns after 1972 learned the lessons taught by McGovern's appreciation of the relocation of power over the nominating process. Differences between campaigns in understanding the impact of rules lessened in subsequent nominations, diminishing its influence on the outcome.

Watergate conditioned the 1976 nominating process of both parties. Nixon's resignation had elevated Gerald Ford to the Presidency but his lack of an electoral base or a constituency amongst Republican activists exposed him to a challenge from within his own party. While the reformed process did facilitate a contested nomination, Ford's unique route to the Presidency, propelled by Watergate, contributes to an explanation of his vulnerability when the contest occurred. By deepening the disreputability of Washington, the Watergate scandal also enhanced the appeal of political outsiders untarnished by experience in the federal government. Jimmy Carter, Ronald Reagan and Jerry Brown, advertising their distance from the political establishment, found a particularly receptive audience in 1976. Carter's election and subsequent shortcomings as President ensured that reverberations from Watergate would extend into 1980 when he sought renomination.

The scope for a variety of outcomes within the reformed rules was demonstrated by the nominating contests of 1972 and 1976. Different from pre-reform nominations, they were different from each other. Issue appeals to the liberal or 'New Left' wing of the Democratic party mobilized a winning faction for McGovern, whilst the opponent whose campaign used the slogan 'Trust Muskie' quickly withdrew after a series of setbacks. Yet four years later Carter based his successful campaign on his personal probity (promising never to tell a lie), defeating several would-be McGoverns who sought to mobilize a liberal constituency with appeals on issues. Nixon's cruise to renomination in 1972 was followed by Ford narrowly avoiding becoming the first President of the twentieth century to be denied nomination by his party.

Variety in the dynamics and outcomes evident in the 1970s proliferated in subsequent years. The victories for insurgents and Washington outsiders was not repeated after the 1980 election. The pre-convention preference of the Democratic superdelegates has been nominated each year since their inception. But the support of superdelegates was not essential to their nominations. Rather it demonstrates that under the appropriate political conditions primary and caucus voters concur with party elites on their preference for the nomination.

In part, the success of insiders in later contests derived from a greater sensitivity to the requirements of the reformed process than their predecessors in the 1970s. Centrist Democrats like Mondale and Dukakis established grassroots organizations. They also recognized the indispensability of the earliest contests and the need to compete in every primary. The political context was also more conducive to insiders. There was no great issue like Vietnam to mobilize liberal activists. Conservative activists, in contrast, had assisted Reagan in winning the Presidency in 1980. Reagan's pursuit of conservative economic and foreign policy aims occupied the political space of the activists, pre-empting opposition to his renomination in 1984. Prosperity and peace solidified Reagan's hold on the Presidency, and advantaged his heir-apparent, George Bush, in 1988.

Campaigns continued to be front-loaded but in the last three contests their results have failed to prefigure the eventual nominee. Both Mondale and Clinton were nominated despite losing New Hampshire. Clinton, Dukakis and Bush (in 1988) were nominated despite losing in the Iowa caucuses. Candidates could offset defeats in these early states if they had regional concentrations of support which delivered victories in states voting in the second phase of the contest. Mondale recovered from a defeat in New Hampshire when the industrial states of the Northeast and Midwest began to vote, whereas both Bush and Clinton were revived by sweeping the cluster of Southern states which voted on the same day, 'Super Tuesday'. Recovery was facilitated by possession of the necessary financial and organizational resources. Their opponents had produced victories in early states by gambling much of their resources in the hope that success would breed success. Whilst retail campaigning could yield success in the early states, with the escalation in the number and size of states in the second phase resources have to be dispersed and media advertising relied upon. Candidates with a 50-state organization and plentiful funds gain the opportunity to recover against opponents who invested heavily from their limited resources in the early contests. Gephardt (who won in Iowa in 1988) and the 1992 New Hampshire winner Paul Tsongas lacked the resources to capitalize on their initial successes.

Cautious media interpretations restrained the impact of some of these early results. Where contests were won by candidates in their home or neighbouring states the result was often predictable and therefore less newsworthy than a surprise win for a candidate playing away from home. Gephardt invested heavily to win in his neighbouring state of Iowa in 1988. His victory was no more than expected and its impact was muted by the media focus on the more newsworthy Republican contest. Despite a modest third place for Dukakis, the Boston press continued to report his campaign favourably, transmitting a positive view of the candidate to the voters in adjacent New Hampshire. On the Republican side, Bush's third place finish in Iowa was interpreted as a possible derailing of the favourite for the nomination. But a Bush counter-attack of negative advertising inflicted a defeat on Dole in New Hampshire, halting the momentum which might otherwise have translated into a surprise nomination.[29] A similarly muted response greeted the Iowa contest in 1992. Harkin's win in his own state was conceded to him by his opponents, who did not mount major campaigns, nullifying its impact. Winning New Hampshire made Tsongas front page news but the press did not judge it the precursor of later success because there were doubts whether his appeal would extend beyond his base in New England.

The centrists and insiders who won the nominations in 1984–92 resembled less their post-reform predecessors, more the nominees of the mixed system. In 1968, the Democrats had nominated a 'New Dealer', former Senator for Minnesota, the favourite of organized labour and the incumbent Vice-President (Hubert Humphrey). Walter Mondale in 1984 was a former Vice-President but otherwise shared the same credentials as Humphrey. In 1988, as in 1960, the Democrats nominated a non-WASP from Massachusetts. Both Dukakis and Kennedy also sought to balance the ticket by choosing the senior Senator from Texas as their Vice-Presidential running mates. There were similarities between those two years on the Republican side. In both years the faithful Vice-President of a President ineligible for re-election was nominated (George Bush and Richard Nixon, respectively). The 1984 process demonstrated that a popular President could be nominated unopposed under the reformed rules, repeating what Eisenhower had accomplished under the mixed system in 1956. Even an unpopular President could escape major opposition under the reformed rules, as the 1992 Republican nomination exemplified. Bush, like Truman in 1948, won the nomination despite widespread disapproval within his own party.

The contribution of the reformed process to deficiencies in Presidential calibre also seems weaker after Carter. Rather than being the model for a new style of Presidency, Carter proved exceptional. None of his successors reproduced his inattentiveness and maladroitness in dealing with their own party's elites. Reagan cultivated such an effective relationship with Congressional Republicans that near-unanimity was obtained when key features of the President's economic programme came to a vote in 1981. Such persuasiveness in the first year of a new administration demonstrated that the reformed process could yield Presidents who were sensitive to the need to build support amongst Washington insiders and adept at doing so. Reagan's legislative triumphs were obtained although Congressional Republicans were irrelevant to his winning the nomination and despite his lack of prior service in Washington.

Like so many of his predecessors, Reagan did not sustain the same scale of legislative successes throughout his Presidency. External conditions became less hospitable to Presidential success as the sense of an electoral mandate faded, the number of Republicans in Congress diminished and the Democrats recovered from the shock of the 1980 election setback to unite against the President's programme. Reagan contributed to his own setbacks by an inflexible commitment to his conservative objectives, an escalating budget deficit and exposure of deficiencies of control and honesty in the Iran Contra affair. Despite the numerous blemishes on the Reagan Presidency, academic commentary remains respectful. According to Richard Neustadt, Reagan left behind 'a temporary glow of seeming mastery'.[30] Louis Fisher also confirmed that Reagan demonstrated that Presidential effectiveness remained possible, showing that 'a person with a good mandate, good speaking skills and a targeted agenda can make the system work'.[31]

Clinton's first year resembled Reagan's in testifying to the speed with which a Washington outsider could establish a rapport with Congress. On almost all of his major initiatives Clinton won majorities in Congress, contributing to a success on votes that since 1952 has only been exceeded by Presidents Eisenhower and Johnson in the year following their elections. Intrinsic to many of Clinton's majorities was an exceptional solidarity amongst Democrats which helped to make 1993 the peak of party unity voting in Congress in 40 years.

Amongst Carter's successors, Bush was the least effective with Congress. Yet he came to the Presidency with a more varied Washington experience than Presidents chosen under the mixed system. He had served as Vice-President, member of Congress, director of the CIA and was the first former national party chairman to become President. Yet Bush never established even a temporary leadership over Congress. His domestic ambitions were modest and some of his greatest successes in dealing with Congress were in having his vetoes sustained, restraining the Democratic majority.

Carter, Reagan and Clinton came to the Presidency with a similar lack of Washington experience. Yet Carter exhibited a naïvety not reproduced by his successors. All three won the Presidency campaigning against Washington but only Carter tried to transform the nation's politics without help from the inside. None of them required the support of party elites to win the nomination but only Carter tried to dispense with their support in governing. To the contrary, Reagan and Clinton devoted themselves to solidifying their parties around them. Their success in doing so demonstrated that party elites do not have to control the selection process to be receptive to Presidential leadership. The variations in performance of the post-reform Presidents indicate that many forces shape the style, skill and conception of the Presidential office. The selection process is but one.

Conclusion

More than 20 years after reform began, the critical conventional wisdom about the new process appears less wise, if no less conventional or critical. There have been no repeats of the McGovern, Carter or Ford nominations. Much the same process that yielded those outcomes subsequently produced a string of nominees who were favoured by party insiders and resembled their predecessors of the pre-reform period.

Where the reformed process differed from the old one was in its accessibility to political movements with a strength in the country that was not reproduced within the party organizations. The reformed process allowed those movements to find expression within the nominating contests of the two parties. Not only has there been no recurrence of the McGovern and Carter nominations, there has been no repetition of the turmoil of the Democrats' last pre-reform convention in 1968. The anti-war movement found expression and representation through McGovern's campaign, the Christian Right via Pat Robertson and post-civil rights era blacks through the two campaigns of Jesse Jackson.

Flawed and unloved though it is, the nominating process is unlikely to be overhauled in the near future. A reversal of the participatory process would be a formidable manoeuvre to execute in a country where openness is a political virtue and elites and backroom deals are vices. As a beneficiary of the reformed process, President Clinton is unlikely to endorse its transformation. Super Tuesday, an innovation Clinton backed whilst Governor of Arkansas, yielded the desired result in 1992, demonstrating that the demands of participation, political moderation and sensitivity to Southern preferences could be reconciled within the post-reform rules. Clinton's journey from obscurity to the Presidency is also likely to fuel the ambitions of a new generation of imitators, enhancing the appeal of the reformed rules to the aspiring Presidents amongst political elites, a further obstacle to a return to a party-dominated process. Political scientists have not learned to love the reformed process but they must learn to live with it for the foreseeable future.

Notes

1 Nelson W. Polsby and Aaron B. Wildavsky, 'Uncertainty and Decision-Making at the National Conventions', in Nelson W. Polsby, Robert A. Dentler and Paul A. Smith (eds), *Politics and Social Life*, Houghton Mifflin, 1963, pp.370–89.

2 For the 1968 Republican convention, see Lewis Chester, Godfrey Hodgson and Bruce Page, *An American Melodrama: The Presidential Campaign of 1968*, Viking, 1969, pp.454–75.

3   Hugh A. Bone, *American Politics and the Party System*, 3rd edn, McGraw-Hill, 1965; V.O. Key, Jr., *Politics, Parties and Pressure Groups*, 5th edn, Crowell, 1964; Austin Ranney and Willmore Kendall, *Democracy and the American Party System*, Harcourt, Brace, 1956; Nelson W. Polsby and Aaron B. Wildavsky, *Presidential Elections: Strategies of American Electoral Politics*, Scribner's, 1964; Aaron B. Wildavsky, 'On the Superiority of National Conventions', *Review of Politics*, **24**, 1962, pp.307–19; for an exception, see the Report of the Committee on Political Parties, 'Towards A More Responsible Two-Party System', *American Political Science Review*, **44**, 1950, supplement.

4   Chester *et al., An American Melodrama*, pp.51–66.

5   Byron E. Shafer, *Quiet Revolution: The Struggle for the Democratic Party and the Shaping of Post-Reform Politics*, Sage, 1983.

6   See ibid.

7   Commission on Delegate Selection and Party Structure, *Mandate for Reform*, Democratic National Committee, 1970.

8   Compendiums of the deficiencies of the new process include Nelson W. Polsby, *Consequences of Party Reform*, Oxford University Press, 1983; Jeane J. Kirkpatrick, *Dismantling the Parties: Reflections on Party Reform and Party Decomposition*, American Enterprise Institute, 1978; James W. Ceaser, *Reforming the Reforms; A Critical Analysis of the Presidential Selection Process*, Ballinger, 1982; George Grassmuck (ed.), *Before Nomination: Our Primary Problem*, American Enterprise Institute, 1985; Jeane J. Kirkpatrick *et al., The Presidential Nominating Process: Can It Be Improved?*, American Enterprise Institute, 1980.

9   James W. Ceaser, *Presidential Selection; Theory and Development*, Princeton University Press, 1979.

10 Quoted in Jules Witcover, *Marathon: The Pursuit of the Presidency, 1972–1976*, Viking, 1977, p.126.

11 Howard Baker, quoted in *Newsweek*, 16 June 1980, p.24.

12 Jeane J. Kirkpatrick, *The New Presidential Elite*, Russell Sage Foundation and Twentieth Century Fund, 1976; Jeane J. Kirkpatrick, 'Representation in American National Conventions: The Case of 1972', *British Journal of Political Science*, 5 July 1975; James I. Lengle, *Representation and Presidential Primaries: The Democratic Party in the Post-Reform Era*, Greenwood Press, 1981; Austin Ranney, *The Federalization of Presidential Primaries*, American Enterprise Institute, 1978.

13 Lengle, *Representation*.

14 William G. Mayer, 'The New Hampshire Primary: A Historical Overview' in Gary R. Orren and Nelson W. Polsby (eds), *Media and Momentum: The New Hampshire Primary and Nomination Politics*, Chatham House, 1987, pp.9–41; Larry M. Bartels, 'After Iowa: Momentum in Presidential Primaries'; Nelson W. Polsby, 'The Iowa Caucuses in a Front-Loaded System: A Few Historical Lessons', in Peverill Squire (ed.), *The Iowa Caucuses and the Presidential Nominating Process*, Westview Press, 1989, pp.121–48, 149–62.

15 William C. Adams, 'As New Hampshire Goes ...', in Orren and Polsby, *Media and Momentum*, p.45.

16 Larry M. Bartels, *Presidential Primaries and the Dynamics of Public Choice*, Princeton University Press, 1988; John H. Aldrich, *Before the Convention: Strategies and Choices in Presidential Nomination Campaigns*, University of Chicago Press, 1980; Thomas R. Marshall, *Presidential Nominations in A Reform Age*, Praeger, 1981.

17 Thomas E. Patterson, *The Mass Media Election: How Americans Choose Their President*, Praeger, 1980; Marshall, *Presidential Nominations*.

18 Theodore H. White, *The Making of the President, 1972*, Jonathan Cape, 1973, p.83.

19 Scott Keeter and Cliff Zukin, *Uninformed Choice: The Failure of the New Presidential Nominating System*, Praeger, 1983; Patterson, *The Mass Media Election*.

20 Kirkpatrick, 'Representation in American National Conventions: The Case of 1972'.

21 Eric L. Davis, 'Legislative Liaison in the Carter Administration', *Political Science Quarterly*, **94**, 1979, pp.287–302; Charles O. Jones, *The Trusteeship Presidency: Jimmy Carter and the United States Congress*, Louisiana State University Press, 1988.

22 Martin Wattenberg, *The Decline of American Political Parties, 1952–1988*, Harvard University Press, 1990.

23 See note 12.

24 John G. Geer, 'Assessing the Representativeness of Electorates in Presidential Primaries', *American Journal of Political Science*, **32**, 1988, pp.929–45.

25 Barbara Norrander, 'Ideological Representativeness of Presidential Primary Voters', *American Journal of Political Science*, **33**, 1989, pp.570–87.

26 Lorna Rae Atkeson, 'Moving Toward Unity: Attitudes in Nomination and Presidential Election Stages of a Presidential Campaign', *American Politics Quarterly*, **21**, 1993, pp.272–89.

27 Walter J. Stone, Lorna Rae Atkeson and Ronald B. Rapoport, 'Turning On or Turning Off? Mobilization and Demobilization Effects on Participation in Presidential Nomination Campaigns', *American Journal of Political Science*, **36**, 1992, pp.665–91.

28 Walter J. Stone and Alan I. Abramowitz, 'Winning May Not Be Everything But It's More than We Thought: Presidential Party Activists in 1980', *American Political Science Review*, **77**, 1983, pp.945–56; idem., *Nominations Politics*, Praeger, 1984.

29 Christine F. Ridout, 'The Role of Media Coverage of Iowa and New Hampshire in the 1988 Democratic Nomination', *American Politics Quarterly*, **19**, 1991, pp.43–58; Bruce E. Cain, I.A. Lewis and Douglas Rivers, 'Strategy and Choice in the 1988 Presidential Primaries', *Electoral Studies*, **8**, 1989, pp.23–48; Bartels, 'After Iowa', pp.141–5, and Henry E. Brady, 'Is Iowa News?', in Squire, *The Iowa Caucuses*, pp.116–18.

30 Richard E. Neustadt, *Presidential Power and the Modern Presidents: the Politics of Leadership from Roosevelt to Reagan*, Macmillan, 1990, p.x.

31 Quoted in *Congressional Quarterly Weekly Report*, 7 January 1989, p.10.

10 The 1992 Presidential Election*

Alan Grant

On 3 November 1992, at the end of another gruelling marathon of an electoral campaign, American voters chose Bill Clinton, the poor boy made good from Hope, Arkansas and Governor of the state that ranked 49th out of 50 in most league tables, as their next President. Clinton, the first of the 'baby-boomer' generation to make it to the White House, took 32 states and the District of Columbia to give him a total of 370 Electoral College votes, a hundred more than he needed to secure an overall majority. President George Bush was well beaten and picked up only 168 votes, mostly from sparsely populated states with small numbers in the Electoral College. Independent candidate and billionaire Ross Perot failed to win any state but obtained 19 per cent of the popular vote, the highest for any independent or third party candidate since 1912. He drew sufficient support to reduce Clinton's tally to 43 per cent, 5 per cent ahead of the incumbent President, but actually 3 per cent less than the Democratic candidate Michael Dukakis achieved in 1988. After defeat in five of the last six Presidential elections, and with talk of the Republicans having an electoral 'lock' on the Presidency, Clinton's victory was sweet music to Democratic ears and ensured that they controlled both ends of Pennsylvania Avenue for the first time in 12 years; with it went the chance at least to end the political stalemate between President and Congress which had been so evident throughout most of George Bush's term of office.

The Nomination Process

It had not always seemed likely that George Bush would become the first elected Republican President since Herbert Hoover in 1932 to be denied a

*This chapter is based on an article by the author that originally appeared in *Parliamentary Affairs*, **46**, (2), April 1993 and is reprinted here by permission of Oxford University Press.

second term. In March 1991, after victory in the Gulf War, Bush enjoyed the highest approval rating (89 per cent) of any President since polling began and he continued to bask in the glory of the Desert Storm campaign well into the late summer, despite a majority of the public disapproving of his handling of the economy. The apparent look of invincibility deterred many of the potential Democratic candidates, such as Governor Mario Cuomo, Senator Bill Bradley and Rep. Richard Gephardt, from declaring their interest in their party's nomination. Only the relatively unknown Paul Tsongas, who had recovered from the cancer that had led him to retire from the US Senate, was brave enough to enter the fray in April 1991 at the height of Bush's popularity. It was only in the autumn of 1991, when hopes of recovery from the recession that had become apparent a year before began to fade, that Bush's ratings declined noticeably and other Democratic contenders, including Bill Clinton, entered the race. Clinton was fortunate in that the big names still not did not wish to fight (Cuomo typically hesitating for months before finally deciding not to enter in December) and the field really comprised the Democratic party's second division. Governor Douglas Wilder of Virginia withdrew even before the primaries started, while Senator Bob Kerrey of Nebraska and Senator Tom Harkin of Iowa left the race in early March 1992 after disappointing showings in the opening contests. Table 10.1 shows the full list of Democratic and Republican party candidates in the 1992 Presidential primaries. Tsongas, who won the first primary in New Hampshire, next door to his native Massachusetts, and a number of other states mostly in the North East, bowed out after 'Super Tuesday' on 10 March, having run out of money and energy. Tsongas had gained a great deal of favourable comment and respect for running an intelligent campaign based on issues which appealed to professional middle-class Democrats. He was the antithesis of what is expected of the modern American Presidential candidate – uncharismatic and not at all telegenic – but his honesty and integrity shone through to the electors.

Although anointed the Democratic front runner by the media early on, Bill Clinton did not emerge decisively from the pack until Super Tuesday, when he swept to victory in the Southern states as well as winning in important Mid-western states which enabled him to demonstrate that he could win votes outside the South.[1] Super Tuesday had been initiated in 1988 by Southern Democrats who had hoped that, by establishing a regional contest on the same day, candidates would be obliged to take more notice of their interests and that their influence would be strengthened in relation to the Northern liberal states. In that year Jesse Jackson's appeal to black voters prevented the emergence of a Southern moderate candidate, although Al Gore did win five Southern border states. In 1992, however, Bill Clinton's victories throughout the South gave him such a boost in delegate support

Table 10.1 Presidential candidates and Presidential primaries, 1992

	Primaries on ballot	Total vote	Percentage	Best showing	
DEMOCRATS					
Bill Clinton (Ark.)	39	10 471 965	51.89	Puerto Rico	(95.6%)
Jerry Brown (Calif.)	39	4 023 373	19.94	Calif.	(40.2%)
Paul E. Tsongas (Mass.)	35	3 644 543	18.06	Mass.	(66.3%)
'Uncommitted'	25	779 895	3.86	Idaho	(29.1%)
Bob Kerrey (Neb.)	30	317 939	1.58	S.Dak.	(40.2%)
Tom Harkin (Iowa)	30	280 324	1.39	S.Dak.	(25.2%)
Lyndon H. LaRouche Jr. (Va.)	31	154 015	0.76	N.Dak.	(22.4%)
Eugene J. McCarthy (Va.)	12	106 376	0.53	La.	(3.9%)
Charles Woods (Nev.)	15	89 037	0.44	N.Dak.	(21.1%)
Larry Agran (Calif.)	18	57 672	0.29	Idaho	(1.6%)
Ross Perot (Texas)	0	41 512	0.21	N.Dak.	(28.4%)
Ralph Nader (DC)	1	35 963	0.18	Mass.	(4.1%)
Louis Stokes (Ohio)	1	29 515	0.15	Ohio	(2.9%)
Others, scattered write-ins	–	147 844	0.73		
REPUBLICANS					
George Bush (Texas)	39	9 512 142	73.03	Puerto Rico	(99.2%)
Patrick J. Buchanan (Va.)	36	2 912 156	22.36	NH	(37.4%)
'Uncommitted'	18	290 118	2.23	S.Dak.	(30.7%)
David Duke (La.)	16	119 942	0.92	Missi.	(10.6%)
Ross Perot (Texas)	0	56 136	0.43	Wash.	(19.6%)
Others, scattered write-ins	–	135 330	1.04		

Source: *Congressional Quarterly Weekly Report*, 4 July 1992, p.71, and 8 August 1992, p.67.

217

that he appeared unstoppable after what Ryan J. Barilleaux and Randall E. Adkins call the 'breakaway' stage of the nominations process.[2]

The only other candidate remaining in the race against Clinton was the eccentric former Governor of California, Jerry Brown, who, in the absence of Jesse Jackson, sought to appeal to the party's radical wing and those disillusioned with orthodox party politics. Brown refused to accept large donations and interest group money for his campaign and appealed instead for small contributions from supporters, using a toll-free telephone number that he publicized at every opportunity. Brown won the Colorado and Connecticut primaries and, despite defeats by Clinton in New York and Pennsylvania after all the other candidates had withdrawn, continued to fight his lone crusade right up to the convention in July, benefiting to some extent from the 'Anyone But Clinton' vote in the 'mop-up' stage of the process.

Bill Clinton's campaign had been dogged by allegations about his private life and avoidance of the draft for the Vietnam War during his student days. In the run-up to the opening New Hampshire primary, Gennifer Flowers claimed in a tabloid newspaper that she had had a 12-year affair with Governor Clinton. This was denied by Clinton but it forced him to go on to the television programme, 'Sixty Minutes', with his wife Hillary, to discuss their marriage and confirm that whatever problems they may have had in the past were now behind them. The allegations did not torpedo Clinton's campaign, as similar charges about Senator Gary Hart had done in 1988, when he was the Democratic front runner. Clinton's responses to the draft question were inconsistent enough to keep the issue running throughout the year, but he managed to survive the New Hampshire primary, coming second to Tsongas with 26 per cent of the vote. The fact that both of these problems were exposed early in the primary season appears in retrospect to have actually benefited Clinton in that their impact was reduced when the Republicans tried to revive them in relation to the 'character' issue later in the year; Clinton was also able to demonstrate his resilience by recovering from this early crisis.

Clinton described himself as the 'Comeback Kid' bouncing back when many commentators had written him off. However, many Democrats had severe doubts about their front runner; only 25 per cent turned out for the New York primary and, of those voting, 29 per cent supported Tsongas, even though he had already withdrawn from the race. Two-thirds of Democrats told pollsters they wished they had an alternative choice. Many felt that the party was landing itself with a candidate who was fatally flawed and who would be destroyed on the 'character' issue when the gloves really came off in earnest in the general election campaign.

History indicates that incumbent Presidents who sail to their party's nominating convention without real challenges usually go on to victory and a second term in the White House.[3] Richard Nixon (1972) and Ronald Reagan (1984) are recent examples. When a President faces substantial opposition for the nomination the divisions so created within the party and the image left among the electorate of a President who is not even fully supported by his own rank and file can, and often do, lead to defeat in the general election. This happened to Gerald Ford in 1976 and Jimmy Carter in 1980. Therefore the significance of Pat Buchanan's challenge to George Bush lay not in the fact that he won a substantial number of delegates or that he won any particular state primary (he did not), but in that it was made at all. Buchanan announced his candidacy in December 1991, following a decision by Bush to sign into law a civil rights bill he had previously attacked as 'quota legislation'. The fact that Buchanan obtained 37 per cent of the Republican primary vote in New Hampshire after attacking the President principally on the issues of the economy and taxation demonstrated Bush's potential vulnerability. Buchanan particularly focused on Bush's failure to keep his 1988 pledge: 'Read my lips; no new taxes'. The fact that Bush's compromise with Congressional Democrats in 1990 in an effort to reduce the federal budget deficit had led, not only to increased taxes, but also to additional public spending with no reduction in the deficit only exacerbated the anger and frustration of the Republican Right. For many conservatives who had never trusted Bush as the heir to Ronald Reagan's political legacy, the U-turn on taxes was a great betrayal. Bush's own admission that the U-turn itself had been a mistake only served to underline to many his lack of consistency and principles.

Bush was also unfortunate in that the primary season kicked off in New England, which had been particularly hard hit by the recession. He seemed unprepared for the degree of bitterness and anger among voters at the scale of plant closures and home repossessions in what had traditionally been a rock-solid Republican state. Media interest in the Republican race declined once it was clear that Bush, despite this discontent in the heartlands, would easily gain the delegates necessary for renomination and, despite remaining in the race, the Buchanan challenge fizzled out. However it was not before damage had been done to the President's standing and lines of attack had been developed that the Democrats could utilize and reinforce later in the campaign.

With the Democratic and Republican parties both moving inexorably towards nominating candidates about whom an increasing number of voters had doubts and reservations and a mood in the country of disillusionment with 'politics as usual', the time was ripe for the emergence of an alternative and unorthodox choice, in the diminutive shape of Texas billionaire, H. Ross Perot. Perot first appeared on the Presidential election scene in the spring, with television interviews given on a number of chat shows and phone-in programmes such as 'Larry King Live' on CNN, which draw mass audiences. These opportunities provided widespread exposure of Perot's message that the country was in an economic mess, that politicians of both parties had fiddled while the federal deficit had climbed into the strato-sphere and that the American Dream for future generations was in serious jeopardy unless something radical was done about it. Perot tapped into an increasingly pessimistic public mood and before long had a huge volunteer army working to get his name on the ballot for President throughout the United States. At the end of May, *Time* featured him on its front cover,[4] and a number of polls showed him leading both the President and Governor Clinton. Although he did not officially declare his candidacy, Perot's claims that he was prepared to put himself at the service of the American people, that he could use his business acumen to get things done in Washington and break the deadlock, as well as his lack of party ties, appealed to many Americans. However the media inevitably began to focus on the man and his background and by the end of June critical stories began to appear, questioning his business practices, his autocratic character and his suitabil-ity for the nation's highest office. Perot clearly resented scrutiny of his personal and business affairs and his lead in the polls began to evaporate. With the Democrats attending their convention in New York City the politi-cal landscape changed once again as Perot announced the end of his non-candidacy on the day of Clinton's acceptance speech. He claimed that this was partly because the Democratic party had 'revitalized' itself and that the parties were now focusing on the deficit problem. He also said that he had no wish to see the election end up in the House of Representatives as the Constitution requires if a three-way split in the Electoral College leads to no candidate obtaining an overall majority. Later in the year he was to make a bizarre claim that he had withdrawn in July because he had learned of a plot by Republican dirty tricksters to disrupt his daughter's wedding, an allega-tion for which he offered no evidence and which raised further question-marks about his personality.

The immediate impact of Perot's withdrawal, coinciding as it did with the week-long publicity for the Democratic convention, was to give a consider-able boost to Clinton's poll ratings. He could now be portrayed as the only real agent for change, and post-convention polls showed him leading Bush by up to 24 per cent. Although his lead was inevitably reduced during the rest of the campaign, Clinton was to stay in front until election day. Of the almost 200 polls carried out between July and November, every one showed Clinton ahead. Perot left behind him a very large number of angry and disillusioned followers, many of whom had never before participated in a political campaign and who felt betrayed by their hero's sudden departure. The enigmatic Perot, however, had a further surprise in store when he announced in October that he was re-entering the race. At that time only 7 per cent of electors said they would vote for him, but during the next month the percentage climbed again, although never reaching the dizzy heights of early summer. Using over 60 million dollars of his own money to pay for advertising slots on television, including 30-minute 'infomercials' during which he lectured millions of voters on the dangers of the deficit and poured scorn on his rivals, Perot undoubtedly made his own unique impact. As he eventually secured 19 per cent of the popular vote across the country, one is left to ponder what might have happened if he had stayed in the race and not withdrawn for a vital period of ten weeks during the summer.

Going into the Democratic convention in July the three candidates were neck and neck in the polls. Perot had stolen the limelight since Clinton had tied up the nomination of his party, appearing as a genuine outsider and diverting media attention from the Democratic challenge to President Bush. The Clinton campaign was determined to 'reintroduce' their candidate to the American people; to show him as a successful Governor, a family man and someone who had succeeded by his own efforts and did not come from a rich or privileged background. They used the 'new media' to get that message across. The candidate answered voters' questions directly at dozens of 'town hall meetings' across the country, each carried live by local television stations. He was interviewed on dozens of satellite and cable channels and campaign staff distributed hundreds of thousands of video cassettes about Clinton and his policies. Clinton made a guest appearance on the Arsenio Hall late night television show, playing his saxophone and wearing plastic sunglasses, as well as appearing on MTV, the cable music network to grab public attention and appeal to young voters. On a more serious level he released a detailed programme, 'Putting People First', which emphasized the economy as the centrepiece of his campaign. Before the convention met, Clinton announced his choice for Vice-Presidential running mate. In selecting Senator Al Gore of Tennessee, Clinton was breaking with the tradition of 'balancing the ticket'. Instead of choosing someone who came from a different part of the country or wing of the party, Clinton preferred a man whom he felt was best qualified for the job. Al Gore, who had campaigned briefly himself for the Presidency in 1988 and emerged unscathed from the media attention, in many respects mirrored Clinton. Both were from the South, in their mid-forties and centrists within the Democratic party. However Gore also complemented Clinton by being a Vietnam veteran, someone with direct experience of Washington politics, an acknowledged specialist in environmental and defence policy and with a settled family background. Gore was also able to reinforce the image of generational change, while the ticket offered a real threat to Republican dominance of the South. The choice of a running mate is the first chance a

Presidential candidate has to demonstrate his decision-making abilities. The reception of Gore by the party and the media meant that Clinton had passed the test with flying colours and polls indicated that doubts among voters about Clinton's fitness for office had been substantially reduced. The contrast with the furore following Bush's selection of Dan Quayle in 1988 and the fact that Quayle continued to be seen as a political liability could hardly have been greater. Asked by pollsters at the end of the campaign whom they would support if they could vote separately for a Vice-President, 62 per cent backed Gore, 28 per cent Quayle with 7 per cent for Stockdale, Perot's running mate.

Fascinating comparisons can also be made between the two national conventions of 1992, held in July in New York City by the Democrats and in August in Houston by the Republicans, as well as with previous conventions. In most recent campaigns the Republicans have appeared united and enthusiastic about their candidate and their conventions have been carefully choreographed rallies designed to take maximum advantage of the free prime time television coverage. The Democrats have frequently appeared divided over their platform and factionalized, with a host of minority groups seeking attention for their sometimes unpopular causes. They were sometimes encumbered by a candidate chosen by the party activists who was too liberal for the tastes of the majority of Democratic voters, let alone those independent and non-affiliated electors whose support is needed to win in November. Democratic conventions have not been as well organized for the television audience, although recent ones have done better than the 1972 fiasco, when George McGovern made his acceptance speech in the middle of the night when most people had already gone to bed. In 1992, the Democratic party, buoyed by Perot's withdrawal and the sudden realization that their candidate might have a chance of winning after all, put on a rare display of public unity and focused on projecting a positive image of the Clinton–Gore ticket. Jerry Brown remained an irritant but he and Jesse Jackson were only allowed to address the convention in non-prime time speaking slots. Clinton was helped by the fact that Jackson, who had been such a significant figure at the 1984 and 1988 conventions and had to be accommodated by the victorious candidate, on this occasion did not have any delegates pledged to support him and therefore was able to exert considerably less influence on proceedings. Privately Jackson complained that Clinton's campaign was pandering too much to white middle-class voters and ignoring the interests of those minority groups he had described as his 'Rainbow Coalition' in previous elections. The Los Angeles riot in May had vividly demonstrated the boiling resentments and the problems of America's inner cities; Jackson argued that the Democrats should not take the votes of such communities for granted. Later Clinton criticized Jackson for his support of a black rap singer who had made a record celebrating the killing of a policeman. In doing so, he symbolically demonstrated his ability to stand apart from the special interests within the Democratic party.

In another break with tradition, and learning the lesson of the Dukakis campaign in 1988, Clinton and Gore were determined to capitalize on their successful convention and lead in the polls by setting out immediately on a coach tour to 'meet the people', one of a number throughout the country during the campaign. This ensured that they would remain in the public eye throughout the rest of July and August and consolidate their position by the time the Republicans convened in Houston. This also established a pattern as Clinton and Gore worked together as a team throughout the campaign, in contrast to Bush and Quayle, who had their own separate schedules and were rarely seen together.

In 1992, it was the Republican convention that turned out to be a public relations disaster, giving the impression of a narrow and exclusive party that was not reaching out to the wider electorate. Worried about the lacklustre performance of the President and the apparent disorganization within both the White House and the Bush campaign team, Republicans gathered against a background of a substantial Clinton lead in the polls and no sign of an economic upturn which would boost their fortunes. The first few days were dominated by the divisive issue of abortion. The Religious Right appeared to control proceedings with their demands for a complete ban on abortion, going further than the President's personal approach to the issue. Many women and young people watching at home were alienated and moderate Republican delegates at the convention were also antagonized. By emphasizing the so-called 'family values' issue, the Republicans were accused of not-so-subtle attacks on homosexuals, single parents and minority groups. Pat Buchanan was given the opportunity to voice his extreme views in a bitter speech that clearly embarrassed many Republican leaders, while only paying lip-service to the cause of re-electing George Bush. Ronald Reagan's appearance at the podium only served to emphasize again the fact that the 'Great Communicator' still held the affection and loyalty of the party in a way that Bush had never managed to achieve. Even Bush's announcement that Secretary of State James Baker would take over the management of the campaign could only temporarily raise Republican spirits. Leaks to the media that Bush would sack his whole economic policy team if re-elected only reinforced the impression of disarray in the White House, while Bush almost casually commented later that Baker would be put in overall charge of domestic and economic affairs in a second term. Bush's acceptance speech was generally well if not rapturously received and he did obtain a 'bounce' in the polls, reducing Clinton's lead to around 10 points, but this was short-lived and by Labor Day in early September the Democrat was ahead by approximately 15 per cent. What is more, the rhetoric and tone of the convention provoked liberal activists and interest groups into producing a flood of large financial contributions into the Democratic party's coffers.

The General Election Campaign

One of the other key lessons learned by the Democrats from the 1988 campaign, when Dukakis frittered away a substantial post-convention lead, was the need to respond immediately to attacks and critical statements by their opponents. Allowing such allegations to go unanswered cost Dukakis dearly and enabled the Republicans to paint a very negative picture of the Democratic candidate. Clinton's team were prepared for similar negative campaigning and commissioned a number of officials to issue immediate and detailed rebuttals of any charges that they felt distorted Clinton's record or position on the issues. They even set up shop in Houston during the Republican convention and, within minutes of speeches being made, had their own side of the story in the hands of the media. Counter-attack within the news cycle every time they were attacked became a key objective.

One Bush commercial concentrated on creating a particularly depressing picture of Arkansas as a place to live while claiming that, as Governor, Clinton had raised taxes and doubled the state's debt. It ended: 'Bill Clinton wants to do for America what he's done for Arkansas. America can't take that risk.' Within hours the Clinton response team had a commercial running that quoted respected sources as a rebuttal of the Bush claims: 'No wonder the *Washington Post* says George Bush is lying about Bill Clinton's record and why the *Oregonian* concluded, "Frankly we no longer trust George Bush".' Clinton, of course, also went on the attack himself, particularly focusing on Bush's record of breaking his pledge not to raise taxes and his claim in 1988 that Americans would feel better off. His commercial concluded. 'Well, it's four years on. How are you doing?'[5] By emphasizing the economy and the 'pocket book' issue at a time of recession, Clinton was as effective with this line as Ronald Reagan had been when he asked a similar question during his televised debate with President Jimmy Carter in 1980.

Bush's campaign was so disorganized that his television commercials did not start running in many key states until mid-September. By that time the Democrats, who had carefully targeted their media buying, had already built up substantial leads in many areas. In an effort to reduce Clinton's lead in the national polls, Bush also wasted valuable resources by buying block advertising across the country, thus paying for commercials in states they knew they had no chance of winning. Bush's campaign team suffered from internal divisions and lacked the organization and experience of the architects of his 1988 victory. They found it difficult to provide a consistent focus on themes that appealed to the voters. In contrast, Clinton's organization, led by James Carville, followed a strategy of concentrating on the twin themes of the economy and the need for change.

As in every Presidential election since 1976, voters were able to view the candidates in a series of televised face-to-face confrontations. In 1992, public interest in the election was considerably higher than in 1988, with 79 per cent of respondents saying they were interested in the Presidential race, compared with 64 per cent four years earlier, and on election day there was a 55 per cent turnout, an increase of 4·5 per cent over 1988. This was in part due to the fact that many broadcasters, stung by criticisms that they had trivialized recent elections by their coverage, did attempt to spend more time analysing the issues and critically examining the claims and counterclams made by the candidates and their commercials. It is estimated that 92 million Americans watched the final televised debate in 1992, compared with 71 million in 1988.[6] For President Bush, lagging in the polls, the debates were seen as the most important opportunity to make a breakthrough in the campaign. However the Bush team managed to give the impression that they were afraid of letting their man in the ring with Clinton (the 'Oxford debater' as Bush called him) by refusing for weeks to agree the number of debates and the rules and procedures. Eventually three 90-minute programmes featuring the Presidential candidates were arranged, with one featuring the Vice-Presidential contenders, all to take place over a ten-day period in mid-October.

In the past, over-rehearsed candidates, constrained by a format of questions and answers from hand-picked journalists within rigid time limits have restricted the opportunity for real debate. The contrived drama, the prepared one-liners and effective sound-bites tend to stay in the memory. In 1992, the first debate was based on the traditional pattern. The main winner was Ross Perot. Appearing on the same platform with the two main party candidates raised his stature, and his good-humoured folksy wisdom played well with the viewers. In addition it was noticeable that in all three debates Bush and Clinton concentrated their fire on each other and at times seemed to defer to the independent candidate in the hope of not alienating Perot supporters and with an eye to eventually winning them over to their own cause. A *Newsweek* poll after the first meeting reported that 43 per cent felt Perot had won, 31 per cent Clinton and only 19 per cent backed Bush. Perot's support in the opinion polls jumped from 7 per cent to 14 per cent almost overnight.

The second debate provided a welcome variation in format, with a talk show setting and the candidates being questioned by an audience of uncommitted voters. Candidates could move around the platform while answering questions in a more informal style, an approach that had been suggested by Clinton and suited him well as he spoke directly to the questioners and set out specific proposals to deal with the wide range of issues raised by the voters. Bush, who was chastened by a voter chiding him for negative attacks on his opponent, appeared ill at ease and on several occasions was caught by the camera glancing at his watch. Viewers began to tire of Perot's hectoring style and lack of specific answers and a CBS poll showed that 53 per cent judged Clinton to be the winner, with Bush gaining 25 per cent support and Perot 21 per cent. It was only in the third debate that Bush gave a combative and forceful performance with a focus on the main themes of his campaign; even then polls indicated that Clinton was judged to have performed better. The Vice-Presidential debate was notable for the fact that Dan Quayle surprised many observers by being a match for Al Gore and for what ranks as easily the most embarrassingly inept performance ever in such confrontations, by Perot's running mate, retired Admiral James Stockdale.

Invigorated by the favourable reaction to his third debate performance, George Bush campaigned across the country in the last two weeks promising to 'give them hell', invoking memories of Harry Truman's 1948 campaign with a whistle-stop train tour. Ross Perot's exposure in the debates and his huge spending on television advertising and 'infomercials' boosted his poll ratings to approximately 20 per cent. Despite his successes in the television debates, Clinton's lead, which had been remarkably consistent since early September, appeared to narrow dramatically in the last week of the campaign. Before the first debate Clinton enjoyed a 13 point lead in the CBS/*New York Times* poll; after the final debate this had been cut to 5 per cent. On the weekend before the election tracking polls of likely voters (as opposed to registered voters) showed Bush within 2–3 per cent of Clinton.[7] It appeared that at long last the negative attacks on Clinton's character and the issue of 'trust' might be paying off.

Bush also received a boost from news that economic growth in the third quarter of 1992 had picked up 2·7 per cent, compared with 1·5 per cent in the previous quarter. However Bush lost momentum in the final days of the campaign. Clinton pressed his attacks on Bush and fresh evidence suggested that the President had not told the truth about his involvement in the Iran Contra scandal. Voters may also have been turned off as the personal attacks by Bush became more shrill and unpresidential: he called Clinton and Gore a couple of 'bozos' and said they were 'crazy'. The final opinion polls (Table 10.2) indicated that Clinton's lead had widened again to 5–7 per cent; on election day his winning margin in the popular vote was 5 per cent. Clinton visited eight marginal states in a frenzied 28-hour campaign tour in a final effort to consolidate his lead and give the voters an upbeat image of

Table 10.2   Final opinion surveys in 1992 Presidential election (%)

	Clinton	Bush	Perot	Undecided/Other
Actual popular vote	43	38	19	
Gallup/CNN/*USA Today*	44	37	14	5
Lou Harris	44	38	17	1
CBS News/*New York Times*	45	37	15	3
Washington Post	43	35	16	6
ABC News	44	37	16	3
NBC News/*Wall Street Journal*	44	36	15	5
Battleground poll	40	36	19	5

Source: *Congressional Quarterly Weekly Report*, 7 November 1992, p.3550.

energy and enthusiasm as polling day began. Bush's final day of election-eering, in contrast, gave the impression of a man who was relieved to have finished his last campaign and who was almost resigned to the inevitability of defeat. As the first results on election night came in from New England the scale of that defeat was apparent. Clinton won many previously solid Republican states which had not voted Democrat since Johnson's landslide in 1964. At the end of the night, Bush's popular vote was the lowest share of the vote recorded by any incumbent President seeking re-election since 1912 and 15 per cent less than he personally achieved in 1988.

The 1992 Vote, Issues and Candidates

Recent Republican successes in Presidential elections have been built on an electorally solid base of prosperous and expanding Western and Southern states which has led many analysts to argue that the party had a 'lock' on the Electoral College. In 1992, these areas gained in the apportionment of Electoral College votes to take account of population movements in the preceding decade. However Clinton picked the lock by winning eight of the 13 Rocky Mountain and Pacific Coast states, including the biggest prize of all, California, with its 54 electoral votes (Table 10.3). The weakness of the Bush campaign is demonstrated by the fact that he had given up hope of winning California early in the summer, despite the state's record of having supported Republican candidates in every Presidential election since 1968. On the day Clinton won California by 14 per cent and led by a ten-point

Table 10.3   Number of Electoral College votes and % of popular votes for Clinton, Bush and Perot

Clinton (Dem.) 370 EC Votes (43%)					*Bush (Rep.) 168 EC Votes (37.4%)*			
	EC	*C*	*B*	*P*		*EC*	*B*	*C*	*P*
Arkansas	6	53.2	35.5	10.4	Alabama	9	47.6	40.9	10.8
California	54	46.0	32.0	20.6	Alaska	3	39.5	30.3	28.4
Colorado	8	40.1	35.9	23.3	Arizona	8	38.5	36.5	23.8
Connecticut	8	42.2	35.8	21.6	Florida	25	40.9	39.0	19.8
Delaware	3	43.5	35.3	20.4	Idaho	4	42.0	28.4	27.0
Dis. Columbia*	3	84.6	9.1	4.3	Indiana	12	42.9	36.8	19.8
Georgia	13	43.5	42.9	13.3	Kansas	6	38.9	33.7	27.0
Hawaii*	4	48.1	36.7	14.2	Mississippi	7	49.7	40.8	8.7
Illinois	22	48.6	34.3	16.6	Nebraska	5	46.6	29.4	23.6
Iowa*	7	43.3	37.3	18.7	North Carolina	14	43.4	42.7	13.7
Kentucky	8	44.6	41.3	13.7	North Dakota	3	44.2	32.2	23.1
Louisiana	9	45.6	41.0	11.8	Oklahoma	8	42.6	34.0	23.0
Maine	4	38.8	30.4	30.4	South Carolina	8	48.0	39.9	11.5
Maryland	10	49.8	35.6	14.2	South Dakota	3	40.2	37.1	21.8
Massachusetts*	12	47.5	29.0	22.7	Texas	32	40.6	37.1	22.0
Michigan	18	43.8	36.4	19.3	Utah	5	43.4	24.7	27.3
Minnesota*	10	43.5	31.9	24.0	Virginia	13	45.0	40.6	13.6
Missouri	11	44.1	33.9	21.7	Wyoming	3	39.6	34.0	25.6
Montana	3	37.6	35.1	26.1					
Nevada	4	37.4	34.7	26.2					
New Hampshire	4	38.9	37.6	22.6					
New Jersey	15	43.0	40.6	15.6					
New Mexico	5	45.9	37.3	16.1					
New York*	33	49.7	33.9	15.7					
Ohio	21	40.2	38.3	21.0					
Oregon*	7	42.5	32.5	24.2					
Pennsylvania	23	45.1	36.1	18.2					
Rhode Island*	4	47.0	29.0	23.2					
Tennessee	11	47.1	42.4	10.1					
Vermont	3	46.1	30.4	22.8					
Washington*	11	43.4	32.0	23.7					
West Virginia*	5	46.7	35.4	15.9					
Wisconsin*	11	41.1	36.8	21.5					

Notes

*States won by Democratic candidate in 1988.

Percentages are of total popular vote, including those cast for minor party candidates. Based on official returns.

margin in the West, building on the gains made by Michael Dukakis in that region in 1988. Despite having two Southerners on the ticket, the Democrats did not sweep the South; seven of the 11 states of the Confederacy went to Bush. Outside their home bases, Clinton and Gore won Georgia by one point and Louisiana by 4 per cent. The South was the only region to give Bush a lead – a bare 1 per cent (see Table 10.4). Clinton's victory was national in its scope, with his taking all of the North-east (11 states plus the District of Columbia) and seven of the 12 Midwest and Plains states.

A key element of the winning Republican coalition has been the blue-collar 'Reagan Democrats', whose votes had been vital in taking a number of important industrial states in the 1980s. However, in 1992, this group went back to the Democratic party by a ratio of two to one, and Bush failed to win in states such as New Jersey, Pennsylvania, Ohio, Michigan and Illinois, which had contributed significantly to his 1988 victory. Suburban voters supported Clinton in preference to Bush by 45 per cent to 37 per cent and middle-income groups moved decisively towards the Democrats, while the traditional elements of their coalition, such as low-income voters and minorities were solidly behind Clinton. Bush's lead among white voters fell from 19 per cent in 1988 to 2 per cent in 1992.

Exit polls showed that Clinton had also succeeded in securing leads among a number of demographic groups that had favoured the Republicans in recent elections. Younger voters (18–29-year-olds), with whom Reagan had enjoyed a 19 per cent lead in 1984, supported Clinton by 10 per cent. First-time voters who favoured Bush by 4 per cent in 1988 this time over-whelmingly preferred Clinton by 18 per cent. The over-60s age group moved from a 21 per cent Republican lead in 1984, to a 1 per cent Bush lead in 1988, to a 12-point advantage for the Democrats in 1992. Bush's 16 per cent lead among male voters in 1988 was reversed to a 3 per cent Clinton majority; among women Clinton secured a 9 per cent lead, compared with Bush's marginal 1 per cent advantage in the previous election. Concentration in the campaign on economic and domestic issues seems to have led to a closing of the 'gender gap' that had opened up in recent elections. In effect Bush's vote almost totally comprised people who had voted for him four years earlier, while Clinton had a much broader appeal; in addition to holding almost all those who reported a 1988 vote for Dukakis he won converts from previous Bush voters as well as a large percentage of those who had not voted four years earlier.[8]

Ross Perot's support varied from 30 per cent in Maine and 29 per cent in Utah (where he beat Clinton into second place) to 9 per cent in Mississippi and 4 per cent in Washington DC. Unlike most independent and third party candidates who have drawn their support from particular regions or groups, Perot was a national candidate in the sense that he won votes from all areas

Table 10.4 Portrait of the electorate 1984, 1988 and 1992

% of 1992 total		Vote in 1984		Vote in 1988		Vote in 1992		
		Reagan	Mondale	Bush	Dukakis	Clinton	Bush	Perot
	Total	59%	40%	53%	46%	43%	38%	19%
46	Men	62	37	57	41	41	38	21
54	Women	56	44	50	49	46	37	17
87	Whites	64	35	59	40	39	41	20
8	Blacks	9	89	12	86	82	11	7
3	Hispanics	37	61	30	69	62	25	14
65	Married	62	38	57	42	40	40	20
35	Not married	52	46	46	53	49	33	18
22	18–29 years old	59	40	52	47	44	34	22
38	30–44 years old	57	42	54	45	42	38	20
24	45–59 years old	59	39	57	42	41	40	19
16	60 and older	60	39	50	49	50	38	12
6	Not a high school graduate	49	50	43	56	55	28	17
25	High school graduate	60	39	50	49	43	36	20
40	College graduate or more	58	41	56	43	44	39	18
49	White Protestant	72	27	66	33	33	46	21

Catholic	27	54	45	52	47	44	36	20
Jewish	4	31	67	35	64	78	12	10
White fundamentalist or evangelical Christian	17	78	22	81	18	23	61	16
Union household	19	46	53	42	57	65	24	21
Family income under $15 000	14	45	54	37	62	59	23	18
$15 000–$29 999	24	57	42	49	50	45	35	20
$30 000–$49 000	30	59	40	56	44	41	38	21
£50 000–$74 999	20	66	33	56	42	40	42	18
$75 000 and over	13	69	30	62	37	36	48	16
From the East	24	52	47	50	49	47	35	18
From the Midwest	27	58	40	52	47	42	37	21
From the South	30	64	36	58	41	42	43	16
From the West	20	61	38	52	46	44	34	22
Republicans	35	93	6	91	8	10	73	17
Democrats	38	24	75	17	82	77	10	13
Independents	27	63	35	55	43	38	32	22
Liberals	21	28	70	18	81	68	14	18
Moderates	49	53	47	49	50	48	31	21
Conservatives	29	82	17	80	19	18	65	17
First-time voters	11	61	38	51	47	48	30	22

Sources: 1992 Voter Research and Surveys exit poll; 1984 and 1988 New York Times/CBS News exit polls.

of the country and a wide range of electors. He did best among white males, younger voters and middle-income groups. If Perot had not been on the ballot, his supporters indicated they would have split evenly, with 38 per cent each saying they would have voted for Bush and Clinton and 15 per cent stating that they would not have voted. Analysis of exit poll data suggests that only Ohio would have shifted its Electoral College vote from Clinton to Bush in Perot's absence.[9] However Perot voters tended to hold views on the role of government that were closer to Republican voters than Democrats.[10] As Perot's attacks were principally against Bush, his campaign may well have damaged the Republican candidate more, but it appears that Clinton would have won the election with or without Perot on the ballot.

Examination of the reasons for these significant changes in voting behaviour points principally to the state of the economy as the key factor. Although nationally the recession was not particularly deep, its duration and the fact that some areas of the country and professional and middle-class groups were affected more seriously this time had major political repercussions. Battered successively by Buchanan, Perot and Clinton, Bush took the lion's share of the blame from the electorate for the loss of the 'feel good' factor. Some 43 per cent of voters said that jobs and the economy were the major influences on their vote, with the budget deficit being seen as the most important issue by 21 per cent. The recession's effects on confidence were widespread, with eight out of ten voters expressing pessimism about the state of the economy and fewer than one in three approving of Bush's handling of it. Voters were concerned about the nation's future economic prospects even when they themselves had not experienced a fall in their living standards. States such as California and those in New England which had suffered most in terms of growing unemployment showed a sharp swing away from the Republicans. Clinton managed to make the election principally a referendum on the economy; for 11 months he maintained a consistent message that 12 years of 'trickle-down economics' had failed, that Bush had lost touch with the people and that it was time for change.

Bush appeared early in the campaign to deny there was a problem, then to admit the economy was 'lousy', but failed to project a clear and coherent strategy for dealing with the issue. News about improved economic growth came too late in the electoral cycle to rescue the President. Other important voter concerns were domestic issues such as the cost of health care and standards in education on which Clinton had campaigned vigorously and offered proposals for reform. The health care issue was closely related to economic concerns; many voters were worried that losing their jobs would also lead to a loss in health care insurance coverage provided by their employers.

In previous elections the Republicans had convinced voters that they were better able to handle foreign policy, would keep America's defences strong and would stand up to the Soviet Union. The collapse of communism and the Soviet Union reduced the impact of foreign policy on the 1992 election; only 8 per cent of electors saw it as the key issue determining their vote. President Bush's high approval ratings immediately after the Gulf War were whittled away as voters' interest and attention switched to domestic issues. Bush's reputation in foreign policy was also eroded by his failure to provide a clear post-Cold War agenda, by his disastrous visit to Japan and by his isolation at the environmental summit at Rio de Janeiro. Most important, however, was the fact that many voters began to ask why the leader who could carry off a military and diplomatic success in the Gulf could not take a more dynamic role in dealing effectively with America's own domestic problems.

The Bush campaign's attempts to focus voter attention on the themes they wanted to emphasize could not divert them from the overriding concern about the economy. After the Republican convention the 'family values' issue was quietly dropped, partly because of the failure to define it clearly but principally because of the negative impact it seemed to be having among young and female middle-class voters. Bush decided to concentrate on two issues: taxation and trust. First, he had to convince Americans that a Clinton Presidency would lead to a substantial increase in taxation for ordinary people and not just the wealthy earning over $200 000 dollars a year, as Clinton claimed. Second, voters had to have their doubts about Clinton's character, which had been raised earlier in the year, reinforced to the point where they would not be prepared to see him as their President. Republicans argued that Clinton had been evasive on the draft issue and that on many other questions he had changed his mind or had tried to be all things to all people in order to win votes, reminding voters that he had been nicknamed 'Slick Willie' by some Arkansas politicians. These twin themes dominated Bush commercials, his stump speeches and his attacks on Clinton in the televised debates. In the sense that Clinton's lead in the polls narrowed as election day grew nearer, it can be argued that this strategy had some success, but it was insufficient in the end to override voters' concerns about the economy and Bush's record in office. Only 13 per cent considered taxation to be the most important factor affecting their vote and, while 40 per cent said they had an unfavourable image of Clinton, 57 per cent viewed Bush unfavourably. What is more, the twin themes of taxation and trust could be readily thrown back at Bush: he had broken his pledge not to raise taxes, could not be relied upon to keep his word and had not told the truth about his involvement in the Iran Contra scandal. Nearly 70 per cent said they did not believe Bush on this issue, which was resurrected in the final days before polling.

One of the key factors in explaining Bush's defeat is the way in which the Republican coalition put together by Ronald Reagan fractured during the Bush Presidency. Without the glue of anti-communism and prosperity to hold it together, the cracks became apparent. By his own actions Bush managed to alienate conservatives (particularly over taxation and spending) but also angered moderates by his appeasement of the Religious Right. His lack of vision and core values meant that he looked as if he did not stand for anything. Conservatives accused him of a directionless pragmatism which resulted in a failure to build on the Reagan achievements of the 1980s. Bush did not capitalize on his earlier popularity and foreign policy successes in order to govern effectively at home. His lack of interest in domestic issues and failure to construct a clear agenda for action led to his being left high and dry when voter attention turned inwards. Early warning signs of discontent, such as the defeat in the November 1991 special Senate election in Pennsylvania of the Republican candidate, Attorney General Richard Thornburgh, were ignored and opportunities to submit an anti-recession package to Congress before the Presidential primaries were missed.[11]

As Gerald M. Pomper has pointed out, although in objective terms the state of the national economy was not desperate and models of the vote based on economic data did actually forecast a Bush victory, for many voters the economic travails of the present were tied to a deeper fear of the future; the President, unlike persuasive leaders such as Roosevelt and Reagan, could provide no solace.[12] In other words, Bush's defeat was certainly not inevitable. The campaign itself made a difference – Bush ran a very poor campaign and Clinton a highly successful one – but Bush's record in office gave the Democrats plenty of ammunition.[13]

Bush's supporters argued that the practical constraints within which he was working – an escalating federal budget deficit and a generally hostile Democratic majority in Congress – limited his room for manoeuvre. The President emphasized the need to break the deadlock of divided government by giving him a new Congress with whom he could work, blaming the Democrats on Capitol Hill for obstructing many of his initiatives. However it was highly unlikely that the Republicans could capture control of Congress in 1992; voters concluded that, if there was to be an end to divided government in Washington, it was a lot easier to change the occupant of the White House. In the event the Democrats increased their majority by one seat in the Senate and, although the Republicans did make some gains in the House, the Democrats retained a large majority of 259–175.

Some historians have argued that every 30 years or so the nation turns away from conservatism and retrenchment to an era of active government and liberal idealism.[14] After the 'New Deal' of Franklin D. Roosevelt and the 'New Frontier' of John F. Kennedy, Bill Clinton put forward the 'New

Covenant'. Undoubtedly Clinton attempted to project himself as the heir to this tradition; he has a clear belief in the ability of government to improve people's lives and he had specific six-point programmes to deal with almost every area of public policy during his campaign. The huge video screens at the Democratic convention showing him as a schoolboy meeting President Kennedy at the White House left a powerful visual image. At the same time, Clinton was successful in picturing himself as a 'new kind of Democrat' and not just another 'tax and spend liberal'. Clinton and Gore had been among the leading members of the centrist Democratic Leadership Council which had been formed in the 1980s to try and win back the middle ground of American politics from the Republicans by distancing the party from old fashioned liberalism. Clinton emphasized that he favoured welfare reform to encourage individual responsibility ('welfare should be a second chance, not a way of life', as his commercial put it); he was for a tax cut for the 'forgotten middle classes' and he favoured capital punishment. In talking of empowering people to solve their own problems he shared the rhetoric of the conservative Right on some issues.

Clinton managed to emphasize the need for change and government action but did not alienate Reagan Democrats and middle-class voters by provoking the fear of tax increases. He spoke of challenges, but did not talk of personal sacrifice being necessary to deal effectively with the problems the nation was facing. The real challenge for the new President was to define his priorities and determine what his 'mandate' for change, which was actually backed by only 43 per cent of voters, actually meant. Bill Clinton promised action on many fronts and, with the constraints of the federal budget deficit and the high potential cost of many of his reforms, the danger was that he had raised expectations that would be difficult to satisfy. To win a second term in the White House, Clinton would have to demonstrate that he was capable of governing successfully, breaking the gridlock in Washington politics and achieving the key objectives he had set himself, particularly in relation to the economy and health care reform. Only then would he be able to build on his successful 1992 campaign by broadening the coalition of support to convert an electoral plurality into a popular majority. In particular, he would have to work hard to convince the sceptical Perot voters of 1992 that he is worthy of their support in 1996, while holding on to the Reagan Democrats, middle-class and young voters who trusted him in this election. Unlike Richard Nixon, who was able to employ a 'Southern Strategy' to appeal to George Wallace's discernible constituency after 1968, Clinton will have difficulties in finding ways of incorporating the diversity of Perot's supporters into a Democratic Presidential coalition in 1996. Bill Clinton ran a highly successful election campaign; he was single-minded, resilient, enthusiastic and demonstrated effective communication skills, great stamina and self-control under fire. He will need all of these qualities in abundance over the coming years.

Postscript on the 1994 Midterm Elections

The 1994 midterm elections can justifiably and without hyperbole be described as historic with the Republicans sweeping to victory across the United States to shift the centre of American politics. The Republicans not only captured control of Congress for the first time since 1954 but also made substantial advances in state capitols and town halls throughout the country. Whereas the President's party has traditionally lost some seats in Congress at midterm, the Democrats suffered the worst defeat of any majority party at this point for 36 years. As most of the new Republican members are committed conservatives the 104th Congress will be considerably more right wing than its predecessor. A different form of divided party control of the executive and legislative branches will exist from that we have seen in recent decades. President Clinton, who had major problems in persuading Congress to go along with his legislative proposals in 1994, is certain to find even greater difficulties in advancing his political agenda when dealing with a House of Representatives that has Newt Gingrich as its Speaker and a Senate led by Robert Dole.

In the Senate the Republicans gained eight seats and were also boosted by the defection to their ranks of Senator Richard Shelby of Alabama. Among those Democrats defeated were Jim Sasser of Tennessee who had hoped to be Majority Leader in the new Congress on the retirement of George Mitchell. Mitchell's seat in Washington state was won by Republican Olympia Snowe, making her the eighth female Senator. The defeat of Oliver North by incumbent Chuck Robb in Virginia and the victory in California of Dianne Feinstein over Michael Huffington, who spent over $28 million of his own money on his campaign, were bright spots on an otherwise dismal night for the Democrats. Although Republican control of the Senate had been seen as a strong possibility the size of the majority was larger than predicted.

In the House of Representatives Republicans' early hopes of control by gaining 40 seats had been diminishing in the final weeks of the campaign as polls indicated a slight improvement in Democratic fortunes. In the 103rd Congress the Democrats enjoyed a comfortable 256–178 advantage; the tide of voter discontent swept the Republicans to a clear majority with over 50 seats gained. Prominent Democrats who went down to defeat included Speaker Tom Foley (Washington) whose strong opposition to term limits hurt him, Dan Rostenkowski (Illinois) who faced corruption charges, and Jack Brooks of Texas, the Chairman of the Judiciary Committee.

At state level the Republicans picked up a net 11 Governorships (with two races too close to be decided on election night) and took control of 10 legislative chambers. Following these elections the Republicans hold more gubernatorial positions than at any time since 1970 and significantly these include seven out of the eight biggest states; the big gains in 1994 were New York and Texas.

Republicans achieved success across the country but did particularly well in the South, the Midwest and the West. Overall Republicans now hold 16 out of 28 Southern and Border Senate seats, seven of the 14 Governorships and 73 of the 139 Representatives. The GOP now has control of the Georgia, North Carolina and Tennessee Congressional delegations for the first time this century. The election confirmed a long term trend of increasing Republican strength in the South, while the party won back the loyalties of many voters in other areas such as the Midwest and West who had defected to the Democrats in the 1992 Presidential election.

Although the scale of Republican successes surprised most observers the political trend had been clear for some time. Republicans had won almost every significant election during 1993 and 1994 and opinion polls indicated unusual strength for the party among electors intending to vote in the Congressional elections. Polls also confirmed President Clinton's poor public approval ratings (48 per cent in the run-up to the elections which was a slight improvement on earlier showings). This was a significant factor affecting Democrats' performance and many candidates chose to disassociate themselves from the President as far as they could and refused offers from the White House to campaign on their behalf. Anti-Clinton sentiment was particularly strong in the South but was also evident elsewhere. The driving force behind Republican gains was, according to exit polls, the voters' identification of Clinton and the Democratic party with big government and higher taxes. Try as he might to convince voters that he represented a different approach, the tax increase for the high income groups in his 1993 budget plan and the scope of his ill-fated health care reform appear to have convinced people that Clinton was not the 'New Democrat' he had claimed to be in his 1992 campaign. Ironically, genuine 'New Democrats' such as Reps. Jim Cooper of Tennessee and Dave McCurdy of Oklahoma went down to defeat along with other moderates, leaving the Congressional Democratic party in the 104th Congress more liberal and urban-based.

Public disillusionment with Washington politics and the way Congress works also seems to have been a major reason for the outcome of the elections. As the majority party for so long (especially in the House) the Democrats took the blame for failing to live up to the promise of ending the deadlock of divided government of the Bush years. Claims of Republican obstructionism, which were to some extent justified, could not hide the fact

Table 10.5   Portrait of the Electorate 1994

% of total		Dem.	Rep.
49	Men	46	54
51	Women	54	46
79	White	42	58
13	Black	88	12
5	Hispanic	70	30
5	18–24 years old	58	42
6	25–29 years old	51	49
21	30–39 years old	47	53
23	40–49 years old	52	48
16	50–59 years old	48	52
18	60–69 years old	52	48
10	70 and older	48	52
5	Less than high school	68	32
22	High school graduate	52	48
32	Some college, but not four years	47	53
22	College graduate	45	55
19	Postgraduate study	54	46
36	From Northeast	52	48
17	From Midwest	44	56
25	From South	45	55
22	From West	59	41
41	Democrat	90	10
35	Republican	7	93
24	Other	44	56
45	Voted for Clinton 1992	87	13
37	Voted for Bush 1992	11	89
12	Voted for Perot 1992	33	67
4	Did not vote for President 1992	46	54

Source: Exit poll by Mitofsky International of New York, reported in *Washington Post* 10 November 1994, p.A33.

that as a result of ineffective leadership and party divisions the Democrats could not deliver the goods on a number of key legislative objectives in 1994. Voter frustration turned out not to be motivated so much by anti-incumbent feelings as some had predicted (no incumbent Republican lost in 1994) but rather by anti-Democrat sentiment directed at the party with power and responsibility.

Despite statistical evidence of sustained economic growth and reducing budget deficits there was an absence of a 'feel good' factor to help the Democrats. Instead exit poll data indicated that crime was the biggest single issue that influenced electors (38 per cent), a concern fully exploited by the Republicans in their campaigns. Other important issues were the economy and jobs (27 per cent), taxes (22 per cent), health care (22 per cent), family values and morality (19 per cent) and education (19 per cent).

The most significant feature of the exit poll responses was the widening of the gender gap in this election. The Republican gains seem to have been achieved with disproportionately strong support among men; they backed the Republicans by 54 per cent to 46 per cent. In the last midterm elections the majority of males had voted Democrat. In contrast, among female voters the numbers were reversed; 54–46 per cent in favour of the Democrats. Many men appear to have been motivated to go to the polls because of the issues such as crime that the Republicans put at the centre of their campaign.

This brief survey provides some of the key data and discusses some of the significant factors explaining the momentous changes resulting from the 1994 midterm elections as a conclusion to this volume on contemporary American politics. More detailed appraisal and analysis will have to wait to a later date.

Notes

1   Pippa Norris, 'The 1992 US Primaries: If It Ain't Broke Don't Fix It', *Parliamentary Affairs*, **45**, (3), July 1992.
2   Ryan J. Barrilleaux and Randall E. Adkins, 'The Nominations: Process and Patterns', in Michael Nelson (ed.), *The Elections of 1992*, Congressional Quarterly Press, 1993, pp.31–3.
3   Alan Grant, *The American Political Process*, 5th edn, Dartmouth, 1994, pp.242–3.
4   *Time,* 25 May 1992.
5   John Underwood, 'A run for their money', *Marketing*, 12 November 1992.
6   Robert Worcester, 'America decides for the devil it did not know', *The Times*, 5 November 1992.
7   CNN/Gallup Poll, 30 October 1992, reported by 'Inside Politics', CNN.
8   Gerald M. Pomper, 'The Presidential Election', in Gerald M. Pomper *et al.*, *The Election of 1992*, Chatham House, 1993, p.141.

9   *International Herald Tribune*, 7–8 November 1992.
10   Everett Carl Ladd, 'The 1992 Vote for Presidential Clinton: Another Brittle Mandate?', *Political Science Quarterly*, **108**, Spring 1993.
11   John O'Sullivan, 'How Bush went out of his way to ensure defeat', *Daily Telegraph*, 6 November 1992.
12   Gerald M. Pomper, 'The Presidential Election', p.147.
13   Paul J. Quirk and Jon K. Dalager, 'The Election: A "New Democrat" and a New Kind of Presidential Campaign', in Michael Nelson (ed.), *The Elections of 1992*, p.83.
14   Arthur Schlesinger, Sr. and Arthur Schlesinger, Jr., quoted in *Time*, 16 November 1992, p.28.

Index